Cars Online For Dummies

Cheat Sheet

Photocopy this page (but only this page!) so you can take it with you when you shop for your car.

Essential New Car Information

Vehicle Identification Number* _____

Dealership Information _____

Year _____ Model _____

Make _____ Color _____

New car price _____(dealer offer)_____(dealer's cost) _____(manufacturer's suggested retail price) *See Chapter 6 for online information about dealer cost.*

Trade-in price target _____ *See Chapter 15 for online information on getting the best price for your current car.*

Insurance _____ Leasing options _____

Financing _____

Accessories and Options _____

_____

Notes _____

Essential Used Car Information

See Chapter 13 for online tips when researching a used-car purchase.

Vehicle Identification Number * _____

Dealership information _____

Year _____ Model _____

Make _____ Color _____

Price _____(dealer offer)_____(dealer's cost)

Insurance _____ Financing _____

Accessories and Options _____

_____

Notes _____

For Dummies®: Bestselling Book Series for Beginners

Used Car Checklist

You can find out the answers to the questions below by obtaining the vehicle's VIN* and then going online to www.CarFax.com. Has this vehicle ever had . . .

Flood damage   Yes___   No___   Were its air bags ever used?   Yes___ No___

Fire damage   Yes___   No___   Odometer fraud report   Yes___ No___

Crash damage   Yes___   No___   Has this vehicle been identified as a lemon?   Yes___ No___

How many times has the vehicle changed hands? _____

What is its salvage history, if any?_____

Does it have its: Gas cap key?___Owners manual?___Repair and maintenance records?___

Did you test all the accessories and features? Air___Heater___Radio___Tape Player___Windows___Locks___Seat Adjuster___Spare Tire___Jack___

During the test drive did you notice any odd behaviors or sounds?___Drifts to one side?___Brakes to one side?___Good suspension?___All lights working?__ Engine has good power going uphill?___Exhaust smokes? (car dealers call this kind of car a *crop duster*)___Smooth shifting?___

Did you have an independent mechanic evaluate the car's condition? Yes___ No___

* Locate a car's Vehicle Identification Number (VIN) on its dashboard, on the insurance or title documents, from the dealer, or online through services, such as www.Autobytel.com and www.Autoweb.com.

The pros of leasing

- Monthly payments are lower than when you purchase a car, and often you make *no down payment*.
- You don't face the hassle of negotiating the value of a trade-in on your next purchase.
- If the vehicle is a lemon or starts experiencing serious problems, well . . . *you* don't own this clunker.
- Signing a lease is usually easier and more convenient than buying.
- You get a nice, new car every two or three years.
- If you like the car and want to keep it, the dealer may offer you a nice deal for its purchase.

The cons of leasing

- If you buy, you own the car.
- You may be stuck with a shocking bill to pay when the lease ends.
- At the end of the normal three-year lease, you must look for a new car.
- Leases are usually complex documents.

Copyright © 2000 IDG Books Worldwide, Inc.
All rights reserved.
Cheat Sheet $2.95 value. Item 0697-8.
For more information about IDG Books, call 1-800-762-2974.

IDG BOOKS WORLDWIDE

Car Buying Online

FOR DUMMIES®

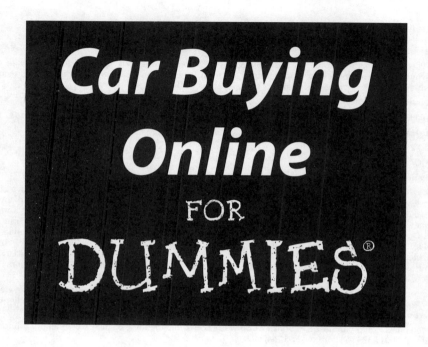

Car Buying Online

FOR DUMMIES®

by Richard Mansfield and Pierre Bourque

IDG BOOKS WORLDWIDE

IDG Books Worldwide, Inc.
An International Data Group Company

Foster City, CA ◆ Chicago, IL ◆ Indianapolis, IN ◆ New York, NY

Car Buying Online For Dummies®

Published by
IDG Books Worldwide, Inc.
An International Data Group Company
919 E. Hillsdale Blvd.
Suite 400
Foster City, CA 94404
www.idgbooks.com (IDG Books Worldwide Web site)
www.dummies.com (Dummies Press Web site)

Library of Congress Control Number: 00-100127

ISBN: 0-7645-0697-8

Printed in the United States of America

10 9 8 7 6 5 4 3 2 1

1O/QW/QX/QQ/IN

Distributed in the United States by IDG Books Worldwide, Inc.

Distributed by CDG Books Canada Inc. for Canada; by Transworld Publishers Limited in the United Kingdom; by IDG Norge Books for Norway; by IDG Sweden Books for Sweden; by IDG Books Australia Publishing Corporation Pty. Ltd. for Australia and New Zealand; by TransQuest Publishers Pte Ltd. for Singapore, Malaysia, Thailand, Indonesia, and Hong Kong; by Gotop Information Inc. for Taiwan; by ICG Muse, Inc. for Japan; by Intersoft for South Africa; by Eyrolles for France; by International Thomson Publishing for Germany, Austria and Switzerland; by Distribuidora Cuspide for Argentina; by LR International for Brazil; by Galileo Libros for Chile; by Ediciones ZETA S.C.R. Ltda. for Peru; by WS Computer Publishing Corporation, Inc., for the Philippines; by Contemporanea de Ediciones for Venezuela; by Express Computer Distributors for the Caribbean and West Indies; by Micronesia Media Distributor, Inc. for Micronesia; by Chips Computadoras S.A. de C.V. for Mexico; by Editorial Norma de Panama S.A. for Panama; by American Bookshops for Finland.

For general information on IDG Books Worldwide's books in the U.S., please call our Consumer Customer Service department at 800-762-2974. For reseller information, including discounts and premium sales, please call our Reseller Customer Service department at 800-434-3422.

For information on where to purchase IDG Books Worldwide's books outside the U.S., please contact our International Sales department at 317-596-5530 or fax 317-572-4002.

For consumer information on foreign language translations, please contact our Customer Service department at 1-800-434-3422, fax 317-572-4002, or e-mail rights@idgbooks.com.

For information on licensing foreign or domestic rights, please phone +1-650-653-7098.

For sales inquiries and special prices for bulk quantities, please contact our Order Services department at 800-434-3422 or write to the address above.

For information on using IDG Books Worldwide's books in the classroom or for ordering examination copies, please contact our Educational Sales department at 800-434-2086 or fax 317-572-4005.

For press review copies, author interviews, or other publicity information, please contact our Public Relations department at 650-653-7000 or fax 650-653-7500.

For authorization to photocopy items for corporate, personal, or educational use, please contact Copyright Clearance Center, 222 Rosewood Drive, Danvers, MA 01923, or fax 978-750-4470.

 is a registered trademark under exclusive license to IDG Books Worldwide, Inc. from International Data Group, Inc.

About the Authors

Just in case you care about such things, **Richard Mansfield** has written 25 computer books, 4 of which became bestsellers: *Machine Language for Beginners, The Second Book of Machine Language, The Visual Guide to Visual Basic,* and *The Visual Basic Power Toolkit* (with Evangelos Petroutsos). His most recent title is *Hacker Attack.* He has written columns and articles in computer magazines, but since 1991 he has focused full-time on writing books. Overall, his books have sold more than 500,000 copies worldwide and have been translated into 11 languages. But that's not the whole story. He's extraordinarily sedentary, preferring to sit and read, write, or program his computers instead of moving around. He realizes that all this goes against the popular health craze, but so far — so good.

Pierre Bourque has had a fascination with cars for most of his life. As a former race car driver who competed in Canada, the USA, and Europe, he has fully enjoyed the pleasures of motoring, both on and off the track, at a high professional level. Pierre's family has been involved in the car industry for a number of years, and he has had the opportunity to own and drive a wide variety of cars, both foreign and domestic, new and used.

Today, Pierre Bourque is the publisher of Bourque Newswatch, Canada's Online News Authority (www.bourque.com). He drives an Acura, and lives in Ottawa, Canada.

ABOUT IDG BOOKS WORLDWIDE

Welcome to the world of IDG Books Worldwide.

IDG Books Worldwide, Inc., is a subsidiary of International Data Group, the world's largest publisher of computer-related information and the leading global provider of information services on information technology. IDG was founded more than 30 years ago by Patrick J. McGovern and now employs more than 9,000 people worldwide. IDG publishes more than 290 computer publications in over 75 countries. More than 90 million people read one or more IDG publications each month.

Launched in 1990, IDG Books Worldwide is today the #1 publisher of best-selling computer books in the United States. We are proud to have received eight awards from the Computer Press Association in recognition of editorial excellence and three from Computer Currents' First Annual Readers' Choice Awards. Our best-selling ...*For Dummies*® series has more than 50 million copies in print with translations in 31 languages. IDG Books Worldwide, through a joint venture with IDG's Hi-Tech Beijing, became the first U.S. publisher to publish a computer book in the People's Republic of China. In record time, IDG Books Worldwide has become the first choice for millions of readers around the world who want to learn how to better manage their businesses.

Our mission is simple: Every one of our books is designed to bring extra value and skill-building instructions to the reader. Our books are written by experts who understand and care about our readers. The knowledge base of our editorial staff comes from years of experience in publishing, education, and journalism — experience we use to produce books to carry us into the new millennium. In short, we care about books, so we attract the best people. We devote special attention to details such as audience, interior design, use of icons, and illustrations. And because we use an efficient process of authoring, editing, and desktop publishing our books electronically, we can spend more time ensuring superior content and less time on the technicalities of making books.

You can count on our commitment to deliver high-quality books at competitive prices on topics you want to read about. At IDG Books Worldwide, we continue in the IDG tradition of delivering quality for more than 30 years. You'll find no better book on a subject than one from IDG Books Worldwide.

John J. Kilcullen
John Kilcullen
Chairman and CEO
IDG Books Worldwide, Inc.

**Eighth Annual
Computer Press
Awards ▷1992**

**Ninth Annual
Computer Press
Awards ▷1993**

**Tenth Annual
Computer Press
Awards ▷1994**

**Eleventh Annual
Computer Press
Awards ▷1995**

IDG is the world's leading IT media, research and exposition company. Founded in 1964, IDG had 1997 revenues of $2.05 billion and has more than 9,000 employees worldwide. IDG offers the widest range of media options that reach IT buyers in 75 countries representing 95% of worldwide IT spending. IDG's diverse product and services portfolio spans six key areas including print publishing, online publishing, expositions and conferences, market research, education and training, and global marketing services. More than 90 million people read one or more of IDG's 290 magazines and newspapers, including IDG's leading global brands — Computerworld, PC World, Network World, Macworld and the Channel World family of publications. IDG Books Worldwide is one of the fastest-growing computer book publishers in the world, with more than 700 titles in 36 languages. The "...For Dummies®" series alone has more than 50 million copies in print. IDG offers online users the largest network of technology-specific Web sites around the world through IDG.net (http://www.idg.net), which comprises more than 225 targeted Web sites in 55 countries worldwide. International Data Corporation (IDC) is the world's largest provider of information technology data, analysis and consulting, with research centers in over 41 countries and more than 400 research analysts worldwide. IDG World Expo is a leading producer of more than 168 globally branded conferences and expositions in 35 countries including E3 (Electronic Entertainment Expo), Macworld Expo, ComNet, Windows World Expo, ICE (Internet Commerce Expo), Agenda, DEMO, and Spotlight. IDG's training subsidiary, ExecuTrain, is the world's largest computer training company, with more than 230 locations worldwide and 785 training courses. IDG Marketing Services helps industry-leading IT companies build international brand recognition by developing global integrated marketing programs via IDG's print, online and exposition products worldwide. Further information about the company can be found at www.idg.com. 1/26/00

Dedication

Richard Mansfield dedicates this book to his roommate and best friend, David Lee Roach.

Pierre: To Buddy

Acknowledgments

Steven Hayes supervised the publication of this book with care and thoughtfulness. He was a pleasure to work with. And sometimes, if you're lucky, you get a really good editor. Kyle Looper is level-headed, understanding, author-friendly, and smart. We were fortunate that he oversaw the editing. A book is always stronger when authors can work in partnership with someone who knows his stuff. The technical accuracy of the book was checked, and improved, by Bill Greffin. Throughout the entire process of publishing this book, none of these fine people became frantic. As far as we know.

Pierre would like to thank his agent Matt Wagner and Waterside Productions for their persistence, perseverance, and indulgence. He would also like to thank Kristine Haselsteiner for her enthusiasm, encouragement, and patience. Many thanks to the hard working professionals at IDG who saw this project through.

Publisher's Acknowledgments

We're proud of this book; please register your comments through our IDG Books Worldwide Online Registration Form located at http://my2cents.dummies.com.

Some of the people who helped bring this book to market include the following:

Acquisitions, Editorial, and Media Development

Senior Project Editor: Kyle Looper

Acquisitions Editor: Steven H. Hayes

Copy Editors: Williams A. Barton, Stephanie Koutek

Proof Editor: Teresa Artman

Technical Editor: Bill Greffin

Permissions Editor: Carmen Krikorian

Associate Media Development Specialist: Megan Decraene

Editorial Manager: Leah P. Cameron

Media Development Manager: Heather Heath Dismore

Editorial Assistant: Beth Parlon

Production

Project Coordinator: Maridee Ennis

Layout and Graphics: Amy Adrian, Gabriele McCann, Tracy K. Oliver

Proofreaders: Laura Albert, Corey Bowen, John Greenough, Susan Moritz, Christine Pingleton

Indexer: Lynnzee Elze

Special Help Amanda M. Foxworth

General and Administrative

IDG Books Worldwide, Inc.: John Kilcullen, CEO

IDG Books Technology Publishing Group: Richard Swadley, Senior Vice President and Publisher; Walter R. Bruce III, Vice President and Publisher; Joseph Wikert, Vice President and Publisher; Mary Bednarek, Vice President and Director, Product Development; Andy Cummings, Publishing Director, General User Group; Mary C. Corder, Editorial Director; Barry Pruett, Publishing Director

IDG Books Consumer Publishing Group: Roland Elgey, Senior Vice President and Publisher; Kathleen A. Welton, Vice President and Publisher; Kevin Thornton, Acquisitions Manager; Kristin A. Cocks, Editorial Director

IDG Books Internet Publishing Group: Brenda McLaughlin, Senior Vice President and Publisher; Sofia Marchant, Online Marketing Manager

IDG Books Production for Branded Press: Debbie Stailey, Director of Production; Cindy L. Phipps, Manager of Project Coordination, Production Proofreading, and Indexing; Tony Augsburger, Manager of Prepress, Reprints, and Systems; Laura Carpenter, Production Control Manager; Shelley Lea, Supervisor of Graphics and Design; Debbie J. Gates, Production Systems Specialist; Robert Springer, Supervisor of Proofreading; Trudy Coler, Page Layout Manager; Troy Barnes, Page Layout Supervisor, Kathie Schutte, Senior Page Layout Supervisor; Michael Sullivan, Production Supervisor

Packaging and Book Design: Patty Page, Manager, Promotions Marketing

◆

The publisher would like to give special thanks to Patrick J. McGovern, without whom this book would not have been possible.

◆

Contents at a Glance

Cartoons at a Glance

By Rich Tennant

page 131

page 7

page 55

page 231

page D-1

page 277

page 263

page 207

Fax: 978-546-7747
E-mail: richtennant@the5thwave.com
World Wide Web: www.the5thwave.com

Table of Contents

Introduction

●●●

*W*elcome to the wonderful world of online vehicles! Many car companies are currently putting all their best, cutting-edge features at your fingertips via the Internet. They're all competing for your money — and, as Martha Stewart loves to say, *that's a good thing*.

This book shows you how to use these great online tools to get the best possible vehicle for the best possible price.

The Internet is both powerful and diverse. It enables you to rapidly and thoroughly explore thousands of options. Comparison shopping for financing, leasing, safety features, accessories — indeed, for any aspect of obtaining a vehicle — becomes far easier if you use the Internet. And as you see in this book, the best part is how *easily* you now can avoid the traditionally tedious aspects of deciding what kind of vehicle you want and then haggling with a salesperson for the best deal possible.

You even find out in these pages how to get several car dealers in your town to bid against each other to offer you the best price! We also show you how to get a loan approval at a great rate in *less than 20 seconds*! These items are only two of the many benefits and techniques that we describe in this book for you to use in purchasing or leasing a car. By using the Internet as we describe in these pages, you can, in fact, quickly accomplish things online that often prove difficult, if not impossible, to do in the "real" world.

Who Should Read This Book

If you have any interest at all in finding out exactly how to best purchase a vehicle — new, used, or classic; car, truck, SUV, or whatever — you now have the right book in hand. Before the advent of the Internet, you normally had to slog around town trying to comparison-shop as best you could, and in the end, you finally settled on a dealer — only to spend a lot of time discovering that the salesman was a *much* better negotiator than you were.

The Internet, however, changes the entire vehicle-buying balance of power (and some dealers are hopping mad as a result). So if you're planning on purchasing another vehicle anytime soon, you picked up the right book.

We tell you *everything* that you need to know to save yourself both time and a surprising amount of money in your quest for a car.

Saying that this book is strictly *For Dummies* is a bit misleading, however, because we know that you're not dumb. In fact, knowing that you can use help in buying a vehicle *proves* that you have brains. (Even the brief bit of negotiation that we ask you to do requires some practice to master — but we're confident that you can handle it.)

How to Use This Book

Vehicle purchase is low on most people's list of favorite pastimes, but this book can change your attitude. In its pages, you find out how to use the Internet to quickly and thoroughly research the information that you need to even the playing field as you enter negotiations. In fact, you see how to largely eliminate negotiations altogether by arranging your (Internet) financing ahead of time so that you already have the check in your pocket as you arrive at the dealership!

By then, you can even know exactly what accessories you want (and what add-ons, such as "prep" or "detailing," are useless to you). You already know whether you want to lease or buy. You already know the price that you should pay and the price you should get for your trade-in. All this information — and more — you can find but a few clicks away if you use *Car Buying Online For Dummies* as your guide.

So no matter where you are in a car-buying situation, take a look through the book, underline important points, and fire up your Web browser so that you can start gathering the information that makes you an effective power customer instead of another loser in the ancient game known as horse (whoops, we mean *car*) trading.

We must, however, alert you right up front: Although you can accomplish 95 percent of the task of buying a car in the virtual world of the Internet, two things remain that you must usually do in person in the physical world: take a test drive and sign some papers after you close the deal. We say *usually*, however, because as you see in this book, you now even have ways to avoid ever going down to a dealership to negotiate (even the little bit that we generally recommend) and sign papers. Some of the cutting-edge online car dealers enable you to make all the arrangements on the Internet itself (supplemented by fax or mail), and then they drive your shiny new chariot right to your front door!

How This Book Is Organized

We divide this book into five main parts. Each of the chapter topics that you see in the table of contents fit into one of five main categories (although sometimes a bit loosely, we do admit). The following sections give you a brief description of each of the book's five main parts.

Part I: Online Car Buying Basics

This part is your get-oriented section of the book. Here, you find some of the main techniques and strategies that you use throughout the book. Chapter 2, for example, is all about using Internet search engines to quickly locate the information that you need. You also lay the groundwork for your purchase by seeing what others are saying about the vehicle you're considering, including the writers of professional reports that you can obtain online.

Part II: Narrowing the Search: Finding the Right Car for You

This part of the book helps you become a savvy — and decisive — car buyer. We walk you hand-in-hand through the first steps that you need to take in buying a car online, and then we explain to you how to use the Internet to determine just how much a new (or used) car costs *before* you head to a dealer and find yourself at the mercy of a clever salesman and a carload of unnecessary, tacked-on fees. We describe how you can get online to narrow down your choices so that you go into a dealership knowing just *what* you want as well as *how much* to pay for it. We even give you tips on how the Internet can help you test-drive a potential purchase (although you usually still need to do the actual driving physically) and even determine just how safe that car may be out on the actual highway.

Part III: Taking the Plunge: Buying a Car Online

In this part, we tell you how to go all the way — actually buying a car online! First we tell you how to secure financing online and then how to use the Internet to decide whether to actually buy or just lease a car. Then we give you the lowdown on buying a new, a used, or a collector car on the Internet — and how to negotiate your deal like a pro. And finally, in this section of the book, we give you tips and pointers on getting the best deal possible for your trade-in, from selling it yourself online to locating Web sites where you can donate your old car for a tax write-off. After you finish this part, you're ready to roll right on over to the dealer, whether you do so in person or online.

Part IV: After You Buy It

Insurance for your new purchase is important — and often a legal requirement — and this part tells you how to find the best insurance deals online. In this section of the book, we also provide you with methods for finding online the exact driver's- and vehicle-licensing requirements for your home state — another necessity if you intend to take your car out for a spin without breaking any laws.

Part V: Keeping Your Car in Good Shape

After you actually buy a car, you want to make sure that it runs well for years to come. This part can help you in that goal by describing how you can obtain service advice for your car online and how to use the Internet to find replacement parts at the best price possible (especially if you own a used or classic car for which parts are hard to obtain). We also describe how you can exhibit pride in your car by joining any of several online organizations, if you're so inclined.

Part VI: The Part of Tens

This part contains only two brief chapters, but you don't want to miss it. These Part of Tens chapters include useful and cool information — ten important warnings (things to watch out for in buying a car online) — and ten additional, valuable tips to help you save money or time. You definitely want to try out some of these pointers.

Part VII: Appendix

This final part of the book provides you with vital information about the book's CD-ROM. If you have questions about any of the terms that we use in this book, about online requirements, or about using the CD, turn here.

Car Buying Online for Dummies Internet Directory

You also see a section of yellow pages in this book — our Internet Directory. In these pages, you find a collection of great vehicle-buying Web sites, with brief descriptions of each, which we organize by topic. (You also find the Directory in an interactive format on this book's CD-ROM. If you're online while using our CD, you can just click any of the links, and your browser takes you right to the Web site that entry describes.)

Conventions Used in This Book

For convenience, we usually employ the word *car* rather than use more clumsy diction, such as *vehicle*. But whenever we do use the word *car*, we also mean it to include SUVs, trucks, and other vehicles. The chapter "Finding Financing Online," for example, includes information on financing cars, of course, but tells you how to finance various other kinds of vehicles as well.

This book includes many step-by-step lists that function similar to recipes in helping you cook up a finished product. Each step starts off with a **boldface** sentence telling you what *you* need to do. Directly after the bold step, you may see a sentence or two in regular type telling you what happens as a result of the bold action — a menu pops up, a dialog box opens, a Wizard appears, you win the lottery . . . whatever.

A special symbol shows you how to navigate menus. Whenever you see a phrase such as "Choose File⇨Save," you want to click the File menu up on the menu bar and then click the Save command in the File menu that appears.

Finally, if we want you to type a certain phrase or word in a text box or field online — if, for example, you're using a search engine — we put that word or phrase in **boldface** type. And whenever we list an online address for a Web site or newsgroup, we put that address in a special typeface: www.dummies.com.

Icons Used in This Book

Notice the eye-catching little icons in the margins of this book. These tiny pictures appear next to a paragraph to draw your attention to items that you may — or may not — want to read immediately. Following are the icons that we use in this book and their meanings:

This icon points you to shortcuts and insights that save you time and trouble.

This icon highlights nerdy technical discussions that you can skip if you want.

This icon aims to steer you away from dangerous situations. Take heed whenever you see it.

Important information that you may want to . . . well, remember . . . displays this icon in the margin.

Where to Go from Here

Where else? Start up your Web browser, turn to Chapter 1 (or any other chapter you see in the table of contents that piques your interest), and get ready to become knowledgeable in the ways of buying a car online!

Part I
Online Car Buying Basics

The 5th Wave   By Rich Tennant

My car is approaching the law of diminishing returns.

You mean it's not worth repairing anymore?

No. I mean the number of times it returns home on its own power is diminishing.

In this part . . .

Okay, you may know something about buying a car, and you probably know a little about getting online (or at least you know someone who does). But just how do you put these two concepts together to figure out how to buy a car online? Well, look no further: This part is your get-oriented section of the book. In the chapters of this part, we introduce you to some of the main techniques and strategies that you use throughout the process of car buying online.

Chapter 1, for example, tells you why you even want to consider going online to buy a car, while Chapter 2 is all about using Internet search engines to quickly locate the information that you need (in researching a car or anything else, for that matter). This part also helps you lay the groundwork for your purchase by describing how to go online to determine what others are saying about the vehicle you're considering purchasing and how to conduct some basic research by obtaining professional reports off the Internet that give you even more data about the car that you may want to buy.

If you're not quite sure where to start, we highly recommend that you thoroughly peruse the chapters here in Part I before striking out on your car quest.

Chapter 1

Why Buy a Car on the Internet?

*L*ots of people don't realize that you can buy a car on the Internet. They figure: How are they going to fit my new Honda into that little FedEx truck? And how much *is* shipping and handling for something that big, anyway?

The word *dummy* in the title of this book is ironic — I don't expect you to actually believe that FedEx delivers the car or truck you buy online. You pick up a vehicle at a traditional dealer in your area (at least for now — see the section titled "Dot-com distribution down the road?" at the end of this chapter).

We still live in a material world, and we're all material girls or boys. But it *is* true that you can research the vehicle online. You can then buy it at a very, very good price.

You can use the Internet to do almost everything that you used to have to do at a traditional dealership:

✔ Narrowing your choice of vehicle

✔ Deciding whether to buy or lease

✔ Arranging financing

✔ Finding the best insurance

✔ Figuring out what your trade-in is worth

In other words, you can do almost all of the preparation for buying a vehicle while online. After the price, the finances, and all the other details are essentially finalized, you can just waltz in, sign a few papers, and drive off in your new vehicle. The bad old days — when you had to spend hours getting sales pitched, negotiated, and distracted by confusing math at the dealership — are over.

Notice the process here: You use the Internet to get price information as well as to arrange financing and, if necessary, insurance. You then visit a local dealer to first test drive and visit again to conclude the process and actually purchase the car itself.

A smart shopper does all the preparation online. Go to the dealer for only two things:

✔ To take a test drive to be sure you physically enjoy the vehicle you've chosen

✔ To complete the final details: signing the necessary forms, handing them the check for the full price (which you've already obtained via online financing), and driving away in your shiny new vehicle

 We use the term *car* in this book quite often, but we also mean that term to include trucks, SUVs, and other kinds of vehicles. Perhaps sticklers for proper diction would want to use the word *vehicle* instead of *car*, but the heck with them.

Avoiding the Dreaded Haggling Process

Most people dislike buying a car because they hate to negotiate. Use the Internet and you don't have to negotiate! What's more, by avoiding the bargaining process, you're likely to save yourself quite a lot of money. Most of us are very bad at negotiating for a new car, and most car salespeople are quite good at it.

Car haggling. You remember it, don't you? You sit around for hours trying to save some money — *and you're dealing with professional negotiators who know lots of ways to wheel and deal.* Don't forget that car salespeople are usually outgoing and personable and enjoy working with people. They're often essentially quite nice. But they have a job to do — a job to do on you.

Buyer's remorse

Almost everyone drives off in their new car with the nagging feeling that they could have saved quite a bit of money if they'd been more shrewd, been in less of a hurry, felt less sorry for the salesperson, or otherwise negotiated better. They're right. They probably could have saved hundreds, if not thousands, of dollars.

Car salespeople are often unfairly portrayed as only slightly more wholesome and reliable than members of Congress. Talk about defamation. Nonetheless, the seller of vehicles is a direct descendant of the horse trader.

In our culture, we have few opportunities to practice bargaining. We live in a sticker price society, and most of us don't attempt to whittle down the price of a TV any more than we would bicker with the electric company to get a lower power rate. We take a package of light bulbs up to the checkout line and never think to offer the clerk 25 cents less than the sales sticker price.

Most of us are forced to bargain only on the big-ticket prices. Because the cost of not bargaining for the price of a house or car can be thousands of dollars, most of us attempt to bargain for those items. But we do a pretty poor job of it.

You walk into a dealership and the salespeople begin immediately to "qualify" you, as they call it. Innocent questions such as "What do you do?" are far from innocent. They're figuring out how to maximize the sale. If you seem stubborn about getting the lowest price for the new car, they'll be a bit stubborn, but yield if necessary. No problem; they can probably make up that loss by jacking up the cost of your financing and giving you a low-ball price for your trade-in.

On the other hand, if you're one of those people who has no idea what the dealer's cost is for the car you're buying, but think that your trade-in is worth a lot of cash, the salesperson can handle you, too. If you focus on getting a high trade-in price, they can slip in all kinds of unnecessary costs like stripes, undercoating, "prep," upholstery guarding, rustproofing, you name it. And they can also hike the finance costs. Get it? They can raise whichever of the four main costs of buying a new car you aren't emphasizing in order to give you a "deal" on what seems to pull your chain. The four main costs are: trade-in, new car price, financing, and the "extras" (undercoating and all the rest).

And this kind of manipulation is only the tip of the selling strategy iceberg. You haven't heard *anything* yet!

Getting a blank check

The greatest thing about buying your car online is that you can avoid the negotiation phase of purchasing the car. Before you set foot on the dealer's lot, you've already researched the value of your trade-in and decided the precise money you'll pay for the new car (and the exact accessories you want), and you even have a blank check in your pocket because you got the loan from an online finance company. See Chapter 10 for details on locating online financing.

Where'd this blank check come from? You fill in a small form on the Internet, and the company sends you an answer in minutes via e-mail. If you qualify for the loan, the finance company sends you a blank check — one of us got ours the next morning via Air Express. The company tells you to fill in the check for any amount up to a maximum (it allowed several thousand more than we asked for). The check is blank because you may want to add a CD changer or something at the last minute. And the loan rates are usually excellent.

Jump In and Try Getting a Price Fast

Do you like the idea of a nice, crisp blank check arriving at your house tomorrow morning? Want to omit haggling from your next car purchase? Then briefly visit a cyber salesroom.

Throughout this book, you can find descriptions of various popular and successful online "showrooms" you can visit, with names like cars.com, carsdirect.com, autoweb.com, CarPoint, and many others. To give you an idea of what virtual salesland is like, go to carOrder (www.carorder.com) for a few minutes. To get there, follow these steps:

1. **Fire up your browser and type** www.carorder.com **into the Address text box. (If you're using Netscape, type it into the Location text box.)**

2. **Press the Enter key.**

   You arrive at the main entrance to carOrder's site, as shown in Figure 1-1.

Figure 1-1:
Go through the "glass doors" into the showroom; there's no salesperson in sight.

Notice that this site offers several features on its home page:

- Financing

- Research

- Leasing rates

- Insurance

- Order tracking

- A chat feature where you can interact with a live person — so much more efficient than the alternative

- Testimonials

- Saved specs (the "virtual garage")

- A 360-degree Exorcist-cam where you can view the entire interior of the car you're interested in

- Purchasing

- A toll-free number you can call, also presumably featuring a live person

3. Scroll down to the bottom of the home page (or press the PgDn key).

You see the other half of the home page, as shown in Figure 1-2.

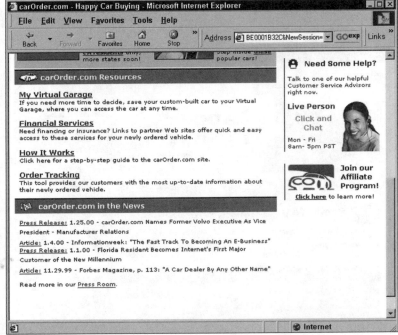

Figure 1-2:
Want to
chat online
with a living
being about
carOrder's
features?
Click the
smiling face.

4. **Click the Build It link.**

   You see the first specifications page, where you describe your location
   and the make, model, and style of the car you want, as shown in Figure
   1-3. Choose whatever car you're interested in.

5. **Click the Configure link.**

   You see the invoice price, the MSRP (manufacturer's suggested retail
   price), and the price you can pay at carOrder. You also see how much
   your monthly payment would be for a purchase or a lease.

   On this page, you can choose the interior and exterior color schemes.
   You can also choose to save this car to your "Virtual Garage" —
   that way, everything you've done is stored so that you can return to
   carOrder in the future and resume where you left off. You don't have to
   retype or reselect options when you visit the site again.

6. **Click the Pick My Options link.**

   On this page you can register yourself if you want. If you choose to register, you'll go through several pages, then resume with Step 7 when
   you've finished the registration process.

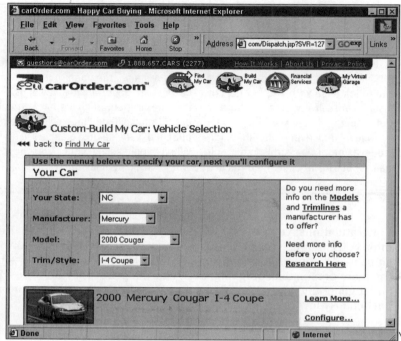

7. **Click the Continue button.**

   You're asked to fill in contact information (name, password, e-mail address, and ZIP code). The ZIP code is used to figure out local taxes and fees like vehicle registration.

8. **Fill in your contact information and click Create my Account.**

   A new page pops up asking you to specify your city and county.

9. **Choose your location and then click the Save these changes link.**

   You're sent an e-mail message confirming your account. You also see the page where options are listed, taxes and any rebates are described, and the cost of such things as the destination charge or title certificate is disclosed.

You're now registered, and you can return to the site any time you want and pick up where you left off. The car prices quoted are guaranteed for a week, but you can always return to the "garage" or "showroom" and change your specs or start a new purchase.

Chatting to be clever

carOrder is clever to provide a toll-free 800 number and live online chats. Either feature allows you to touch base with another human and to reassure yourself if you're having any doubts about leaping into the world of cyber-shopping. I believe that eventually shopping online will seem as natural as strolling through the local mall — but for now, many of us are people who need people. The Internet represents a major transition, but behaviors of the past are still important to many of us. Remember that the first automobiles back in your great-grandfather's time had a little metal gadget attached to the car just outside the driver's door. When people asked what it was for, the answer was "Why, that holds the whip."

Congratulations; you've just cybershopped for a new car! In a matter of minutes, you can receive a price quote. Try doing that in the real world of dealerships made from brick and mortar. Nothing against salespeople — many of them are personable, outgoing, even charming. But they do have a job to do, and it generally doesn't involve giving you a final price quickly or offering a particularly low price, either.

What's Down the Line Online?

One of the best things about buying and selling things on the Internet is that you can eliminate the middleman (and the money the middleman adds to the cost).

This can mean that: a factory outlet is actually the factory (not some mall that calls itself a factory outlet); that a warehouse sale actually sells stuff from a warehouse; and that "wholesale direct" is just what it says.

When buying a new car on the Internet, the middleman you eliminate is the car dealership.

Local dealers providing online quotes

Of course, there's a big difference between buying a book or shirt online and buying a truck. For one thing, the truck can't be sent by overnight FedEx.

However, the problem of distribution is being solved in several ways. Most online car-purchasing services function as dealer-referral services. You describe your wants on the Internet, and then one (or several) local dealers make offers — either sending you e-mail with price quotes or getting in touch with you over the phone.

The important differences between this approach and the traditional car purchase process are that you get price offers without having to drive around to visit different dealers and you don't have to haggle.

Dot-com distribution down the road?

Another tactic that may have a big impact in the near future is the possibility that dot-com car-selling sites may create their own network of dealerships around the country. Several online organizations are currently reported to be contacting automobile manufacturers requesting approval of dealership acquisitions. The owners of some dealerships have apparently already agreed to sell to Internet companies. Online companies face few problems raising financing — many dot-com companies are awash with cash. We wouldn't have imagined that AOL could *buy* Time-Warner!

Clearly, this trend toward online companies' ownership of local dealerships, if it develops, would shake the long-established auto sales industry to its foundations. However, the Internet has a way of reshaping almost every commercial venture — from travel agencies to booksellers. Only a couple of years ago, many people were regretting the trend where local bookstores were being put out of business by mega-stores such as Borders and Books-a-Million. Now the mega-stores tremble as online book sales increasingly eat into their bottom line. Where, oh where, will it all end?

As a result of the empowerment we customers are now getting from information we can gather on the Internet, many car dealership owners have, as the English put it, their pants in a twist.

Naturally, classic dealerships often seriously resent the intrusion of the Internet into their tried-and-true sales systems. Buyers walking into a car showroom knowing what the dealer paid or, worse, already having received a firm price have removed one of the important points of negotiation that traditionally favored the dealer. In the past, salespeople could use the price of the new car as a useful selling point. Increasingly, though, the selling price is no longer a variable that can be fiddled with during the sale.

Now the very ownership of car showrooms is perhaps in doubt. Manufacturers can refuse to award a dealership for reasons ranging from inexperience selling autos to inadequate financial backing. Manufacturers have always had broad discretion in the awarding of dealerships.

Why resist reality?

As someone wise once said, it's impractical to resist reality. And all signs point to the Internet as the wave of the future. If one or more online car-selling sites manages to set up a dealership network, you could arrange your financing, the car price, and every other element of the car purchase entirely online. If you're like most people, you would prefer not to have to undergo the tedium and strain of the sales struggle at the dealership.

The car dealership of the future may well resemble a simple warehouse rather than the glass-and-gloss showrooms of today. Here are the steps that direct online dealers can take to drive down the cost of a new car:

- Eliminate salespeople and their commissions

- Drop newspaper advertising (it costs around $300 per car!)

- Set up a warehouse in a low-cost rural area

- Avoid having to build a fancy showroom

- Stock cars on an as-needed basis (a car sitting on a dealer's lot runs up around $300 per car in finance payments before it's sold, on average)

All these moves cut the cost of a car. Choose a car online and it's driven to your door from that low-rent country warehouse sitting out there between your town and the next town. Of course, this system of cybersales does leave out the important test drive, where you see if you are actually comfortable in the real-world vehicle. But there are ways around this limitation: perhaps a trial period to see if you feel right or a simple trip down to the local traditional dealership to kick the tires and take a test drive around town.

As I describe in detail in Chapter 5, you always want to take a test drive just to ensure that you and the car are physically harmonic. But you can accomplish everything else (including saving yourself headaches, time, and money) in cyberspace.

Chapter 2

Smart Searching

• •

• •

N o other research tool has ever come close to the Internet's sheer breadth and depth of information. What's more, much of that information is in a constant state of flux. The process is similar to how the stock market continually revises itself so that it's always up to date.

This chapter shows you how to use the Internet to search for information. You can find out how to locate places where you can purchase, repair, insure, or otherwise efficiently deal with vehicles. And the way that you can best find all these things on the Internet is by using its many search engines. In this chapter, I tell you how best to use some of the best — and most popular — search engines available to scour the Web for all the information that you can possibly want about buying your very own car online.

(And while you're searching for the perfect vehicle, don't wrap yourself up so much in your quest that you forget that you can locate all kinds of other data on the Internet — expert health advice, millions of recipes, and information on any subject on earth. Finding out how to get the most out of the Internet's search engines benefits you long after you save money on your car insurance or buy that great new truck at a great price.)

Using Online Search Engines

Online information gathering nearly always begins with *search engines*. Numerous search engines are out there in cyberspace, and many of them are excellent and swift.

How search engines work

Using a search engine is generally quite easy. You type a word or phrase such as *Lincoln Town Car* into a text box and then press Enter (or click a Go or Search or similar button). Almost immediately, a list of links appears on-screen. These links are the matches (or *hits*) that take you to Internet sites containing information relevant to your search phrase. You can click any link to visit its particular site. Then, if you don't like what you see, you can just press the Backspace key (or click the Back button in your browser) to return to the list of hits and try another one.

Search engines provide hundreds (or thousands, in some cases) of hits almost instantly. How do they do it? They don't actually look all across the Internet after you press Enter to start the search. Instead, they're constantly looking, day after day, for information — some of them for years now. They build databases of links, which they continually update because Web pages are notorious for changing frequently.

Little robotlike programs known as *spiders* automatically and ceaselessly roam the Internet, sending back information to the search engine's databases (and may return information on that vintage MGB Spyder you've been searching for). After you start a search, the engine simply displays a handful of the best links from its database that relate to your search phrase.

How do the engines rank Web pages so that they know in which order to display the hits in the list of links that appears? Following are some common ranking criteria:

- How often your search word or phrase appears in the page or site. A site that uses the word *BMW* only once is less likely of interest to you than is a site that uses it 48 times.

- Where in the pages the search phrase appears. The more times that it appears near the beginning of the document, the more relevant the document is to your search.

- How popular the page is — in this case, how many other sites link to it. (Google, among others, uses this technique.)

Searching 800 million pages

An article in the journal *Nature* offers some revealing statistics about the scope of information on the Internet, which is why search engines are so vital to your quest for online info (not only for that about the automotive world but for *anything*):

✔ Approximately 800 million Web pages exist.

✔ On those pages, you find approximately 180 million images.

✔ Scientific or educational sites make up only about six percent of Internet data.

✔ Eighty-three percent of all the pages on the Web are commercial.

Nonetheless, all this information is useless unless you can access it — and can do so quickly, without needing to sift through page after page of data to find what you need. That's why, fortunately, so many search engines are available today. What's more, they're almost unbelievably rapid, and — even better — they're also free!

You're sure to find that buying a vehicle is far easier (and less expensive) if you do all your homework ahead of time. And thanks to its search engines, the Internet is now an ideal research tool for any prospective car — or truck, or motorcycle, or SUV — buyer.

Combining Engine Power

Experts calculate that even the best search engines tap into only around 15 percent of the total available pages on the Internet. If you use several different engines, however, you can boost your coverage to more than 40 percent. Other surveys report different results but agree that no search engine completely covers the entire waterfront. By combining the power of several search utilities at once, however, *meta-engines* can help automate the search process. That way, you don't need to run several engines yourself — or retype the search criteria for each different engine.

Go for GO Express Search

The *GO Network Express Search* engine is one such meta-engine that you may want to consider. It not only engages other popular engines in its search, but it also boasts some excellent features that you may not think about otherwise.

The GO Network Express Search engine is probably one of the best freebies on the Internet, at least in my view. (It's a part of the InfoSeek search-engine service.) GO offers several significant advantages over most other search engines. For one, it enables you to scroll through the hits so that you don't need to keep using the Backspace key or the Back button on your browser's toolbar to return to the hit list to click another link. In most search engines, you see a list of the hits, you click a likely link, and then you're at that site. If it's not exactly what you're looking for, you can click the Back button or press Backspace to return to the search engine's list. GO cleverly avoids this wasted time.

A second big advantage is that pages in the hit list automatically load in the background. While you're checking out one of the links, others next in the list are loading onto your computer. After you click the next link (or click GO's Next button), the next site appears on-screen right away. GO already loaded it in the expectation that you may want to view it. This thoughtful feature is most useful to people who don't yet have a high-speed Internet connection such as a cable modem or DSL.

Installing GO Network Express Search

GO Network Express Search is actually a program that you download from the Internet and install on your computer. It adds itself to your browser and puts an icon on your Windows system tray (near the clock at the bottom-right corner of your screen).

Follow these steps to download and install the GO Network Express Search engine:

1. **Access the GO Web site by typing** `express.go.com` **into the Address text box of your browser and pressing Enter.**

   You now see a page describing the Express Search engine. (By the way, if you use Netscape Navigator as your browser, the name of the text box in which you type the address is *Location* rather than Address.)

2. **Click the Download button.**

   The Windows File Download dialog box appears, asking whether you want to run or save this program.

3. **Click the Save This Program to Disk option button and then click OK.**

   The dialog box closes and a Save As dialog box appears.

4. **Choose the location on your hard drive where you want to save the exp_setupIE.exe file.**

   The exp_setupIE.exe file is the file that installs the GO Express Search engine software on your computer.

5. **Click the Save button.**

   The Save As dialog box closes, and the File Download dialog box appears.

6. **Wait until the 1.06MB file downloads onto your hard drive and then click OK to close the dialog box (if it doesn't close itself) after the download is complete.**

7. **Open Windows Explorer.**

8. **Locate the exp_setupIE.exe file in the folder in which you chose to save it in Step 4 and double-click its name.**

   The setup program runs.

9. **Follow the instructions that the GO Network Express Search engine's setup program provides to install the search engine on your computer.**

Giving Express Search a trial run

To try out Express Search, double-click the Go icon in your system tray (near the bottom-right corner of your screen, where your clock is). You see a screen similar to the one shown in Figure 2-1.

Type the phrase **new buick** into the express search's Search For text box and press Enter to start the search. You see a list of results (various Web sites that match your search phrase) within a few seconds, as shown in Figure 2-2.

Notice the information at the bottom of the express search page. It tells you which search engines are responding to your query. These statistics appear only if the program finds few hits in response to your search. You may want to make some adjustments to the engine if you don't find many hits, such as permitting a longer search time or modifying your search phrase.

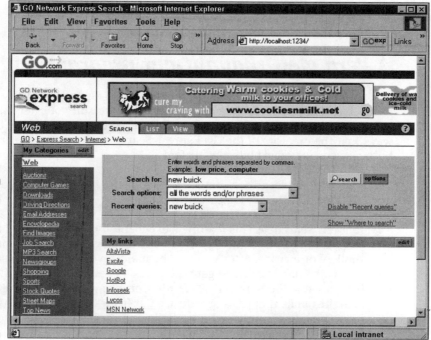

Figure 2-1:
The excellent GO Network Express Search meta-engine is off and running.

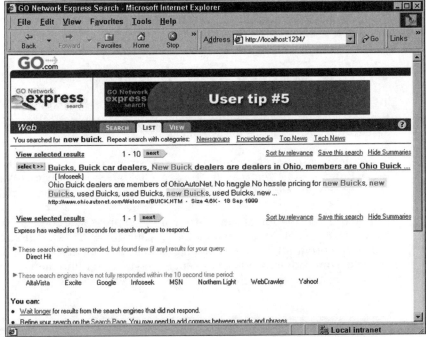

Figure 2-2:
Searching
for *New
Buick*
results in
hits such as
these in a
matter of
seconds.

A very well-thought-out program

You're likely to notice that the GO Express Search engine is nothing if not cus-
tomizable. You can adjust it in many, many ways to suit your needs. It's also
full of features that you may find useful. Take a look at some of the thoughtful
ways that the creators of the GO Express Search engine make life easier for
both novice and expert Internet surfers.

The following list describes some of the interesting features that you may
want to try out in the GO Express search utility:

✔ **Related Searches:** This feature is excellent. It provides you with alternative search terms — intelligently defined categories that you may not
think of otherwise. After you see them, however, you can quickly figure
out which one is going to get you the exact results you want. If I type **car
insurance** in the Search For text box, for example, some of the Related
Searches links that GO suggests are Car Insurance Quotes, Classic Car
Insurance, Car Insurance Rates, Collector Car Insurance, Canadian Car
Insurance, Car Insurance UK, and Insurance Rates.

✔ **Limiting the search to a category of engines:** On the left side of the main GO Network Express Search screen, you see a list of engine categories such as the following: Web, Auctions, Computer Games, Downloads, Driving Directions, E-mail Addresses, Encyclopedia, Find Images, Job Search, MP3 Search, Newsgroups, Shopping, Sports, Stock Quotes, Street Maps, Top News, Weather, White Pages, and Yellow Pages.

If you're interested in Egyptian history, for example, you can probably obtain more useful information by choosing the Encyclopedia category of engines than by searching the entire Web.

✔ **Save Searches:** If you use particular searches often, you can save them for the future by clicking the <u>Save this search</u> link.

✔ **Recent Queries:** This feature saves all the searches that you perform in a particular category. GO divides these searches by category. If you click the Encyclopedia category, for example, only searches within that category appear.

✔ **Highlighting:** This feature highlights the search terms that GO Network Express Search finds within the Web pages that it locates as a result of your query. This feature makes locating the actual paragraph or section of interest in a long document quite easy.

All in all, I think you're certain to find that downloading and experimenting with GO Network Express Search is well worth your time — especially after you see how much time it saves you in searching through the myriad pages of the Web for a great deal on a new car.

You may want to also check out another free search utility that you can download and run from your computer. Discovery (from AltaVista) not only enables you to search the Web, but it can search your hard drive as well (replacing the Windows Find utility on the Start button menu). Discovery also searches your e-mail archives, creates tree diagrams of Web sites, and highlights hits. As does GO Network Express Search, Discovery can really facilitate your online search for the perfect new or used vehicle. You can download Discovery at `www.discovery.altavista.digital.com`.

Other Engines of Note

Everyone has a favorite search engine. The GO Network Express Search engine that I describe in the preceding sections is especially powerful and well-organized and I recommend it highly. I also have good results in using Google (at `www.google.com` on the Web) and NorthernLight (at `www.northernlight.com`). Both use various kinds of intelligence to provide you with useful hits. All the engines that I mention in this chapter are also solid. Give them all a try.

The embarrassment of riches

The Internet can easily overwhelm you with a blizzard of sites that "match" your criteria. It's an embarrassment of riches. You want your search engines to cover as much of the Web as possible — this practice provides better, more accurate, and more recent data.

Typing **Arizona**, however, and getting 276,033 Web pages matching that criterion is what the French call an *embarras de richesses*.

You can't possibly read through all those matches, so the better engines rank the results in one way or another. Some do so by the site's popularity (how many other people have gone to that site, or how many other Web pages link to that site). Others rank sites by how closely the phrase in your search matches a phrase in the title (and then the body text) of a site. Other ways to rank sites exist, but a search engine's ultimately popularity depends on both the breadth of its coverage and the quality of its ranking method.

In the section "AND, OR, and NOT: Narrowing Your Searches" later in this chapter, I describe some techniques that you can use to assist the search engine in providing you with precisely the information you're after. In the following section, I take a look at a few of the most popular engines.

Everybody's favorite search engines

Many excellent search engines are available on the Web. Following are some of the most popular, in no particular order: HotBot, Go2Net (MetaCrawler), AskJeeves, MSN (Microsoft Network), Google, Yahoo!, WebCrawler, AltaVista, DirectHit, Snap, NorthernLight, Excite, Infoseek (GO), Netscape, and GoTo. (I'm leaving out a couple famous ones that I don't think are all that useful because they haven't kept up with the latest search technology.)

Different search engines have different strengths. The following list offers my own recommendations:

- For interpreting natural English questions ("Where can I find out about Buicks?"), try *AskJeeves*. It's particularly good for beginners because it's very easy to use.
- For speed and a newsgroup search feature, try *AltaVista*. (For pure newsgroup searching, however, use `www.newsgroups.langenberg.com`.)
- For speed and the sheer number of Web pages that it covers, few engines can challenge *HotBot*. It also maintains a good reputation for accuracy.
- Some search engines are famous for ranking results according to site popularity. *Google* and *NorthernLight* are two such engines.
- Meta-engines — such as *MetaCrawler*, *MetaFind*, and *GO* — provide you with results from several *other* search engines.

✔ For children, *AskJeeves For Kids* (at www.ajkids.com) is probably the easiest to use.

✔ To get the most wide-ranging (and often the most pertinent and useful) list of hits, try *InfoSeek*.

✔ *NorthernLight* is good if you come up empty after using other search engines. (It sometimes can find matches for extremely specific and rare topics, such as recipes for Albanian carrot pie.)

✔ *Yahoo!* isn't actually so much a search engine as it is a way to "drill down" for information. It organizes its sites by various categories the way that a library groups its books. Yahoo! is very popular, however, and it can prove a good place for beginners to look around.

Try various sites and see which ones you like best.

If you don't know the exact address of a Web site — the full www.whatsitsname.com — don't panic. In Microsoft Internet Explorer, you can just type the name into the Address text box and then press Enter. To locate the GoTo engine, for example, just type **GoTo** and press Enter. Explorer lists the likely sites for you in the Search panel on the left side of the browser, as shown in Figure 2-3. The default site that appears is surprisingly often the one that you want. If it's not right, try looking down the list of alternative possible matches. If you want to locate Lycos, for example, type **Lycos** in the Address text box.

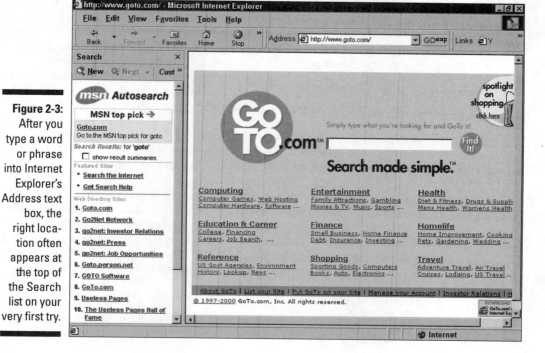

Figure 2-3: After you type a word or phrase into Internet Explorer's Address text box, the right location often appears at the top of the Search list on your very first try.

AND, OR, and NOT: Narrowing Your Searches

Don't be put off by the idea of *Boolean logic*. It's something you've always known and used — you probably just never realized that it had such a great name.

Boolean logic expresses or evaluates relationships between things primarily by using the ideas of *or*, *and*, and *not*. The statement, "Ask Jim *and* John to go with us to the beach," for example, differs from "Ask Jim *or* John to go with us to the beach."

Many search engines enable you to use Boolean expressions. You can, therefore, refine a search by using the words *and*, *or*, and *not*. Sometimes you must capitalize these terms, however, so go ahead and use *NOT* rather than *not* — just to stay on the safe side.

Bill Clinton OR Hillary, for example, returns a large number of matches (including Edmund Hillary, the first person to climb Mt. Everest; Hillary Swank, the actress; and so on).

If you don't use any of the Boolean words (*AND*, *OR*, and *NOT*), the phrase defaults to *OR* anyway. Most engines interpret the phrase *Bill Clinton OR Hillary* as the same as *Bill Clinton Hillary* or *Bill OR Clinton OR Hillary*. This kind of search phrase produces the largest number of matches.

Using the phrase *Bill Clinton AND Hillary* returns fewer hits because the matches must contain *both* Clinton and Hillary (or Bill). In other words, Edmund Hillary and Hillary Swank and any other Hillarys don't appear in the resulting list as matches (unless the text mentions the actress or explorer in connection with Clinton — pretty unlikely).

Bill Clinton NOT Hillary (or in some engines you must use *Bill Clinton AND NOT Hillary*) is an even narrower search because it eliminates any site that mentions Hillary while showing matches to Bill or Clinton.

Putting quotes around a phrase — for example, *"Bill Clinton and Hillary"* — narrows your search the most (although some engines don't permit this use of quote marks). The engine returns only those sites that include the *exact* phrase. You can use the phrase *"President's salary,"* for example, and get a list of only those sites that tell the tale about Mr. Clinton's paycheck. After I ran this particular search, I got the following information at my fingertips:

- ✔ The President's salary is $200,000 per year, plus expense allowance.

- ✔ The Vice President receives a salary of $171,500.

More than I make, plus I don't get any expense allowance. But a president does work harder — I must give him that.

You can also chain several Boolean phrases or quoted phrases together, as in the following example:

"John Lennon" *AND* **"Paul McCartney"** *AND NOT* **Yoko** *OR* **Ono**

Some engines use the + symbol rather than the word *AND* (Lennon + McCartney + Starr + Harrison). Similarly, they use the – symbol instead of the word *NOT* (Lennon–McCartney). Some engines also require you to separate search words by using commas. Each engine explains its format, although most work in a simple, straightforward manner, as I describe earlier in this chapter.

Chapter 3

Tapping Into the Online Owner's Network

· ·

In This Chapter

▶ Locating useful newsgroups

▶ Asking experts for their opinion

▶ Posting response messages

▶ Searching newsgroup messages

▶ Avoiding spam

▶ Trying a chat group

· ·

*Y*ou know what they say in the movie business: Word of mouth makes or breaks a film, no matter how much money the studio spends to promote it. Autos are a far bigger purchase than a movie ticket, but the opinion of friends and acquaintances can have an impact on any buying decision.

Many professional reviewers have to avoid blunt comments about lousy autos because they write for magazines or other media that depend on advertising from the manufacturers of those lousy autos. Sure, nearly all media maintain a "wall" between their editorial and advertising staffs. But the softening of criticism goes on all the time. *It's rotten* is replaced with *it can be improved*. Most of us learn to read between the lines when reading commercial reviews.

No such interpretation is required when listening to the angry owner of a lemon or the proud possessor of a first-rate machine. And thanks to the Internet, you don't have to rely on a small, skewed sample of opinions held by your friends and neighbors. Go online and you can tap into the candid views of thousands of people who are willing to tell you exactly what they think about that car you're considering. In this chapter, we show you how to talk to car owners and other experts and how to find information about specific topics that interest you.

People are often even more blunt online than they are in person. Something about typing your thoughts anonymously into a keyboard feels safe. It's less personal, less dangerous than talking directly to live people who may disagree with you, have a short temper, or carry a concealed weapon. Nobody has ever been shot dead for typing something inflammatory into their computer. (As far as we know.)

So for reasons both economic and cybernetic, you'll find a wide range of blunt opinions online. The drawback is that you cannot always know how qualified these people are — do they really know much about cars, or are they just grumpy or euphoric by nature? Yet in spite of this inherent massive subjectivism, you can learn a lot online about the various strengths and weaknesses of various models. If most people in a newsgroup or chat room are wild with praise for the new Saturn, that says something good about the car.

Word of mouth should not, of course, be your only source of information. We've filled this book with a variety of useful sources — professional reviews, car tests, government reports, dealers, insurance crash stats, even the manufacturers themselves. But the opinions of the man or woman in the street should factor into any intelligent buying decision. No other source is as subjective, but no other source is as frank, either.

You can find two primary sources of owner opinions online — newsgroups and chat rooms. We'll start with the largest and most active collection of online personal commentary, the newsgroups devoted to car talk in all its variety. You'll find that newsgroups are probably more useful. Chat groups, while live, tend to quickly descend into dating games, and worse. Nobody knows why.

Locating the Right Newsgroup

A *newsgroup* is an ongoing discussion about a single, usually quite narrow, topic. For example, you can participate in newsgroups devoted to Mexican cooking, the technical aspects of DVD, the culture of the island of Malta, and, of course, Hondas, Saturns, Volvos, and most any other car you can think of.

Newsgroups work like electronic bulletin boards. People "post" messages on the newsgroup that you can read and respond to if you want. Each original message and the various responses to it are grouped together into what's called a *thread*. This grouping makes it easy for you to look through the topics under discussion in the newsgroup and then read through only those threads that interest you.

Connecting to the experts

One of the best benefits of looking through newsgroups is that experts are often prowling around. You can ask a highly technical question and many times get an excellent answer.

For example, I recently saw the following message on the Ford Focus newsgroup. The header of the message was *Torque Curve for SPI engine vs. Zetec* (a *header* is a short description of the topic of the thread — think of the header as the headline) and the message ran:

> *Does anyone know the difference in shapes of the torque curve between the two engines? Since I am most interested in low-end torque, I was wondering if the SPI was comparable to the Zetec at low rpm.*
>
> *Are there any other notable differences between the engines except for the double camshaft in the Zetec?*

Several people responded and offered solid answers, and that's a technical question if ever there was one.

So if you start a new thread by asking *Does anyone have any serious complaints about the Focus?* you're likely to get an eyeful of opinions ranging from disgruntled ex-Ford salespeople to knowledgeable master mechanics. Take everything with a grain of salt, but do consider the answers you get to your questions and the opinions you read in the various threads. Collectively, the replies in a thread often represent an honest, accurate commentary.

Finding newsgroups

Locating newsgroups is easy. In this section, we demonstrate how to use Microsoft's e-mail and newsreader utility, Outlook Express, to search for and subscribe to as many newsgroups as you wish. After you subscribe to a newsgroup, you can read the messages posted by others and post your own original messages or reply to existing messages. Other newsreaders such as the Newsgroups function in Netscape Communicator have subscription features that work similarly to those in Outlook Express.

Follow these steps to join (or subscribe to) the Mercedes newsgroup — you have expensive tastes, don't you?

1. **Start Outlook Express and log on to the Internet.**

   You see either the Outlook Express Inbox or the main Outlook Express page, depending on which options you chose when you set up the program.

2. **Choose Tools⇨Newsgroups or press Ctrl+W.**

You see the Newsgroup Subscriptions dialog box, as shown in Figure 3-1.

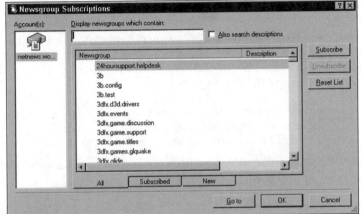

Figure 3-1:
Use this
dialog box
to locate
newsgroups
that interest
you.

If this is the first time you've ever used the newsgroup feature, you'll see the Downloading dialog box shown in Figure 3-2.

Figure 3-2:
The first
time you try
to look at
newgroups,
Outlook
Express is
getting the
latest list of
all available
newsgroups.

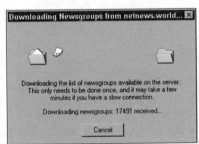

As you can see in Figure 3-2, there are more than 17,000 newsgroups you can subscribe to. You can also force Outlook Express to reload the latest list of newsgroups at any time by clicking the Reset List button in the Newsgroup Subscriptions dialog box.

From time to time when you switch to the Newsgroup feature in Outlook Express (as you do in Step 2), a message is displayed telling you that new newsgroups have been created since you last visited. You are asked if you want to see the latest newsgroups and, if you agree, their names are down loaded and you can then choose to subscribe to any that are of interest to you.

3. **Type the word *Mercedes* into the Display Newsgroups which Contain text box.**

As you type each letter of the word *Mercedes*, you'll see the newsgroups that match your entry, parallel to your typing. For example, when you type in the first letter *m,* you see all newsgroups beginning with *m*. Then, when you type in the following *e,* you see all newsgroups that begin with *me*. This continues until you see only alt.auto.mercedes and perhaps one or two other newsgroups with the word *mercedes* in their titles.

4. **Double-click alt.auto.mercedes in the Newsgroup Subscriptions dialog box.**

A small icon appears next to alt.auto.mercedes in the list box. This icon signals that you have now subscribed to this newsgroup.

5. **Click the OK button.**

The Newsgroup Subscriptions dialog box closes and you're back in Outlook Express, as shown in Figure 3-3.

6. **If you don't see the Folders pane on the left side of the main Outlook Express window (as shown in Figure 3-3), choose View⇨Layout and click the Folder Bar check box.**

7. **If a small dash (–) icon appears next to the Newsgroups folder in the Folders pane, click that icon to open the folder and display the list of newsgroups to which you've subscribed.**

Notice the number in blue in parentheses next to each newsgroup. It tells you the number of messages in that newsgroup that you have not yet read. If you want to know the total number of messages in the news-group, look at the status bar on the bottom of the window. It tells you the number of messages you've downloaded, the number unread, and the total number of messages in this newsgroup.

8. **Click alt.auto.mercedes in the Folders pane.**

You see the messages in the newsgroup.

9. **Click any message to view that message's contents or click any + icon next to a *thread header* (the title of a multiple-message conversation) to expand the header.**

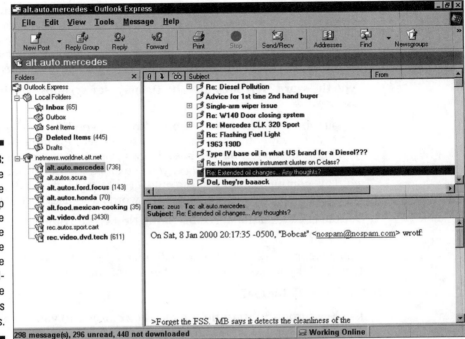

Figure 3-3:
Click the
name of the
newsgroup
in the
Folders pane
to see the
message
titles (head-
ers) and the
messages
themselves.

Whether you need to expand headers, whether you see the currently selected message, how many messages are downloaded each time you view a newsgroup, and other variables are determined by the settings you choose in the View⇨Layout and Tools⇨Options menus.

The number of messages (or, indeed, personal e-mail messages) that you can download or view depends. As new messages are added to a newsgroup, older messages are discarded to conserve storage space on the servers that your ISP maintains. More than 20,000 newsgroups, each containing hundreds of messages, exist — you can imagine the storage problems. In any case, from time to time you'll click a message — perhaps one with a topic such as "Overboost solenoid valves" that you're dying to know more about. But when you click to try to view it, you're told that the message is no longer available. No problem. Just click the New Post button on the Outlook Explorer toolbar (or choose File⇨New⇨News Message) and ask your question about over-boost solenoid valves or whatever is bothering you. Someone will likely answer that the turbo doesn't need replacing if the valve is the only problem.

Replying to messages

If you want to reply to the currently selected message in an existing thread, click the Reply Group button on the Newsgroup toolbar, shown in Figure 3-4. (If you don't see the Newsgroup toolbar, right-click the menu bar and then click Toolbar from the pop-up menu that appears to make the toolbar visible.) To start a new thread, click the New Post button. To send e-mail to the author of the currently selected post, click the Reply button. (This button should be labeled *E-mail* rather than *Reply*, but you just have to live with this quirk.) Sending e-mail allows you to respond privately to the author of the message — your e-mail message is not displayed in the newsgroup for others to see. Finally, if you want to forward a message over e-mail to a third party, click the Forward button.

Figure 3-4:
The main
Newsgroup
toolbar in
Outlook
Express.

Searching for topics

Assume that you're interested in seeing all messages on a particular topic. Easy. Click the Find button on the Outlook Explorer newsgroup toolbar. The Find Message dialog box appears. In the Message text box, type the topic you're interested in, perhaps **overboost solenoid valves.** Click the Find Now button, and all messages containing that phrase are displayed. Double-click any of the displayed messages to read them.

Avoiding spam

You may have heard of crawlers, bots, spiders, or other creatures that tirelessly and constantly roam the Internet gathering e-mail addresses to send back to their masters.

The masters of these nasty beasts are spammers — people who e-mail millions of messages each day, hoping to get a .01 percent response to their offers as they selfishly clog the Internet lines and slow things down for the rest of us. A response of .01 percent is plenty. Imagine 100 people a day sending *you* $25.

How *alternative* becomes *mainstream*

Originally, the *alt* designation was supposed to signify that a newsgroup was an *alternative* newsgroup — freewheeling, independent, unofficial, anything-goes. Alt was used in the same sense that people used to use *alternative newspaper* to describe free spirits who didn't toe the corporate line or yield to pressure from politicians, wealthy people, or advertisers. However, just as the idea of alternative news became mainstream over time, the *alt* designation has been so widely used that it now has little

meaning. This phenomenon — the larger culture assimilating, and blurring, distinctions — is hardly surprising. It happens all the time. For instance, most Internet addresses ending with *.com* indicate commercial enterprises, to distinguish them from .gov (government), .edu (academic), and so on. However, these days everyone and their grandmother is using .com in their Internet address. It's become more generic and widespread.

But how, you ask, can they even get a .01 percent response to their absurd come-ons? When I worked for a magazine publisher, the circulation director explained mass mailing to us. Some people are lonely, some are confused, some have lost their minds entirely, and another group simply wants to be used. Mass mailings harvest their return largely from this unhappy crowd.

But it's worth it. Lonely, confused, mad, or masochistic — they sometimes still have Visa cards that work. Most of us understand what's going on when we get e-mail like this:

Richard Mansfield Has Won $10,000,000,000,000!!!!!!!!!!! (. . .it will say on your check if you win our contest).

But other poor souls (about .01 percent, it turns out) don't understand, and they send money to make their dreams come true. Many state governments are currently taking legal action against this kind of stuff when it happens via junk mail. So far, Internet users aren't protected.

When you first installed Windows, you probably used the Internet Connection Wizard, which asked for your Internet news e-mail address. And, trusting soul that you are, you typed in your true e-mail address.

Rethink this move. True, by including your e-mail address, you make it possible for other newsgroup readers to reply to your messages via e-mail rather than posting a reply on the newsgroup.

But putting your true e-mail address onto public newsgroups also attracts those roaming spiders like a fly batting against a web. (Spiders travel the web, get it?) As a result, you're likely to start receiving more junk mail than you previously did.

I urge you to provide a fake e-mail address here. A strange name like *Z* will do. *Z* or *Zorro* or some other obvious name confounds spiders, but also alerts others on the newsgroup that they need not try to e-mail you. They can always post a public reply to your newsgroup message. However, your fake name must conform to Internet punctuation. It cannot simply be *Zorro*. It must be *Zorro@anygroup.net* or some variation.

Alternatively, if you do want to let newsgroup members send you e-mail, here's a trick you can use. Change your e-mail address (as described in the following section), but don't disguise it totally. For example, if your real e-mail address is John12@aol.com, type it in (in Step 4 in the following section) as, for example, John12hotdog@aol.com. Then, at the end of every message you post to a newsgroup, add this line to clue the other newsgroup members as to how they can send you e-mail:

If you want to send me e-mail, remove the hotdog.

Disguising your e-mail address

Follow these steps to change your newsgroup e-mail address:

1. **Choose Tools⇨Accounts while looking at a newsgroup in Outlook Express.**

   The Internet Accounts dialog box appears.

2. **Click your active newsgroup account. (It's probably already selected; if so, you can skip this step.)**

   Your newsgroup account is selected (highlighted).

3. **Click the Properties button.**

   The Properties dialog box appears.

4. **Change the Email Address text box from your actual e-mail address to some synonym, such as *Turnblad@Tracy.net* or *MmeDeFarge@hairnet.net*.**

5. **Click OK.**

   The Properties dialog box closes.

6. **Click Close.**

   The Internet Accounts dialog box closes.

One further warning

One more point while we're on the subject of avoiding spam. Spammers nearly always write something like this in their messages: "If you do not want future mailings from us, reply to this address. . . ." You may think that spammers are considerate to offer to remove you from their mailings. But always remember that spammers, like telemarketers, are, by definition, *in*considerate.

Trust me: *Never ever* reply to any spam e-mail! Replying identifies you as a live, active e-mail account. (And, worse, a person innocent enough to trust spammers.) Your address is then transferred to the special verified chump database that is sold at a premium to spammers. This golden list contains only those people trusting enough to react to spam. Expect a serious increase in your spam activity. At that point, the only cure is to change your e-mail address with your Internet Service Provider and notify all your correspondents to update their address books with your new address.

Chatting Them Up

A source of car-buying information that's similar to newsgroup messages is the online chat. The main difference is that a chat is in real time — the other people are sitting at their computers at the same time you are, and you can get instant feedback to questions you pose or comments you make.

However, the interaction in a chat room has two primary weaknesses for those serious about researching a car:

- ✔ Fewer — often far fewer — people are available to read your message (and usually the message will not be preserved for future viewing, though there are exceptions — see the Tip later in this section).

- ✔ Chat rooms all too often degenerate into singles bar behavior or worse. No matter what their purported topic, a chat room is frequently viewed as a trolling ground for meeting people rather than exchanging information.

Where do you find chats? Try searching in AOL or use your favorite search engine such as Yahoo! — search for the words *car chat*.

Here are some chat locations to get you started. Just type these addresses into the Address text box of your Internet browser and press the Enter key:

```
www.auctioncarsonline.com/chat.htm
www.c5-corvette.com/C5_Chat.htm
www.classicar.com/chatsforums/chat/
www.yocar.com/chat/chatmain.tpl
```

Some newsgroup message boards and chat room transcripts are archived. For example, several years' worth of recipes and discussions are archived on the Big Green Egg Web site, a gathering place for barbecue fans (`biggreenegg.com/wwwboard/wwwboard.shtml`). To locate archived messages about automobiles, search for *car chat archive* or similar terms such as *auto* or *chevy*.

Chapter 4

Basic Research: Getting Online Reports

. . . .

In This Chapter

▶ Basing your research on sound information

▶ Finding the pros who know online

▶ Employing car magazines' online sites

▶ Checking out some offbeat sites

▶ Discovering who you can trust on the Internet

. . . .

*Y*ou want to be a cunning consumer, a savvy seller, or a brainy buyer, don't you? The Internet is by far the greatest research tool ever devised. It changes constantly — so its information remains up-to-date. The Internet is also massive. One of the better search engines, Northern Light, maintains 208 million pages of data. Other engines claim in excess of 300 million pages. And to make this mass of information useful, several excellent search engines can guide you to what you're looking for intelligently and rapidly (see Chapter 2).

This chapter explores some of the most reliable sources of objective information about cars that you can locate online: respected automobile critics; famous test labs and reviewers, such as Consumer Reports and Edmund's; government reports; and court rulings. The information you'll gather from these sources is invaluable when you're deciding which car is best for you. Chapter 3 explores how to gather word-of-mouth opinions; this chapter covers how to collect research from the professionals.

Reviewing Car Publications

Advertising people sit around for weeks thinking up the perfect phrase: *Where's the beef?*, *Don't squeeze the Charmin,* and the now-trademarked word used by Wal-Mart, *Always*. You wouldn't believe how much money is spent on a 30-second car commercial designed to convince you that you can not only drive a particular SUV up Mount Everest, but that you'll also look breathtakingly beautiful doing it.

This advertising is fake, and on some level, everyone knows it's fake. It's your job to dig beneath appearances and hype to find out as much as you can about the real value of the auto you're thinking of buying. To find this information, you should look for reports, reviews, and driving tests. Some of the best sources of objective information are independent car publications. These sources conduct extensive tests on automobiles, exploring everything from turning radius to radio tuning.

Reading Consumer Reports online

Give Consumer Reports (www.consumerreports.org) credit for some of the very best car reviews available anywhere. The Consumer Reports (CR) site, shown in Figure 4-1, includes special features such as tips for buying a new car, a leasing quiz, a description of their testing process and their test track, and used car advice. However, CR's specialty is its famous auto reports. Alas, they're not free. But in this case, you do get what you pay for.

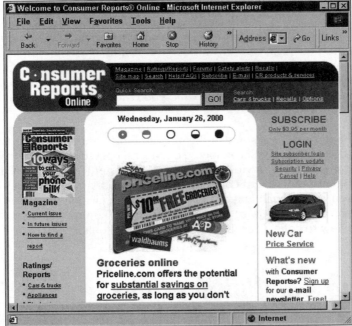

Figure 4-1: Consumer Reports' automobile tests and ratings are famous for their objectivity and thoroughness.

For $12 ($10 per additional report requested at the same time) you get: the invoice price (the dealer cost); the typical sticker price (manufacturer's suggested retail price); additional costs of the factory-installed options; any rebates or incentives; CR's recommendations about what optional equipment you should purchase; CR's safety ratings analysis; similar cars you may want to consider; and suggestions on negotiating the best deal for this car.

It's $12 well spent. Free price quotes are available elsewhere online (see Chapter 6), but they don't provide some of the additional information you get from CR. For $24 a year, you can look at everything CR tests for that whole year.

Consumer's Union, the publisher of Consumer Reports, has its own distinct Web site at www.consumer.org.

This site specializes in governmental actions, recalls, court cases, environmental issues, and similar topics. For instance, at the time of this writing, a series of interesting articles titled "The Risk of Rollover in Some Sport-Utility Vehicles and Consumer Union's Testing for Such Risks" appears there. These reports are free.

Checking Out Edmund's

Featuring the three famous magazines — New Cars Prices & Reviews, Used Cars Prices & Reviews, and Used Cars & Trucks Prices & Ratings — this site also offers a wide variety of information, including road tests, vividly written reviews, Town Hall (online discussion groups on all aspects of vehicle ownership), the "deal of the month," and a useful New Car Buyer's Workbook (available for $9.95; specific to the auto you're interested in). Many people consider the Edmund's reviews to be among the most reliable and thorough; find them at www.edmunds.com.

Pricing from Pace

The Pace Buyer's Guides have been published since 1974. Now they're online at www.carprice.com.

You'll find free price information and other auto data at this Web site. If pricing is your main interest, this site is extremely comprehensive. However, it also includes a variety of additional information, including calculators, recalls, rebates, insurance information, warranty information, tips, negotiation suggestions, motorcycle information, and other data. This is an efficient, quick, easy-to-navigate, and valuable site. Give it a look.

Intelligence from IntelliChoice

Since 1987, IntelliChoice has been publishing auto reports in the award-winning *The Complete Car Cost Guide*. Find it online at www.intellichoice.com.

You'll be able to compare vehicles side by side, and a Spanish language version is available. You can also learn about current rebates and incentives, try the finance calculator to plan your purchase intelligently, find out all about pre-owned vehicles, and much more. IntelliChoice, an independent research firm, also announces its IntelliChoice awards annually. The firm projects that these vehicles will be the best values based on factors including price, depreciation (which can vary considerably among makes and models), repairs, financing, and maintenance. Historical data are used to create projections for a five-year period.

Autos from AutoByTel

Best known as an online car-buying service, AutoByTel is also a good source of automobile and truck reviews. You'll likely be pleased with the accuracy and depth of their coverage at www.auto-reviews.com/reviews/autobytel.htm.

Finding Online Pricing

Your goal in researching pricing online should be to come to a fair and equitable price. You want to give the dealer and salesman a fair profit, but you don't want to lose your shirt. The feeling that you may end up paying too much for a car is what can make the buying process uncomfortable.

Luckily, you can get pretty accurate information about how much automobiles cost online. The more you find out about what the dealer is paying for the car, the better prepared you are to give the dealer a fair return on investment that doesn't cramp your pocketbook.

Prices and more from Kelley Blue Book

Kelley Blue Book is a venerable, respected institution that's now available online. Here you can find out the invoice price that the dealer pays for each type of vehicle, along with the cost of various options.

And Kelley Blue Book serves as a one-stop resource for automobile information as well. From within the site, you can find insurance quotes, vehicle reliability data, and some of the best, most comprehensive automotive data at www.kbb.com.

Using the Black Book

Available since 1955, the Black Book specializes in providing "the latest wholesale prices direct from the auction lanes." Its publishers claim that one of its great strengths is up-to-the-minute pricing.

Sale prices are checked at auctions daily, then added to the Black Book database. A complicated process is used to determine price, taking into account such effects on an auction as weather, current popularity of the model, quantity of a given model that was for sale at the auction, and other factors.

This service is quite similar to the highly responsive price shifts that occur on the stock market, where values move virtually hourly.

Check out their site at www.blackbook.net.

Checking Out Car Magazines Online

Online you'll find both sites for traditional print magazines, such as Car and Driver, and also Internet-only magazines. Both varieties can be helpful when you're gathering information.

Car and Driver

At www.caranddriver.com, you can find tests, reports, reviews, buyer's guides, archives, lists of the 10 best cars and 100 best roads, concept cars, shows, and various other information from the well-known publisher.

Motor Trend Online

Data from this publisher is yours to peruse online at www.motortrend.com/bl/bl_f.html. Reviews, news, links and other features are yours for the clicking. Note that this site, and the Road and Track site, are both particularly aimed at the enthusiast market. Some everyday cars are ignored. Also, you'll find limited information if you're a non-subscriber.

Road and Track

Yet another magazine publisher creates a presence online. Find it at `www.auto-reviews.com/reviews/road_and_track.htm`.

Auto Week

This site offers some fast-breaking news because it's a weekly publication. It also includes respected reviews about driving, with consumer commentary. Try it at `www.autoweek.com`.

Other magazines online

We mention the sites of several famous car magazines, but many more are online. Some are sites offering electronic versions of their newsstand paper counterparts. Others are all-electronic— no paper involved

Online-only magazines are often referred to as *zines*. One such zine is AutoZine. AutoZine (`home.netvigator.com/~europa`) is an interesting site that publishes independent reports (no ads, and, as the author says, ". . .no income. In other words, I do it just for fun."). It covers a wide variety of vehicles. Established in September 1997, it includes photos, ratings, reviews, specs, and additional information.

Use your favorite search engine to locate any of the following online magazines that interest you: Autofacts; The Autonaut; Autopedia; All Auto Online; American Automobile Association; Autoweek Online; CarMag; CarSound Magazine; C.A.R.S. Unlimited; Car Talk with Tom and Ray; Eric Anderson's Car Crazy; Kit Car Buyers Guide; Popular Mechanics Auto; Top Gear Magazine; TURBO Magazine; Turbozine; Vette Vues Magazine; WheelBase; and World of Wheels.

Microsoft's CarPoint

Launched in 1995, CarPoint is one of the oldest, largest, and most comprehensive sources of information about cars on the Internet. The site gets over 3 million unique visitors every month. (Uniqueness is important because some Web sites inflate their activity by counting every visitor, even repeat connections.) Find CarPoint at `carpoint.msn.com/home/New.asp`, as you can see in Figure 4-2.

Go to CarPoint to find substantial information, including

- ✔ Classifieds.

- ✔ Troubleshooting.

- ✔ Automotive reviews.

- ✔ Specs.

- ✔ Prices.

- ✔ Safety reports. You'll find ratings based on more than 250,000 incident reports annually from the Automotive Information System's Identifix program.

- ✔ Reliability ratings.

- ✔ Buying services for both new and used cars with no-haggle quotes.

- ✔ A Side-by-Side Compare feature that lets you contrast the specs of two new or used cars.

- ✔ A payment calculator to let you figure loan payments, total cost, interest rate, loan duration, and down payment. CarPoint offers the current interest rates from more than 2,700 lending institutions.

- ✔ A power search where you type in your desired cost and type of vehicle, and models meeting your criteria are listed for you.

Keeping track of your car's maintenance

Also, take a look at the Personal Auto Page, where you can track your auto's maintenance and repairs, as well as see the current value of your vehicle. Microsoft says that 500,000 consumers have used this feature alone. With the Personal Auto Page, you can see when seasonal maintenance is needed, when it's time for an oil change, and so on. You can even request to be sent e-mail when scheduled maintenance is required or if any reports or recalls have been issued relating to your vehicle. And Microsoft says that soon you'll be able to use a pricing utility that will automatically estimate service and repair costs, comparing various options for you.

Microsoft's MSN claims that CarPoint has more than 3,500 affiliated dealers nationwide and that hits to this site each month trigger more than 145,000 leads, resulting in more than $600 million in car sales. That's an impressive e-commerce activity level. CarPoint can give you data on more than 10,000 models and boasts listings of more than 100,000 used (or *pre-owned,* as dealers prefer to call them) cars.

Try the Exorcist 360-degree head twist

One cool tool you can find at CarPoint is the 360-degree video, as shown in Figure 4-3. You're able to "walk around" the outside of many new car models and also sit inside and "twist" your head in a complete circle, just like Linda Blair, and see *all* the interior details.

100 top ten lists

Would you enjoy seeing what the experts consider the ten best vehicles in many different categories? Want to know which cars are most often stolen or considered the best of the best by Consumer Reports? CarPoint has collected 100 top ten lists at carpoint.msn.com/WindowShopping.asp.

Among the top ten lists you'll find are:

- Gen Xers' Top Ten (J.D. Power and Associates list of automotive preferences of 20- to 34-year-olds)
- AAA Picks Its Top Cars (the famous awards given in 12 classes)
- CarPoint's Top Ten (the cars that were selected as CarPoint's New-Car Buying Service 1999 Top Ten)
- IntelliChoice's Best Overall Values (used vehicles rated Best Overall Value by IntelliChoice, Inc.)

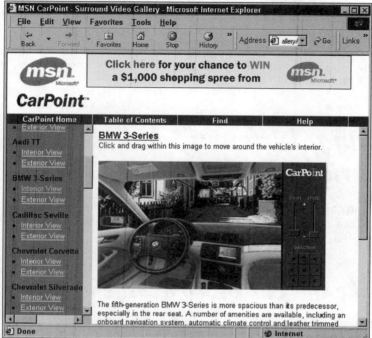

Figure 4-3:
You control
the zoom
level, the
speed, and
the direction
when you
"sit" inside
a car and
watch a
360-degree
video.

✔ Get the Most Bang for Your Buck (the most affordable horsepower powerhorses)

✔ Top Ten Towing Rigs (thinking of getting into hauling?)

✔ High Rollers' Top Ten Cars (if money is no object)

✔ Consumer Reports picks their "Best of the Best"

✔ Top Ten Fuel Misers (the ten thriftiest cars)

✔ America's Most Loved New Cars (in 15 categories)

✔ Most Popular Foreign Cars

✔ America's Top Ten Bestsellers (hint: they're trucks!)

✔ America's Most Stolen (the cars that thieves love most)

✔ Car and Driver's 10 Best

✔ Four-Wheel-Drive Systems

You can find these and many more, including convertibles, muscle cars, cars priced over $100,000, SUVs, vans, and trucks.

AuHo? "The Automobiles Homepage"

For discussions, archives, photos, specs, and links to reviews (CarPoint, Edmunds) on a wide variety of makes and models, check out AuHo? at `www.auho.com/98cars/FordExplorer.html`.

Interesting, Different, and a Couple of Downright Funky Sites

Just in case you're one of those who likes to go off the beaten path to round out your more conventional research, here is a handful of intriguing suggestions that may be just what you're looking for.

Take the Car-O-Scope psychological test

Do you want to know if you are driving, or considering, a car that harmonizes with your personality? Don't fight your own character by trying to fit into a vehicle that is just plain wrong for you. The Car-O-Scope test promises to "help you determine if you're driving a car that fits your psychographic profile." Try it at `cartalk.cars.com/Survey/Results/Psychographics`.

Visit the manufacturers themselves

You can, of course, risk visiting the Web sites of the automobile manufacturers. You'll find a good deal of sizzle, as you might imagine, and no biting, or even very objective, reports. But for completeness of specifications and glamorous color photos, nothing beats the home site of a car's own maker. If you've already made up your mind about the car you want to buy, look up its manufacturer's description so you can feel good about the great machine you're about to own. The creators of the car do their best to put their product on a pedestal.

Ford Motors

See Ford products at `www.fordvehicles.com`.

General Motors

General Motors has a Web site at `www.gm.com`.

Try GM's Buypower feature, as shown in Figure 4-4. It includes research, a way to specify which features you want in a car, dealers' inventories, and allows you to schedule a test drive and ask a dealer for their best price (better also check out the other sources of "best prices" as well).

Gillet Vertigos, Solectrias, Twikes, and 1,000 others

Do you want to visit a less mainstream site than Ford or GM? Interested in something like a Gillet Vertigo, a Solectria, or a Twike?

Find the Web sites, and 800 numbers, of everything from Subaru to Steyr-Daimler-Puch at `autopedia.com/html/MfgSites.html`.

If you're French. . .

Respected French-Canadian journalist Denis Duquet has been writing about cars for 20 years, or as he puts it: "Denis Duquet est chroniqueur automobile depuis 20 ans. Professeur d'histoire ancienne venu au journalisme automobile par un curieux concours de circonstances, il en a fait son unique gagne pain depuis 1982." If you understood that, find out what else he has to say at `www.duquet.com/`.

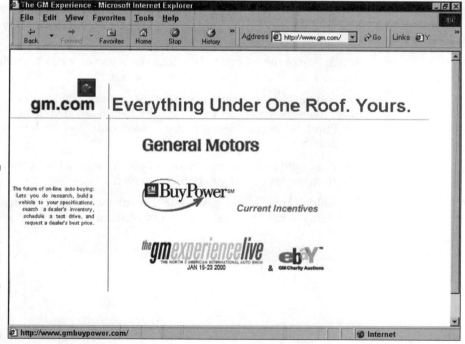

Figure 4-4: The General Motors site's BuyPower feature calls itself the "future of online auto buying."

About.com

This Web site is a good source of links to other sites for all kinds of information, discussions, books, awards, repair histories, museums, parts, dealers, and loads of other topics of interest to car buyers and owners. The information at this site itself is broader than it is deep, but it's deepening all the time. Give it a try: `cars.about.com/autos/cars`.

Car Secrets Revealed

Car Secrets Revealed is said to be among the most-visited automotive sites on the Internet, and you'll find issues raised here that are rarely covered elsewhere. Do you feel you're getting ripped off on repairs or insurance? Are you worried that the new car you're about to buy may turn out to be a lemon? Automotive consultant Corey Rudl's book may be just what you're looking for. You can get a taste of the book online at `www.igs.net/carsecrets`.

The site sells the book, but you may want to explore other intriguing topics here, including these teaser descriptions the site provides of some of the points covered:

✔ One thing you *must* do so you'll never buy a lemon.

✔ Learn how every dealer gets a secret rebate on every car they sell . . . their most guarded secret is revealed.

✔ Which day of the month to buy/lease gets you an extra $400 discount *instantly* (no, it is not the last day of the month).

✔ Are you paying the lowest car price? No, you're not! You'll be shown the exact dialogue you must use to get the best deal on your new or used car. Purchase in confidence that you have obtained the lowest price possible.

✔ Discover hidden bogus extras and double-charging tricks that can cost you thousands . . . and you'll never know it.

✔ The hidden truth about government seizure auctions (you know, drug lord cars) — can you really buy a Corvette for $200 as they advertise?

Who do you trust?

In this chapter — as all throughout this book — you read about many different Web sites. Some of them are selling services or products. How can you know which sites are reliable and which may cause you grief?

A number of utilities online ask you to describe the product that you're looking for and then search the Web for all merchants selling that item. The utility then provides a list of those merchants' names, ordered by price. MySimon is one of the most famous comparison shopper utilities: www.mysimon.com.

If you compare online merchandise, you'll often find quite a range of prices. But the lowest price isn't always going to make you a happy camper if

✔ The merchandise is inferior

✔ The shipping and handling is costly

✔ It takes two months for the online merchant to get around to sending you what you paid for

The easiest solution is to only deal with e-commerce sites that have a good reputation in the real world. For example, if you've had a good experience buying things from Wal-Mart, you can assume that you'll have an equally good experience purchasing from the Wal-Mart online site.

Is the Better Business Bureau online? Not yet. But there are a couple of other resources. First, you can check out BizRate at www.bizrate.com.

BizRate contacts a sample of shoppers at each e-commerce site it rates and then compiles their responses to questions about their satisfaction. Each site is then rated (up to five stars) and given an on-time index as well. Some ratings are also provided by BizRate's staff.

When you select a product on BizRate, you get a thorough narrative description of the merchant involved, plus a five-star ranking for each of the following consumer-satisfaction categories:

✔ Ease of ordering

✔ Product selection

✔ Product information

✔ Price

✔ Web site

✔ On-time delivery

✔ Product representation

✔ Customer support

✔ Privacy policies

✔ Shipping and handling

An alternative to BizRate is Consumer Reports (www.consumerreports.org), which focuses on products but also rates merchants as well. Consumer Reports charges a $3.95 monthly fee for unlimited online access to its massive, and continuing, consumer research. Also look at the Consumer Reports site for their e-ratings, which provide customer satisfaction ratings for more than 50 of the most popular e-commerce organizations.

Got a Lemon?

A lemon is a new vehicle that has one or more serious defects, but these defects are not found in all vehicles of this model (therefore, there will be no recall to correct the problem). Perhaps somebody forgot to secure the oil pan on your brand new car, so after a few miles the engine began to chew itself to pieces. What can you do?

A site named Autopedia boasts a number of valuable resources, including a complete listing of the lemon laws by state. If you suspect that you bought a lemon, here's where you can begin the process of getting a fair shake: `autopedia.com/html/HotLinks_Lemon.html`.

Part II
Narrowing the Search: Finding the Right Car for You

In this part . . .

The chapters here in Part II help you narrow down your search for your dream car and give you plenty of pointers aimed at making you not only a savvy but a decisive car buyer — someone who knows just what *you* want and not what the dealer wants you to want. After all, your goal is to find the perfect car for your needs at the best price for your budget — not to help a crafty car salesperson put his kids through college on your buck.

In Chapter 5, therefore, we walk you hand-in-hand through the initial steps in the process of buying a car online. Then, in Chapter 6, we show you how to use the Internet to determine the fair market price of a new or used car — what you want to insist on paying *before* a dealer tacks on a trunkload of unnecessary fees. Chapter 7 helps you narrow down your choices through online research so that you know what kind of car you want as well as how much you're willing to pay long before you head to a local dealership. We even tell you in Chapter 8 how you the Internet can help you test-drive a vehicle before you ever sit down behind the wheel to do the actual driving. And in Chapter 9, we cover some sources for online safety tips that help you keep that car operating safely out on the actual highway.

Chapter 5

The First Steps in Buying a Car Online

*1*n this chapter, I assume that you've already done some of your preliminary online research, checking out the wide variety of buying options at your disposal thanks to the Internet. After you narrow down your choice a bit, basing your decisions on price, style, safety, and whatever other criteria matter to you, you can then take the first steps toward actually making your purchase.

You need at this point to think about several important questions. Do you want a new or used car? How do you choose and approach a dealer? What are your financing options? How can you avoid getting hit with "dealer-prep" or other last-minute extra costs? Should you consider an extended warranty? You don't need to make final decisions about many of these topics just yet, but they need to become part of your thinking. Consider this chapter, therefore, an introductory overview of topics that I cover in depth in later chapters. First, I look at one of the most fundamental issues: Is your car going to be new or used?

Choosing Between Brand-New and "Previously Enjoyed"

Car dealers employ all kinds of euphemisms for used cars: "pre-owned," "certified," "previously enjoyed," "golden opportunity" — anything but *used*. And yet used vehicles are often among some of the best, smartest auto purchases that you can make. In this section, I consider your options in purchasing a used car, starting with your worries.

Maybe, for example, that used car you're considering was found floating around for a couple of days in a river, but someone cleaned it up. Maybe it flipped down an embankment and was totaled, but then someone pounded back into shape with rubber hammers and repainted it. Did someone rewind the odometer at some point? Did it ever burst out in flames? How can you know for sure whether you're getting a good deal on such a vehicle or getting taken to the cleaners?

You can get answers to these questions via Carfax (at `www.carfax.com`). Carfax can provide you with complete reports on all used cars for a two-month period. The two-month subscription is only $19.95, and these reports can alert you to a variety of potential problems: flood damage, salvage history, odometer fraud, major accidents, and other such problems. You can have your questions and concerns. Was the car ever totaled? Did it ever catch fire? How many times has the car changed hands? Just enter the Vehicle Identification Number (VIN) and your ZIP code at the Carfax site. (You can locate a car's VIN on its dashboard, on the insurance or title documents, from the dealer, or online through services such as Autobytel.com and Autoweb.com.) And if you're selling a used car, the Carfax report can serve as a valuable selling tool that demonstrates the integrity of your own car.

The eternal question: Money

People never seem to resolve certain disputes: renting versus owning a house; leasing versus buying a car; buying a new versus a used car . . . and whether the toilet paper hangs from the back or front of the roll.

You may think, as most do, that buying a used car is cheaper than buying a new car. Actually, the two can often turn out quite close in overall cost per year. Don't forget that a used car is likely to require higher maintenance, command a higher interest rate on a loan, and have less resale value if you trade it in. These factors are easy to overlook if you merely consider how much cash you're shelling out at the dealer's showroom (and in the monthly payments) for two otherwise comparable vehicles. And don't forget the hidden factors: Driving a four-year-old car is, for example, less impressive to the neighbors. It's also more annoying because things keep breaking down and you must either do without the radio, the heater, or some other feature — or spend the time and money to repair it.

Calculating your own new versus used costs

AOL maintains a set of auto-buying calculators that can help you figure out various loan options. You can find these calculators at the following Web address:

```
www.aol.com/webcenters/autos/home.adp
```

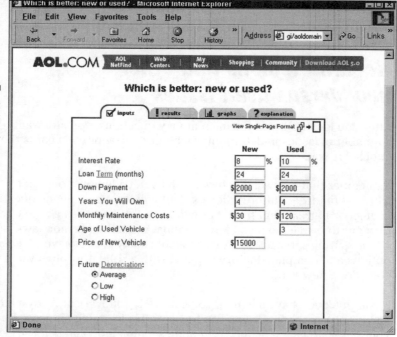

Figure 5-1:
Use this handy AOL calculator to estimate the total costs (not the merely obvious costs) of purchasing a new versus a used vehicle.

The AOL calculators can help you answer the following additional questions:

✔ How expensive of a car can you afford?

✔ Should you buy or lease?

✔ What is your down payment going to be?

✔ What are your monthly payments going to run?

✔ Should you finance or pay cash up front?

✔ Should you consider getting a home-equity loan (and using it to pay for your car with cash up front) instead of getting a car loan at a higher effective interest rate? (Interest on a home-equity loan is the only tax-deductible interest available to most people.)

✔ How long of a loan period do you want?

✔ What about a cash rebate versus dealer-financing? Sometimes you have to calculate the better deal for you between a manufacturer's rebate and a special low finance rate.

I deal in-depth with these various issues throughout this book, but the AOL calculators are invaluable tools if you're close to a final decision and are ready to plug in actual numbers.

Reeking lemons and other new versus used issues

After you look coldly at the main money questions, you still want to consider a number of issues in determining whether a new or used car is the best choice for you.

Remember that a new car *is* new . . . if it's not a lemon, you don't need to worry about frequent breakdowns. And you have no nagging question about neglect or ill-treatment from a previous owner. And even if a new car does turn out to be a lemon, you have a fallback position: Lemon laws can assist you in getting satisfaction. You can also usually expect several leasing options and complete factory support with a solid, thorough warranty if you consider a new car.

If you think you have a lemon, you can try to follow Dear Abby's advice and just make lemonade. Or you can be proactive by going online to find out if your car is, in fact, a lemon. Your state's lemon laws can be accessed at Autopedia. Just go to the following Web address:

```
autopedia.com/html/HotLinks_Lemon.html
```

As Autopedia announces on its home page, "Welcome to the most comprehensive Lemon Law information site on the Internet. Winner of Yahoo Internet Life's 4-Star Award, with complete coverage of all Lemon Law Statutes in all 50 states."

Know your rights. Fight, fight, fight! Don't take it anymore!

That special smell

Whenever you compare the benefits of buying a new versus a used car, one of the first qualities some people consider is the smell — that unmistakable new-car smell. Rumors that dealers use spray cans containing air fresheners of that smell aside, most people find something wonderful about a brand-new car's odor. (A used car may also have an odor, but you usually can't tell what it is. Maybe nasty mud from a river?)

For some people, however, the decision is already made: Buying something that strangers have already used is simply out of the question. And who can blame them? There's something special about owning a brand new car with all the latest goodies and a full warranty. If you possess the must-buy-a-new-car mindset — and the money to indulge it — skip to the section "Test-Driving in Real Time."

Other considerations

Used cars have their advantages: You have a much lower initial cash outlay, as well as lower monthly payments. That huge first-year depreciation hit was already absorbed by the poor chump who bought the car new. And used cars don't exhibit that strong, artificial new-car smell, although they may give off other smells that you can't identify.

For an even greater, in-depth discussion of all the considerations in buying a new car, see Chapter 12; for exhaustive coverage of the issues that buying a used car involves, see Chapter 13.

Finding a Dealer

Whenever you're ready to buy, you ideally want to find a dealer near enough to your home that you don't experience any inconvenience if you need to take the car back in for maintenance. Just about every large dealer has a Web site — you should visit a few, as most describe the services the dealership offers. Check also with the Better Business Bureau and ask around to see what kind of a reputation the dealer has with ordinary people.

Finally, check out the policies of the dealership's service department. It may be important to you, for example, that the service department provides a shuttle service to get you to work after you drop off your car in the morning and then pick you up at the end of the day. If so, make sure that you know whether this service is available before you settle on a certain dealership to make your purchase.

Test-Driving in Real Time

As great as the Internet is for research, for timeliness, and for its depth of information, you simply must get off your chair and actually drive the car you're considering. No virtual reality substitute exists (yet) that can replace getting the total feel of the actual car on a road.

In previous chapters in this book so far, I tell you how to listen to the opinions of other owners in newsgroups or chat rooms; I also tell you how to conduct comparisons by using various online resources such as Consumer Reports and Edmund's reviews. In the preceding sections of this chapter, I show you methods of calculating whether to get a new or used car. After you think carefully about these and many other issues, you're likely to narrow down your search for a vehicle to one or two models. At that point, you need to actually sit down in the driver's seat and go for a spin.

What seems to me to be a solid suspension with good, tight steering may well come across to you as a bumpy ride that requires a wrestling match to parallel park the car. So instead of simply following my recommendations, expert as they may be (ahem!), you want to go to a local dealer and start your own relationship with a salesperson as soon as possible.

I suggest that you form such a relationship relatively early in your quest because you may well return to this same dealer to buy your car. But during the test drive phase, you want to establish a couple things with your contact at that dealer. Tell the salesperson that you're researching your purchase on the Internet and that you aren't buying anything today; make sure that you add, however, that you do intend to ask for that salesperson by name if you decide to return to this dealership to buy. This tactic may head off some of the more dramatic sales tactics you may otherwise face during a test drive.

Another major point: Concentrate during your test on getting the feel of the car. Does it suit your physical needs? (The new Volkswagen Beetle, for example, has a headspace limitation in the rear seat — a fact that you must consider if you have a couple of really tall basketball-playing teenagers.) If the salesman is distracting you from experiencing and feeling the car, say so. Ask whether you can just focus on the driving experience at this point and talk later. Some dealers even permit customers to take test drives alone!

Finally, make sure that you parallel park and that you drive the car on all kinds of roads (bumpy, curvy, hilly, freeway, and wherever else you're likely to use this vehicle). In other words, put the machine through its paces. After all, you want to make sure it can handle all the driving conditions that it will be subjected to if you ultimately buy it.

Getting the Cash for Your Car

After you decide on a car, you must figure out how to pay for it. Chapter 10 goes into this topic systematically, but I consider it briefly here, too.

Rule #1: Try to secure your financing *before* you haggle over the actual price of the car you want. Some of the nicest buildings in your town are the banks. Why? Because lending money can be a very lucrative endeavor. Auto dealers, too, understand that they may not make much on the actual sales price, but they can indirectly make up for it with a dealer-friendly financing agreement.

You can generally expect that the more the car you're buying costs and the better your credit history, the lower the interest rate you will be able to get. So you want to obtain a copy of your credit report to ensure that all the information contained in it is accurate. If you find any errors in the credit report, you want to contest them immediately. (Surprise – credit ratings *can* contain errors.) You can get a free credit report (if you sign up for a trial membership in the CreditCheck Monitoring Service) at FreeCreditReport.Com (www.freecreditreport.com).

You can also pay $7.95 for a report from Experian, or pay $29.95 for a merged triple-source report from three major credit bureaus: Equifax, Trans Union, and Experian. These reports are available at QSpace (www.qspace.com).

As is the case with other aspects of buying a car, you want to try various lending sources to comparison shop for the best deal. If you belong to a credit union, see what its best deal is. Try your bank. Head online and visit LendingTree.Com (www.lendingtree.com) and PeopleFirst.Com (www.peoplefirst.com). Ask the dealership what it can offer. You might even want to consider a home-equity loan so that you can possibly deduct the interest on that loan from your taxes; bear in mind, though, that with a home-equity loan, you risk losing your home if you default on the loan.

Beware of Sudden, Last-Minute Surprise Costs

Most people are so used to sales taxes that they tend to accept odd, additional charges on almost any purchase as normal. You buy a radio at Radio Shack. It costs $30, according to its price tag. At the checkout, however, you owe $32.10. But you don't bat an eye because you understand that the store almost always tacks the tax onto any purchase that you make.

Similarly, figuring out just what *shipping and handling* ("S&H") means if you try to buy something online or through a catalog can often prove confusing. Something very small or lightweight can cost a lot to have shipped to you. Over time, though, you just get used to the retailer adding on such extra costs whenever you buy something.

Tacking on extra charges is rampant in America. You expect it these days. But to avoid a last-minute surprise in buying a car, insist on getting the dealer's best price, *including all charges,* before you agree to the deal.

Refuse to accept any dealer's last-minute attempt to tack on any extra costs for ADP (additional dealer profits) or ADM (additional dealer markups), a "dealer prep," a "market adjustment," or any "jack-up boosters." And believe it or not, all these items (except the last one, which I made up) are real.

Some dealers claim to give you their best price, but then, just as you're ready to sign the contract and drive the car home (and you're probably in love with it by that time), they casually mention that, of course, you also owe them the modest ADP, ADM, dealer prep, or whatever they're calling this extra fee. Such charges, however, simply amount to additional dealer profit — and your loss.

Many dealers and salespeople are, of course, fine, honest, and direct individuals. Others are highly adept at shifting things around and care little about integrity. (In this section, I'm talking about those who fall in the second category and not the good, honest people.)

Remember, too, that some car salespeople practice their more questionable "skills" on customers; many of them practically go to school to learn how to vague out, slide around, fog, and otherwise work psychological ploys to get money out of you. You, however, didn't go to school to learn how to buy a car (although this book can serve as a good substitute for such formal training).

Many salespeople are willing to do whatever's necessary to get their hands in your wallet. They'd twirl around in their chair or set fire to your shoe if such ploys could get them extra money. If you object to an ADP charge, the salesperson may look at your wife or significant other with a slight smirk or a raised eyebrow as if to say, "Are you with this cheapskate?" If you offer less than the suggested retail price, some salespeople may even start yelling at you. But often that smirk alone does the trick. You don't want to appear as if you don't know that an ADP is "always" part of the cost. You don't want to seem cheap.

Well, just go ahead and seem cheap. Refuse any extra charges that show up at the last minute — no matter what the salesperson calls them — after you already ask for and agree on a price with the dealer up front.

Many people, on the other hand, pay whatever the dealer asks them to pay. They never haggle; they don't know what the car is worth; and they have more dollars than sense. They haven't read this book or any other book like it. They're the big spenders, and they make the dealership thrive and the salespeople's commission fat. Such folks consider bargaining beneath them, unpleasant, and vulgar. Don't be one of these people.

Another group of buyers is somewhat more savvy and willing to engage in some haggling. But they still agree to dealer prep, undercoating, sealant, or rustproofing costs or otherwise don't get the best possible deal. Stay out of this group, too.

The best group (the one in which you want to count yourself) comes armed with enough smarts and information to get the lowest price possible. The dealership doesn't get as much of money from these people as they do from those in the other two groups. If you place yourself in such company, you're likely to find the salespeople smirking at you. But for my money, getting smirked at to save $800 is just fine with me.

Warranties and Service Contracts

These days, the most common new-car warranty lasts for 36 months or 36,000 miles, whichever comes first. This kind of warranty covers almost everything, except such items as tires that usually require more frequent replacement. Warranty information on all new-car models can be found at most of the major car-buying sites, such as CarPoint (www.carpoint.com) and cars.com (www.cars.com).

Your problem is to decide whether to extend the original warranty by purchasing what's usually known as a *service contract* (or *extended warranty*). Generally speaking, you don't want one of these extensions. You may notice that whenever you buy a DVD player, a washing machine, or some other electronic item or appliance, the salesperson usually asks whether you want an extended warranty. Does the salesperson offer you this option because he's your friend and wants the best for you? Think again. Salespeople make lots of money on these "insurance" policies. So do car dealers. Unless you get *very* good coverage for a reasonable price, avoid the extended warranty cost. The dealers do their homework. The odds, as they almost always do, favor the house. (In other words, you generally lose money on such "deals.")

Insurance against fire damage to your house or against huge medical expenses or a liability lawsuit — these kinds of major insurance offer you rational and valuable protection. They can protect you from being wiped out financially in a disaster, and the cost of those kinds of insurance is generally quite reasonable. Nothing that's likely to fail in your new automobile, on the other hand, is likely to destroy you financially. So consider any extended warranty that a dealer offers you strictly on its merits. If you can get thorough coverage for a good price, so much the better. It may be worth your consideration. If not — and that's usually the case — don't.

Chapter 6

Dealer Prep: Researching the Best Price and Other Necessary Homework

In This Chapter

▶ Finding good sources of price quotes online

▶ Locating coupons and rebates (for the careful shopper)

▶ Finding a good local dealer

Car buyers are becoming more knowledgeable all the time. A CNW Marketing/Research data quote in a recent issue of *USA Today* indicates that the average discount off the sticker price for new cars was 5.1 percent in 1985. It leapt to 11.3 percent in 1999. People are finding out the dealer's cost for the vehicle before they enter the showroom and negotiating the price upward from there. (In the past, the reverse was true. People started at the sticker price and worked their way down.)

The average actual selling price for a car (with a $20,000 sticker price, for example), was $18,980 in 1985 and $17,740 in 1999. The popularity of the car affects how deep a discount you can try for. Discounts on wildly popular SUVs and full-sized pickups, for example, averaged only around 7.7 percent off the sticker price in 1999, but discounts on sports cars averaged 19.1 percent.

This chapter is about dealer prep — some preparations that *you* want to make before going to a car dealer. Assume that you've seen an ad online or in the paper and you like the price that it quotes. Now, arm yourself for your visit to the dealer. Use the Internet to find out what this vehicle cost the dealer. If you do go to the dealer right away, consider it just a scouting mission. Make a friend among the salespeople and take a look around, maybe take a test drive or two, but read the rest of this book before actually signing on the dotted line.

The first step is getting an accurate dealer cost for the vehicle you're thinking about. As usual, you want to comparison shop, even among online price quote sources. Get a quote from several reliable Internet services. They're (usually) free. They're (generally) objective. And they're well worth your time to obtain. You can walk into the dealership and know precisely what you should pay for the car. Imagine, for example, that you want to buy a 2000 Lincoln. We show you how to price such a vehicle by using a number of online resources in the following sections of this chapter.

If you're like Henry Kissinger — master negotiator, lone cowboy, and otherwise fine, fine deal-maker — skip this section. You can just march right into a car dealer and have the dealer pay *you* to take a shiny new Porsche off his hands. (Make sure that you add the buyer-prep and buyer-profit fees to your take.)

If you're not a powerhouse haggler — if the whole idea of bargaining makes you nervous — you may want to check out the referral services that we also describe in this chapter. (You get a no-further-negotiation best price; you call the special noncommission contact at the dealership; the contact fills out the paperwork while you're on your way; and after you arrive, you simply provide your signature several times and drive off in your new car.)

Pricing Vehicles Online

One of the best ways to prepare yourself before going to a dealer is to get price quotes for the vehicles that interest you from any of several online sources. In the following sections, we describe some of these online resources and give you a few tips on how best to use them in your dealer-prep work.

Finding a price at Autoweb

To use Autoweb — one of the better sites for accurate pricing information — to find out the price you should pay for a new car (and even take steps toward an actual purchase), follow these steps:

1. **Go to the Autoweb Web site by typing** www.autoweb.com **in the Address text box of your browser.**

   The Autoweb home page appears, as shown in Figure 6-1.

2. **Click the New Autos link under the Research heading at the top of the left column on the Autoweb home page.**

   You access a page where you can specify the make and, optionally, a price range and style (SUV, sports car, and so on) for the vehicle that you want (see Figure 6-2).

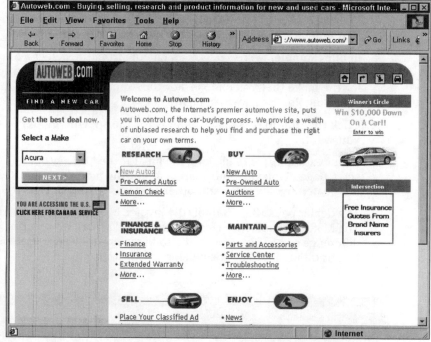

Figure 6-1:
Start your
search for
auto price
quotes
on the
Autoweb
home page.

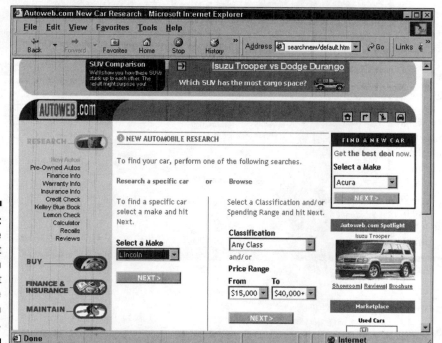

Figure 6-2:
Choose the
vehicle that
you want in
the Select
a Make
drop-down
list box.

3. **Click the down-pointing arrow next to the Select a Make drop-down list box and select the make of the vehicle that you want from the list that appears; then click the Next button under the list box.**

   In our example, we're selecting a Lincoln from the Select a Make list box. A list appears displaying the various models that are currently available for the make that you choose. For the example, the list is of the available 2000 Lincolns, as shown in Figure 6-3.

4. **Click the link in this list of models for the specific model of car that you want.**

   In our example, we're clicking the link for the '00 Continental. You now see a page displaying information about the model you chose, including the dealer invoice price and other costs, as shown in Figure 6-4.

   The dealer pays $36,103 total (the invoice cost plus a destination charge). The MSRP (manufacturer's suggested retail price), however, is $38,880, a difference of $2,777. Be prepared to bargain within this difference if you go to a traditional (offline) dealership.

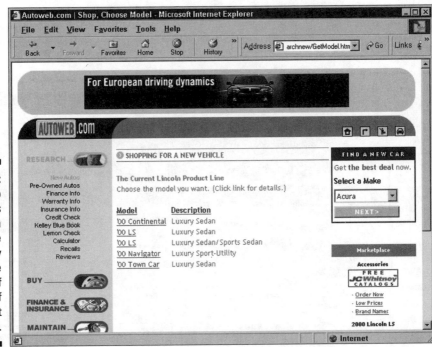

Figure 6-3: Autoweb provides you with a list of all the currently available models of the make of car that you want.

Figure 6-4:
The results of your price search are in. The particular model shown here costs the dealer $35,408, plus a $695 destination charge.

5. Click the Buy button.

You can now click check boxes to indicate which, if any, of the available options you want — phone, CD player, or power sunroof, in the example of the 2000 Continental. You also choose exterior and interior color schemes and any series (model), as shown in Figure 6-5. (In this example, the only series available for the 2000 Lincoln Continental is the sedan.)

6. After you choose your options, click the Next button.

You go to the Autoweb page where you can fill in contact information, payment information (cash, finance, or lease), how quickly you want to accomplish this transaction (two days, one week, a month), and whether you have a trade-in. You can also request a free insurance quote for the car. (See Figure 6-6.)

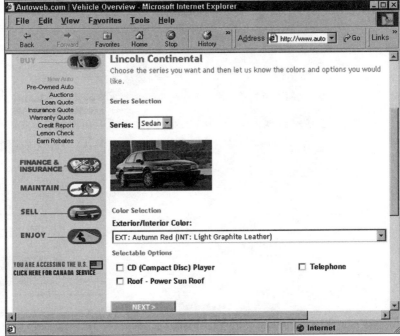

Figure 6-5:
You specify options and color schemes on this page of the Autoweb site.

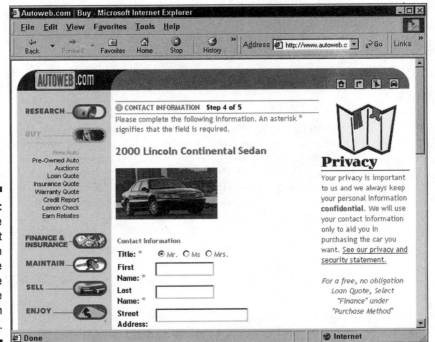

Figure 6-6:
You provide your contact information on this page if you're buying the car from Autoweb.

7. **Fill in the requested information and click the Next button.**

   The confirmation page appears, informing you of any Autoweb.com deal-ers in your area. If none are in your area, the confirmation page tells you that Autoweb is sending your request to carOrder.com, as shown in Figure 6-7. This organization provides you with pricing and availability data. If you agree to buy the vehicle, the company delivers it to your home or office at no charge.

   If more than one dealer in your area has the car that interests you, you can request quotes from all of them. Always comparison shop whenever you can. Remember that for now, you're using the Internet to get an accurate price, then going to a local dealership to do a bit of haggling. In the future, though, it's likely that complete vehical purchasing will become more common — from start to finish — on the Internet itself.

   If you agree to the price at the dealership and are ready to close the deal, you probably meet with a fleet manager (who doesn't pressure you because he's not on commission). The sale should go very smoothly for you. In fact, the sale is already a done deal by the time that you go to the dealer — all you need to do is sign the forms.

8. **If you're asking for an insurance quote, click Next to see your options for getting responses from several insurers.**

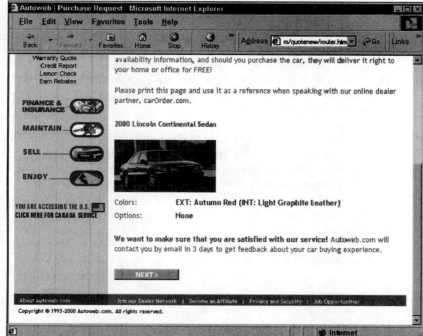

Figure 6-7:
Autoweb
gives you
confirmation
of your
request for
a quote on
this car.

Finding other online pricing sources

Take the time to comparison shop by getting price quotes from other solid sites in addition to Autoweb. The following list describes several such sites:

- AutoVantage (www.autovantage.com)
- CarPrices (www.carprices.com)
- Consumer Reports (www.consumerreports.org)
- Edmund's (www.edmunds.com)

Some of these sites charge a fee, while others provide prices quotes for free. But you always want to get quotes from more than one source. We don't have the space in this chapter to take you step by step through the process of getting quotes from each of these sources, but these sites are generally well-designed and you can expect to experience little or no trouble in navigating them.

Comparing apples to apples

We tried pricing the 2000 Lincoln Continental sedan that we use as an example in the section "Finding a price at Autoweb," earlier in this chapter, at AutoVantage. We ended up with a quote of $35,408 for the dealer cost (somewhat less than that at Autoweb) and a $38,880 manufacturer's suggested retail price (the same price that Autoweb quotes). Prices vary, so you really want to try several sources and, as we keep hammering away, *comparison shop*. Remember that the lowest price isn't always the best deal. Sometimes you get a better result overall by considering other elements of the sale: extras, interest on the loan, and so on.

What's more, some price-quote Internet sources are more specific than others about the model that interests you. Simply asking for a quote on a 2000 Lincoln, for example, doesn't differentiate between the various models and styles that Lincoln offers, which the following list names:

- Continental
- LS Shift
- LS Automatic
- LS V6
- LS V8

> ✔ Navigator
>
> ✔ Town Car, Cartier
>
> ✔ Town Car, Executive
>
> ✔ Town Car, Signature

The moral: Make sure that you get quotes for the exact car that you want if you access the various Web sites that offer price quotes.

Using Sam's Club's services

Another good resource for new car purchases is the Web site for the Sam's Club Auto Program (www.samsclub.com). You can get quotes there and also find dealers who belong to the program, but you must be a member of Sam's Club to use its features. In addition, you can determine the value of your trade-in, read vehicle reviews, find out about warranties and financing, and even get RVs and boats at this Web site.

The service is free. You submit a questionnaire to www.samsclubauto. com/Home.asp. The data that you provide on the questionnaire then goes to the nearest dealer who sells you the auto you request. The dealer must be a member of the program, and the Sam's Club Auto Program must specifically select each dealer, basing the decision on the club's CSI (customer-satisfaction index), the dealer's selection of vehicles, and the dealer's agreement to offer low prices and refrain from haggling. Dealers pay an advertising fee to belong to the program.

Checking Out Coupon City at CoolSavings

Various rebates are available, but you must know about them to get the cash. Many price quote sites alert you about rebates, but you can find other kinds of savings. The Web offers a cool site known as CoolSavings — and it's not just for cars. You visit it, find coupons, print them on your printer, and use them. The coupons available at the site do often include vehicle coupons, so you want to see what the site's offering. You may not get a $2,000 rebate offer on a car, but you still may end up getting a free pair of binoculars. (Binoculars? Sure — if you need a pair, why not get them for free? Check it out.)

To use CoolSavings, follow these steps:

1. **Go to the CoolSavings Web site by typing** `www.coolsavings.com` **in the Address text box of your browser.**

    You see a welcome page and a form to fill out, as shown in Figure 6-8.

2. **Fill in the form with the information that it requests and click Submit.**

    A second form appears, asking for some information on your personal situation, as shown in Figure 6-9. You need to answer only those questions that display an asterisk, but unless you're the head of the CIA or a senator, go ahead and cooperate. (You're unlikely to discover later that foreign agents are using this information to spy on your life, don't you think?) And if you do cooperate, you get more coupons. And more coupons equals more savings. Plus CoolSavings promises to keep everything confidential.

3. **Fill out the second form and then click the I'm Done Here button (unless you want to add a second person to this account — and if so, click the Add Shoppers button instead).**

    A list of free stuff appears for your hungry little consumer eyes to peruse, as shown in Figure 6-10.

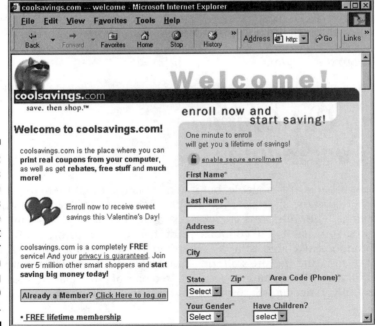

Figure 6-8: Fill in this form at the CoolSavings Web site and get coupons for bargains on everything from cars to baby stuff.

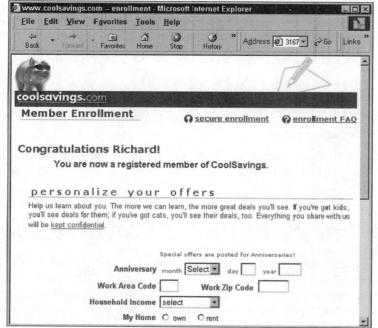

Figure 6-9:
This
CoolSavings
form asks
for personal
information
so that you
can receive
more
coupons.

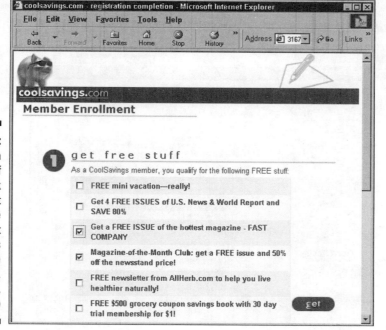

Figure 6-10:
You can
click any of
these check
boxes to get
the free
stuff that
CoolSavings
lists. (Notice
the pig logo.
Appropriate,
huh?)

4. **Click the check boxes next to the items that you want to receive (for free!) and then click the Get button (to actually *get* the free stuff that you request).**

5. **Click the Enter button to go into the CoolSavings site itself.**

   You now see all the bargains that you can access from the CoolSavings site, including other sites such as AutoVantage, as shown in Figure 6-11.

6. **Click a category in the Browse list of links to locate offers in that particular category.**

   For the purposes of this book, select the <u>Automotive</u> link. You then see the list of CoolSavings' automobile-related offers, as shown in Figure 6-12.

Getting Car Prices from CarPrices.com

As you may guess from its name, you can get price quotes from the CarPrices.com Web site (at `www.carprices.com`). Go there and you see a home page similar to the one shown in Figure 6-13. The following sections describe what you can do and what information you can find on this Web site.

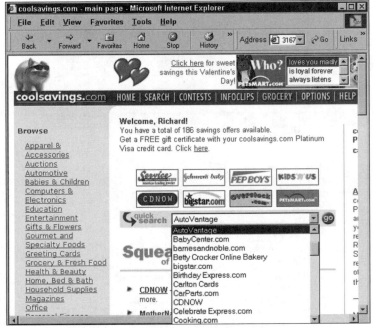

Figure 6-11:
At the main
CoolSavings
page, you
can choose
a category
in which to
browse for
bargains or
pick a
specific
Web site
from the
Quick
Search list.

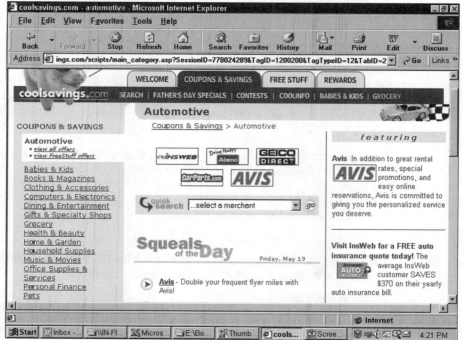

Figure 6-12:
Look at the list of offers that you can access after choosing a Browse category on the CoolSavings main page and then choosing any that interest you.

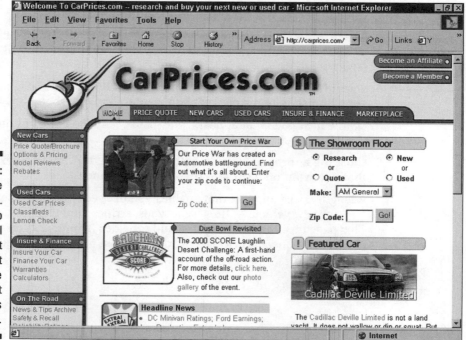

Figure 6-13:
The CarPrices. com Web site is well named, but you can get much more than just price quotes there.

Starting a Local Price War

Along with prices, reviews, rebate info, insurance, financing, warranties, and other data, you can also use CarPrices.com's Start Your Own Price War feature. Type your ZIP code in the text box, click Go, and see what happens. (*Note:* At the time of this writing, this service is available only for San Diegans, but we expect it to go national soon, perhaps even by the time that you're reading this book.)

You can try the demo version of the Price War before taking the full plunge. To experience a demonstration Price War, follow these steps:

1. **Go to the CarPrices.com site by typing** www.carprices.com **in the Address text box of your browser.**

   You see the CarPrices.com home page (refer to Figure 6-13).

2. **Type your ZIP code in the text box under the Start Your Own Price War area and then click the Go button next to the text box.**

   You see a page briefly describing the Price War feature and testimonials from happy Price War users.

3. **Click the <u>Click here to test out a demo version of the Price War</u> link at the bottom of the page.**

   You see a preview page explaining how the Price War works.

4. **Click the Start The Price War Demo button.**

   The first step (of three) in the Price War procedure is to specify the make, model, year, and style of the car that you want to buy, as shown in Figure 6-14.

5. **Select from the appropriate drop-down list boxes the make, model, year, and style of the car that you want to buy and then click Continue.**

   On the next page that appears, you can specify the colors of the car that you want, as shown in Figure 6-15.

6. **Click the appropriate radio buttons for the exterior and interior colors that you want on a car and then click Continue.**

   A lengthy page appears that enables you to specify all possible options on your new vehicle — tires, seat types, stripes, and many other extras. This page describes each option and provides its price. If you select any of these options, CarPrices.com adds the cost to the price it quotes for the car.

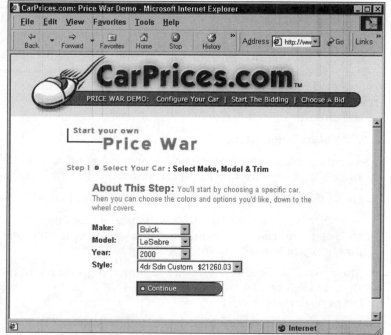

Figure 6-14:
The first step in using CarPrices. com's Price War feature is choosing the specific car that you want to purchase.

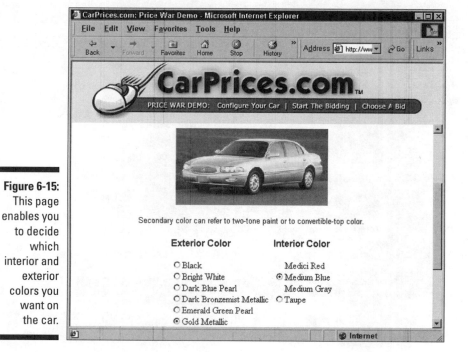

Figure 6-15:
This page enables you to decide which interior and exterior colors you want on the car.

7. **Select the options that you want for your car, if any, and click Confirm Options.**

   You next see a list of the options that you select in Step 7. You can modify the options at this point or start the actual Price War. A brief description of the Price War feature appears on this page, as follows: "We get honest, reputable dealers to bid against each other for the sale of this car. Each dealer offers the lowest price they can. You just sit back and choose."

8. **Click Start The Bidding.**

   A contact information page appears for you fill in data about yourself. You also specify how quickly that you want to buy this car.

9. **Fill in the information that the page requests and click Continue.**

   The Price War now officially begins. It lasts one business day and usually ends at 4 p.m. You receive an e-mail message after the bidding is over that tells you to look at a Web site to see the bids.

   After your Price War is over, you see something similar to the results shown in Figure 6-16, where each bid — #1, #2 and #3 — represents a different dealer's best offer.

Figure 6-16:
The Price War ends, as you can see from the results in this demo version. Choose the bid that you like best.

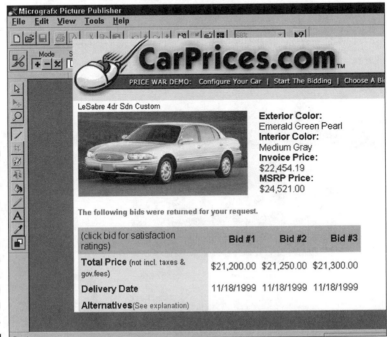

Locating a Local Dealer

It's possible that you might be able to get good pricing information from your local dealer, online. At the very least, you can probably view their price quotes, and compare them with the other sources of good price quotes described in this chapter.

To find the Web site of your local dealer or other online information about local dealers, look at the bottoms of their ads in the classifieds of your local paper. As is true of most other savvy merchants, auto dealers usually include the address of their Internet sites right in their ads. (If a dealer doesn't include a URL in the ad, perhaps he doesn't yet recognize the effect of the Internet on modern commerce.)

Contacting the NADA for dealer information

You can also locate local dealers by contacting the National Automobile Dealers Association (NADA) at www.nada.org on the Web.

Follow these steps to locate a dealer near you by using the NADA Dealer Locator engine:

1. **Go to the NADA home page by typing** www.nada.org **in the Address text box of your browser.**

   You see a page similar to the one shown in Figure 6-17. (I say *similar* because Web pages change all the time.)

2. **Click the <u>Consumer Information</u> link on the left side of the page.**

   A list of additional links appears.

3. **Click the <u>Find a Dealer (Dealer Locator)</u> link in the list.**

   A small form appears, where you can specify a make, and your state, city, and the ZIP code. If you want to specify a relatively large area, provide only the first few digits of the ZIP code, such as **272**, for example, rather than **27263**.

4. **Select a manufacturer from the Make drop-down list box and type the name of your city.**

5. **Select your state from the drop-down list box.**

6. **Click Activate the Search.**

   The results of the search appear, displaying the contact information for all dealers matching your criteria.

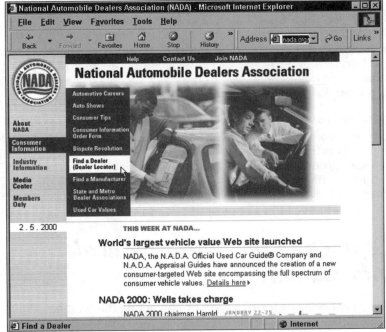

Figure 6-17:
Access the
National
Automobile
Dealers
Association
Web site for
information
on careers,
shows,
conflict
resolution,
and many
other topics.

The <u>Consumer Information</u> link on the left side of the NADA home page also includes a link that connects you to a list of state and local dealers.

Exploring AutoNation

AutoNation (at www.autonation.com on the Web) is the largest automotive retailer chain in the country. (It even saves you the trouble of doing lots of price research because it posts no-haggle prices online for its entire inventory.)

AutoNation currently manages 270 Web sites for its various dealerships around the country and maintains more than 400 franchises in 23 states.

Try AutoNationDirect.com to see what the company has to offer. (Their Internet address is www.autonation.com but their complete, formal name is AutoNationDirect.com.)

Chapter 7

Narrowing Your Choice of Vehicle

. . . .

In This Chapter

▶ Exploring the money questions

▶ Considering safety features

▶ Researching gas mileage

. . . .

A prepared shopper is likely to get the best deal. If you do your homework, you not only get the best price, but you also get a car that fits your lifestyle, is safe, gets good mileage, boasts a strong warranty, and has good resale value.

In this chapter, we show you how to ferret out some of the important details that you need to explore before plunking down your hard-earned cash for a new or used car — safety features, gas mileage, and a vehicle's resale value. Amazingly, some people spend hours shopping for clothes or a TV costing a few hundred dollars but drift unprepared into a dealer's showroom and simply hope for the best when making a $20,000 purchase. They go on intuition and advertising campaigns. Many simply want to avoid haggling and to get out of there as quickly as possible with a car that they like.

First impressions are okay, but you don't want them to form the basis for an expensive purchase. By buying this book and actively using the Internet, you're unlikely to become a victim of a poor car purchase. You can quickly access all the knowledge that you need to ensure that you're happy with your car for all the years that you own it.

Exploring the Money Issue

First, you need to determine how much car you can afford. More important, you need to find out how much car the *bank* says that you can afford. How much do you want to get for your trade-in? And, by contrast, what is the dealership willing to give you for your car? In this section, we mull over these and other questions.

Remember, too, that you must let reality creep into your calculations, even if your imaginary (and wishful) estimates must crash and burn in the process. Start narrowing your vehicle choices by determining what you can afford to pay for a car, using the following information as your guide.

Calculating the monthly payment that you can afford

If your gross household income is $40,000 per year and you're currently paying off a $1,333 per month mortgage, you simply can't afford a new car. You're already maxed out on what lenders usually consider a reasonable debt load. In general, lending institutions figure that you can handle total debt of up to 40 percent of your gross income.

To determine how much you can afford in a car, you just need to do a little arithmetic. (Don't run for the hills; it's just arithmetic — not algebra — and your calculator can handle it easily.)

To think like a bank and calculate how much of a monthly payment you can afford for your new car, just follow these steps:

1. **Add up all your monthly debt payments — your rent or mortgage, credit card payments, and any other debt that you're carrying.**

   If you have a $1,019 monthly mortgage payment and approximately $50 per month in credit card payments, for example, your total debt load is $1,069.

2. **Multiply the total monthly debt load by 12 to figure your annual debt payment. (We won't use this figure in the calculations, but it's sure interesting to know.)**

   Using the example for the preceding step, $1,069 x 12 = $12,828 in total annual debt payments.

3. **Multiply your annual gross income (before taxes and expenses) from all sources by 0.4.**

   This example household earns $40,000 per year in gross income, so the annual debt load can run as much as 40,000 x 0.4, which is $16,000.

4. **Divide the result of Step 3 by 12 to get your monthly maximum debt load.**

   For the example we're using, $16,000 ÷ 12 = $1,333.

5. **Finally, subtract your current monthly debt payment (which you cal-culate in Step 1) from your maximum debt payment (from Step 4).**

   The result is the maximum monthly car payment you can comfortably handle. For our example, $1,333 – $1,069 = $264.

Determining the cost of your payments

If you know the final cost of your new car, the interest rate, the amount of your down payment, any rebate, the likely trade-in value of your existing car, any money you still owe on your current car, and the number of months of the loan, you can try an online calculator, such as the one available at LendingTree (at www.lendingtree.com on the Web). Go to the site and then click the Auto Loan link on the LendingTree home page, as shown in Figure 7-1:

Fill in the form that you find on this page, as shown in Figure 7-2.

Click the Results tab, as shown in Figure 7-2, and your monthly payment appears, as shown in Figure 7-3.

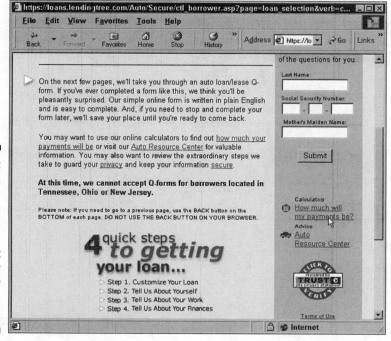

Figure 7-1: Click this link on the LendingTree auto loan start page to figure out the monthly payment for a car you're considering.

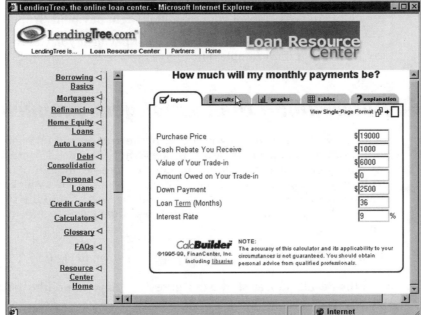

Figure 7-2:
These
variables
determine
your
monthly
payment.

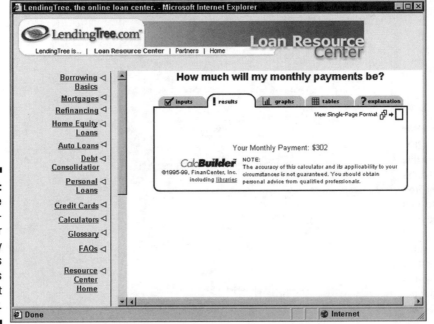

Figure 7-3:
The
payment-
calculator
utility
displays
your results
almost
immediately.

Getting an online financing quote

Chapter 10 covers financing in-depth, but if you want a quick quote, try LendingTree (at www.lendingtree.com on the Web) or one of the other sources of online financing. (At the time of this writing, the company can't accept loan applications from people living in Ohio, New Jersey, or Tennessee.) You must fill in your financial data, but the site is secure. The site uses several layers of security, including a secure server communications layer, firewall protection, encryption (SSL), VeriSign, and passwords.

After you fill in your data, you can also return to query the site about a different loan and you will not need to retype all that information a second time. You can instead request the Loan Xpress feature (click the Loan Xpress link on the home page), which, after verifying you're really who you say you are (by asking your SS number and your mother's maiden name), supplies the information.

After you finish filling out the form, click Submit and the site sends your information to lenders in the LendingTree Network. A lender may require you to complete an application or discuss the information on the Q-form (the name of the LendingTree form that you fill out) before making you a loan offer.

To get car loan quotes from Lending Tree's Network, go to www.lendingtree.com on the Web and follow these steps:

1. **Click the <u>Auto Loan</u> link on the LendingTree home page.**

   You see the Auto Loan page.

2. **Click the Continue button.**

   The first form appears; this is where you fill in data about the car that interests you.

3. **Fill in the form and click the Continue button.**

   Another form appears, in which you provide information about yourself — where you live, your monthly rent or mortgage, and so on.

4. **Fill in the form and click the Continue button.**

   On this page, you describe your job and salary.

5. **Fill in the form and click the Continue button.**

   If you indicated any student, personal, credit card, or other loans on the previous page, you describe them on this page.

On this fourth page of the loan form, LendingTree offers you the opportunity to save your place so that you can return to this location if something goes awry (for example, if you're disconnected from the Internet, you click the Stop button, or you accidentally hit the Enter key before completing a page). Go ahead and save. The site generates and displays a password for you, along with instructions on how to resume work later. You can then resume at this location without needing to retype all the previous information. If you want to restart, just go to the LendingTree home page at www.lendingtree.com and click the Finish My Q-Form option. The site will prompt you for your password and Social Security number.

6. **Fill in the form and click the Continue button.**

   You see a page where you can review some of the primary contact and financial data. You also read some legal information.

7. **Click the <u>Submit My Information</u> link.**

   Your information goes off to LendingTree.

Safety First: Checking Your Car's Record

A major question for many of you is how safe the car is to which you're attracted. Online research can quiet your fears in this area — or frighten you out of your ever-lovin' wits. But be honest: You don't want a car that's unsafe, do you? (And don't forget that a car with a good safety record can lower your insurance costs along with your anxiety level.) The following sections tell you how to go online to determine how safe you're going to be in that new or used car you're considering buying.

Used car safety statistics

A good place to find answers to your questions about recent used cars is Liberty Mutual's Web site (at www.libertymutual.com). This site can tell you about your prospective car's theft, injury, and collision statistics. It compares your prospective car against 335 vehicles in 7 styles for the years 1995 through 1997. After you specify the car's make and model, you see that car's claim statistics.

To find out how the car that interests you compares with other cars, follow these steps:

1. **Go to the Liberty Mutual Web site by typing** www.libertymutual.com **into your browser's Address text box.**

   You see a page with the title How Does Your Family Car Measure Up?

2. **At the bottom of that page, select your make from the drop-down list box.**

   Select, for example, BMW.

3. **Click the Submit button.**

   You see a second page asking you to select the model of your car.

4. **Select your model from the drop-down list box.**

   Select, for example, 318 4D.

5. **Click the Submit button.**

   The results now appear for all three categories. A result of 100 is average (for all makes and models). A result of 200, therefore, is twice as bad as average (or, put another way, 100 percent worse than average), and a result of 90 is ten percent better than average. A higher number is worse.

New-car crash tests

Not much data about theft or injury for new cars exists online yet, but you can find collision data, which derives from deliberate collisions that various research groups conduct to determine how cars stand up. Some tests, for example, involve driving a car directly into a concrete barrier at 35 mph. The testers then see what happens to the vehicle and to the crash-test dummies inside it.

Other, perhaps more realistic, tests drive two cars at each other somewhat off center, as if the drivers are swerving to avoid a collision. This second kind of test is probably closer to what happens in the real world. But from whatever kind of test it comes from, you can find a lot of good information online about the structural stability of the vehicle you're considering buying. Try the following Digital Dealer Web site, for example, for crash-test information:

```
http://digitaldealer.com/Consumer_Info/
    NewCarInformation/crashtest.htm
```

The National Highway Traffic Safety Administration

The U.S. Government is often an excellent source of certain kinds of objective data about vehicles. Try the following site for safety data: www.nhtsa.dot.gov.

This Web address accesses the Web site of the National Highway Traffic Safety Administration (NHTSA), a division of the U.S. Department of Transportation. NHTSA has a variety of responsibilities that fall under the general heading of reducing the overall number of vehicle crashes in the U.S. and reducing the effects of those crashes that do occur.

The agency's Web site is a great source of crash-test data, recall notices, safety alerts, and related information. One drawback: The site reports only on cars built after 1995. For crash tests of earlier models, see the section "CrashTest.com," later in this chapter.

The government purchases new cars every year and crash-tests them to see the results of head-on collisions. After these tests, it rates the cars from one star (the least safe) up to five stars. But when comparing crash test results, you need always to compare cars in similar weight classes — don't compare tricycles with tanks, for example, to exaggerate just a bit.

The famous crash-test dummies — with embedded sensors — register the impact of the crash on their legs, heads, and chests. The government also conducts a pass/fail test at 30 mph into a rigid, unmoving barrier. The law requires this test, and no one can sell any vehicle that fails the test in the United States.

The AAA Foundation for Traffic Safety

The AAA Foundation for Traffic Safety studies why motor vehicle crashes happen and endeavors to show everyone how to avoid unsafe situations. Visit them at www.aaafts.org.

CrashTest.com

CrashTest is an independent auto-safety testing organization that boasts considerable depth for those with an interest in used cars. Most other safety testing organizations publish data only for recent models. CrashTest offers NHTSA data going back as far as the 1970s. The site also boasts a feature that enables you to see the crash statistics on two different cars at the same time. You can find the CrashTest.com Web site at www.crashtest.com.

Insurance Institute for Highway Safety

The Insurance Institute for Highway Safety describes itself as "an independent, nonprofit, research and communication organization . . . wholly supported by automobile insurers." The Web site, which you find at www.hwysafety.org, includes vehicle crash-test data on recent models.

Getting Good Gas Mileage

If ongoing expenses are important to you, consider the gas mileage of any car that you're thinking about purchasing. With gas prices lower than $1 a gallon in past years, you may have considered this expense a non-issue. But prices are going up all the time, and if you do a lot of driving, the money you save when driving a more fuel-efficient car may well interest you.

Magazines and other publications include vehicle specifications in their online reports on cars; one of the most prominent specs is a car's gas mileage (MPG). So if you're looking up a car on, say, CarPoint's Web site (at `carpoint.msn. com/home/New.asp`), you can use its Find a Car utility to get this information. Just choose the make and model from the drop-down list boxes and then click the Go button. After the car's page appears, it looks something like what you see in Figure 7-4.

To locate the MPG figure, click the <u>Engines, Transmissions and Fuel Economy</u> link shown near the bottom of Figure 7-4. You then see the pertinent info, as shown in Figure 7-5.

Figure 7-4:
A vehicle's CarPoint page is your gateway to loads of data, including its gas mileage.

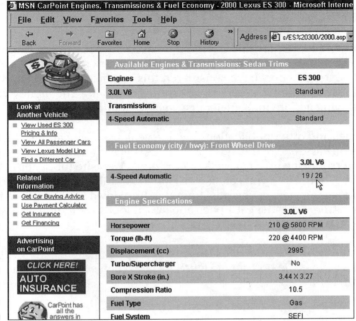

Figure 7-5:
Here are the
city and
highway
MPG figures
for the car:
19 in the
city, 26 in
the wide
open
spaces.

Calculating your car's mileage per gallon

Follow these steps to figure out your auto's gas mileage:

1. **Fill the car's gas tank to the top.**

2. **Write down the miles that currently appear on your auto's odometer.**

3. **Drive a week or two — or however long you need to — until your gas gauge shows that your gas tank is one-quarter or less full.**

4. **Fill the tank to the top again.**

5. **Write down the number of gallons that appear on the gas pump.**

6. **Next to the gallons, write the miles that appear on your auto's odometer (in case you want to calculate your mileage the next time you fill up).**

   Now you're ready to make your calculations.

7. **Subtract the miles that you wrote down in Step 2 from the current odometer reading.**

   This calculation gives you the number of miles you've traveled since the previous fill-up.

8. **Now divide those miles that you get (in Step 7) by the number of gallons you just pumped (in Step 5).**

   If, for example, your odometer shows that you drove 400 miles between Step 2 and Step 6 and you needed to buy 15 gallons to fill your tank, you can figure that your mileage per gallon of gas is 400 divided by 15, or 26⅔ miles per gallon.

Save it yourself

If you love gas-guzzlers, check out the following Web site for tips on how to conserve gas from Shell: `http://shellne.com/btrmiles.html`. At this site, you can find such suggestions as how to avoid lead-foot acceleration, how to avoid unnecessary loads (such as carting around several bowling balls in the trunk even though you haven't bowled in months), how to keep up with the maintenance schedule, and so on.

Chapter 8

Test Driving on the Internet

The car that you decide to buy is an important decision — not one to take lightly or to make without checking every possible detail you can about the car. Remember that you're going to spend a large amount of your time in your car — often early in the morning (possibly before you've had that first cup of coffee or tea) or after work when you're tired. You want this environment to be as comfortable and agreeable as possible.

You want to go down to a dealer and actually test drive any vehicle that you're considering purchasing, of course. You can do *most* things on the Internet when buying a car, but you can't get into it and feel the seats, or see how it handles on corners.

As I discuss in Chapter 5, getting the actual *feel* of the vehicle is essential before you commit yourself to it for several years. (After all, you wouldn't marry someone you'd just met on a TV show, now, would you?)

The Internet, however, can provide you with information about what to look for in a "real-world" test drive. Or you can find data to substantiate your assessment of a vehicle after the fact. You can, for example, read other people's descriptions of their experiences driving the same car. Their comments may even suggest ideas to you — certain preferences of which you aren't even aware.

I remember reading a while back, for example, about how much someone liked the drink-holders in a particular car. I suddenly realized that for years I'd put up with trying to balance a bottle next to the emergency brake or with buying those funky little plastic holders that hang off the window well and bang against it. Obviously, I'd still buy a great car even if it didn't have drink-holders, but with all other things equal, I'd certainly prefer one with a place where I can set my 7-Up.

Another tactic for obtaining more information about a vehicle is to use the AOL Decision Guide utility (see the "Understanding Lifestyle Factors" section, later in this chapter, for more information on the AOL Decision Guide); it can help you narrow your automotive choice by asking a series of questions about your personal needs and wants.

RateItAll Rates Everything

You may pick up some ideas of your own about purchasing a vehicle from hearing or reading about the experiences of others online. Consider, for example, visiting www.rateitall.com, where people regularly sound off about all kinds of products — from graduate schools to their favorite authors (see Figure 8-1). And, of course, you can find plenty of car talk on this Web site.

Click the <u>Cars and Vehicles</u> link on the RateItAll home page. You then see a list of vehicle categories. Click <u>SUV</u> or whatever category of vehicle interests you. You find ratings of up to five stars, along with comments about the vehicles

Figure 8-1:
The
RateItAll
.com site
enables
people to
air their
opinions
about all
kinds of
products
and
services,
including
cars.

in question. You can sort the comments by gender and age (to determine what the people most like you think) or sort them by rating. You can also add your own comments or even suggest a new topic.

If You Live in Milwaukee (Or Anywhere Else)

You can also find online ratings for dealerships in your local area — candid opinions written by your very own townspeople. If you live in Milwaukee, for example, you can check out the Web site that you find at www.dealerreview. webhostme.com.

This is someone's personal Web site (unsupported by lots of corporate dollars) that the owner maintains in his spare time, but he says that he hopes to expand it to cover all of Wisconsin.

Search the Internet to see whether you can find a local or state site similar to www.dealerreview.webhostme.com in your area, where people can comment on their experiences with dealers in your area. (See Chapter 2 for information about the best online search strategies to use in your car buying quest.)

This Milwaukee site includes dealer history, a rating for each dealership, and comments from readers. You can add your own comments as well. Expect sites such as this one to spring up all around the country, because . . . well, it's a *really* good idea. A dealership-rating site enables you to amplify your word-of-mouth information and recommendations way beyond your immediate circle of friends, co-workers, and acquaintances. Remember, however, that personal opinions are highly subjective. But they're also highly candid. Just as you can expect frank talk about a dealership around the office coffee machine, you can also expect it at such locations online.

Trying Consumer Democracy

For a good source of experiences and opinions from others who've tried and tested the vehicle that you're considering, check out the Consumer Democracy Web site (at www.consumerdemocracy.com/cars.htm).

Here you find all kinds of opinions on various topics relating to cars. (You find information about many other consumer items as well because Consumer Democracy doesn't focus only on cars. You can also find opinions and experiences relating to printers, toys, golf, and much more.) Consumer Democracy provides stats, reviews, acclaim, criticism, ratings, comparisons, warnings, and other kinds of discussions and reports about nearly every type of vehicle that you can want.

To access Consumer Democracy's car reviews, follow these steps:

1. **Go to** `www.consumerdemocracy.com` **by using your browser's address feature.**

    You see a page similar to the one displayed in Figure 8-2. Scroll down to the sample reviews to see if the information looks good to you.

2. **Click the <u>Cars</u> link on the Consumer Democracy home page (or choose <u>SUV</u> or <u>Truck</u>).**

    As shown in Figure 8-3, you see a few sample reviews, and you're invited to visit the full site.

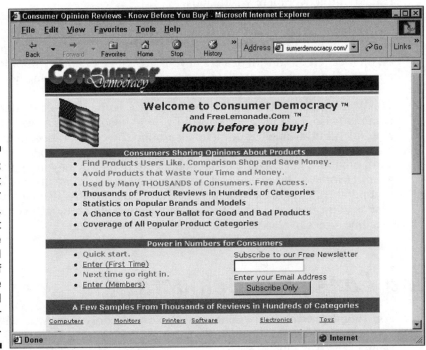

Figure 8-2: At Consumer Democracy, you'll get the unvarnished opinions of people who've lived with your car.

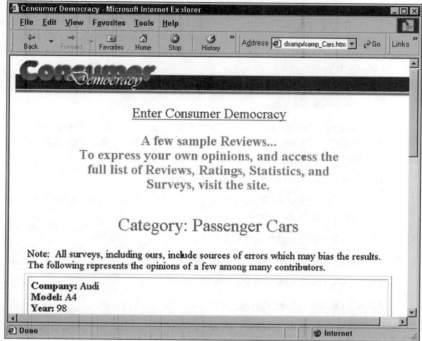

3. **Click the <u>Enter Consumer Democracy</u> link.**

   You must agree to a User Agreement to continue.

4. **Click the <u>I agree</u> link to go to the registration form.**

   You see a form where you briefly describe some aspects of yourself.

5. **Fill in the form and click the Submit button.**

   You see a welcome page.

6. **Click the <u>Click here to make your contribution</u> link.**

   You are asked to provide a review of a product of your choice that you're familiar with—to help others make their buying decisions.

7. **Fill in the review form, describing why you like, or don't like, a consumer product. It can be a car, a computer, whatever you have an opinion about.**

8. **Click the Submit button.**

   You now see a list of reviews of items in the same category in which you just submitted your review. The reviews are listed from best (five stars) to worst (one star). At the bottom of the list you can request to order the list by manufacturer.

You can always search a list like this one by using the search feature in your browser. For Internet Explorer users, just press Ctrl+F, then fill in the search term you're interested in. To see all 27" televisions, for example, type 27". Click the Find Next button and keep on clicking it to see each match.

9. **Click the <u>Go To Consumer Democracy Home Page</u> link at the top of the reviews page.**

   You're now in the main page. On this home page you can select the Popular Products feature, offer more opinions, view others' opinions, or search for a particular item, as shown in Figure 8-4.

10. **Click the Browse Categories link.**

    You see a list of broad categories. To view reviews for a Lexus, for example, continue as follows.

11. **Click the <u>Transportation</u> link.**

12. **Click the <u>Automobile and Truck</u> link.**

13. **Click the <u>Passenger Cars</u> link.**

14. **Click the <u>View Reviews</u> link.**

    At this point you can locate the car you're interested in by pressing Ctrl+F and searching for the model or make.

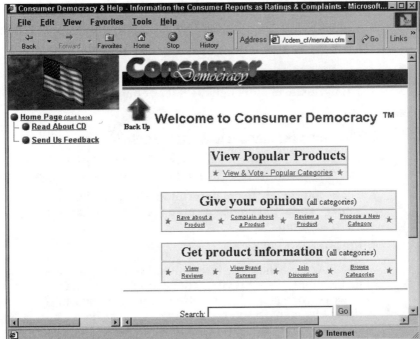

Figure 8-4: The Consumer Democracy home page.

Live Chat for Instant Answers

As I explain in Chapter 3, you can join online chat rooms to discuss cars in real time. The following sections suggest some good sources for online conversations, particularly for car talk.

For the woman motorist

The concept may not be totally PC, but some sites devote their information to women only. Even if you're not a woman, you still may find some information of use to you at the Woman Motorist site (at www.womanmotorist.com on the Web). The site isn't chauvinistic, however — you do find reviews there by both men and women.

As you can see in Figure 8-5, this site offers a complete panorama of varied topics, including reviews, maintenance, tips on buying a used car, safety, a glossary, Q&As, new-product features, and, of course, a chat feature.

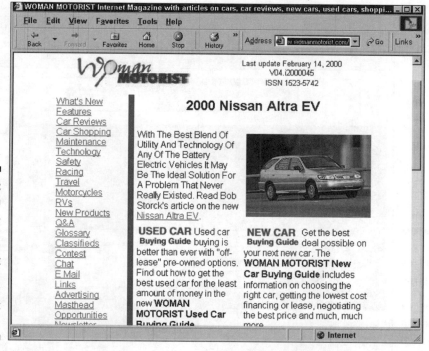

Figure 8-5: For women only (well, mostly), the Woman Motorist magazine site includes a chat feature.

The chat feature also connects to the Talk City site (see the following section) and is open 24 hours a day. Coordinators are online all the time to answer questions. The Auto-General chat room is always open for wide-ranging discussions of topics relating to automobiles, and the Auto-Garage chat room is for specially hosted discussions of all things automotive.

Talk City delivers

Talk City (at www.talkcity.com on the Web), a famous site, offers quite a bit of online activity (see Figure 8-6). You can find chat rooms, famous people leading discussions, polls, photo galleries, and much more at this venerable, active site.

Click the Autos link in the What Interests You? area in the middle of the screen, and you access the Auto interest page, as shown in Figure 8-7.

Click the View a list of Auto chats link. You see a list of the currently active discussions for this category and the number of participants in each, as shown in Figure 8-8.

Figure 8-6:
Talk City is a good place to get instant information on cars.

Figure 8-7: On Talk City's Auto page, you can select categories, choose a "neighborhood," or view a list of currently active auto chats.

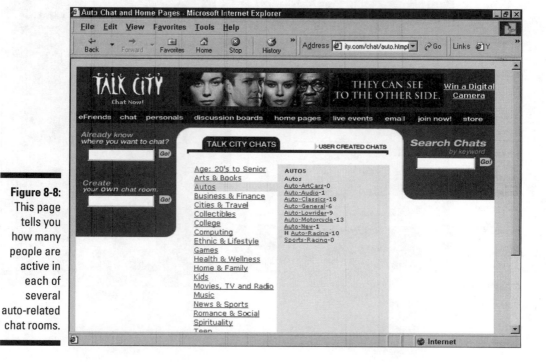

Figure 8-8: This page tells you how many people are active in each of several auto-related chat rooms.

As you can see in the example shown in Figure 8-8, 18 people are talking about classic cars, 6 about autos in general, 13 about motorcycles, and a few others about various other topics. (But what's going on in the Auto-Audio room, where only *one* person is talking?)

If you choose to enter a chat, click the appropriate link. You then see the page shown in Figure 8-9.

Registered members get some nice "prizes" at the Talk City site: free e-mail and a free home page. You can still chat, however, even if you don't want to register at this time. Choose a user name, and you see a message asking whether you want to download the Talk City chat software. Agree. The download only takes a few seconds, and you then find yourself right there in the chat, as shown in Figure 8-10.

Another interesting feature of the Talk City chats is that you can create a chat room (topic) of your own. Just click the Create A Room button in the lower-right corner of the chat page, and you're off and running. You can then sit around in your new chat room (as the *one* person in Auto-Audio is doing in Figure 8-8) and hope that others join you in your new discussion topic.

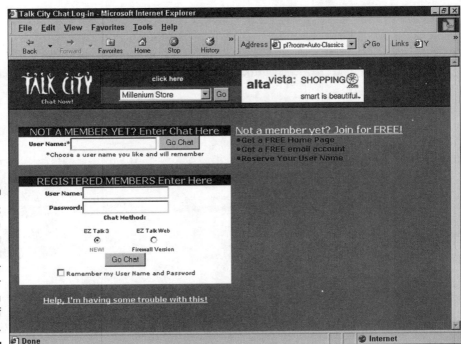

Figure 8-9:
This page enables you to enter a chat or register as a member of Talk City.

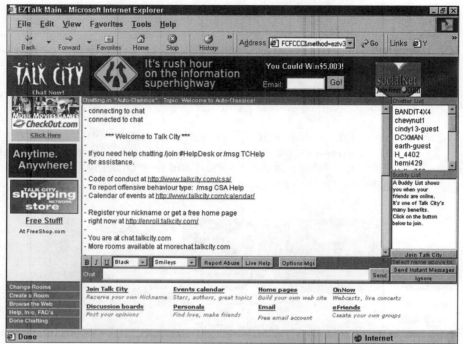

Figure 8-10:
The Auto-Classics chat page at Talk City.

Locating other popular chat centers

Many competing chat centers and message boards reside out there in cyberspace. You can give any of them a try to see whether any particular one is currently a hotbed of car talk. The following list offers a brief rundown of some of the most highly rated gab sites on the Web:

- ✔ www.remarq.com includes an active auto message board.

- ✔ www.powwow.com offers both chat and instant messaging (including voice messages).

- ✔ www.topica.com focuses on e-mail lists of people with various special interests, including — you guessed it — vehicles. As TopicA puts it, "TopicA's service helps you easily find people, discussions, and information on virtually any topic."

- ✔ www.askme.com boasts more than a million visitors a month who pose — and answer — nearly every question under the sun. You can also browse through its archives of more than 125,000 past questions and answers.

AOL, the popular choice

You can find one of the biggest and oldest chat centers around within America Online. You find a *lot* of chatting going on there. And, just as you can at Talk City, you can start your own chat room to discuss the topic of your choice (such as a room that you design specifically for Honda owners) to solicit opinions on that particular make of vehicle you're eyeing.

And while you're on AOL, don't forget to visit its Auto Center. Click the Keyword button (at the top right of the main AOL screen), type **Auto** in the Keyword dialog box that appears, and then click the Go button. You access a window much like the one shown in Figure 8-11.

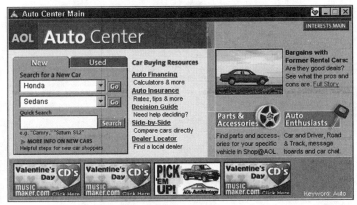

Figure 8-11: AOL's Auto Center is your gateway to a variety of tools.

Understanding Lifestyle Factors

How you live, what you enjoy, *who* you are in your own eyes — these factors can prove significant in choosing something as important (and with as many variables) as your personal automobile.

To increase your odds of forging a happy marriage between your personality and the car that you buy, I suggest the following course: After you ask others in chat rooms how *they* feel about *their* cars, ask yourself some questions. Your answers can help you assess the views that others express and, therefore, determine whether what others like about a car corresponds to your own values in a vehicle. To help you in asking the right questions, I recommend that you try the AOL Decision Guide.

Click the Decision Guide link on the AOL Auto Center screen (refer to Figure 8-11; you find this link in the middle of the screen, under the heading Car Buying Resources). A profiling feature then appears to help you decide what car is best for your lifestyle and personality type, as shown in Figure 8-12.

A list of lifestyle types appears at the bottom of the Decision Guide screen (refer to Figure 8-12): Commuter, College Freshman, Executive, Soccer Mom, Sport Driver, Weekend Warrior, and Jealous Nerd. Well, *Jealous Nerd* doesn't really appear in the list, so if that description fits you, you can't just click one of those predefined lifestyle types to see the car that fits your type. If, however, you're a soccer mom, you can go ahead and click that link. (If you do click the Soccer Mom — or any other of these preset options — and then decide to set up your own custom profile instead, you can click the Return to Start button to get back to the beginning of the profiling feature.)

To fill in your personal profile, follow these steps:

1. **From the Decision Guide start page, click the Q&A button (refer to Figure 8-12).**

   The process of creating your custom lifestyle profile begins with the Car Type page, as shown in Figure 8-13.

2. **Select the check boxes describing the model year and car type that interest you.**

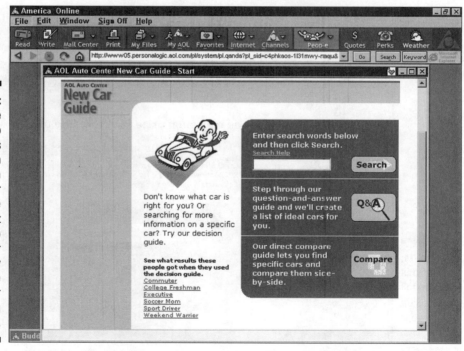

Figure 8-12: The entrance to AOL's Decision Guide, a feature for people smart enough to factor their personality and lifestyle into their car-buying decision.

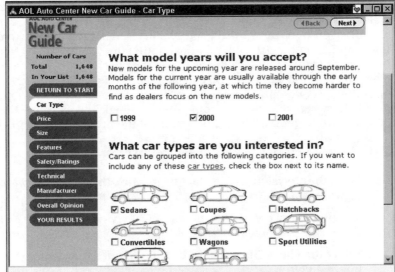

Figure 8-13:
This screen
of the
Decision
Guide is
where you
define the
car type and
model year
you're after.

3. **Click the Next button (at the top-right corner of the screen).**

   The Price page appears, as shown in Figure 8-14:

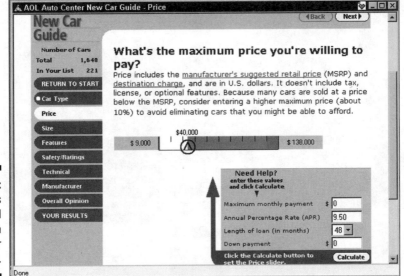

Figure 8-14:
Use this
page to tell
the Decision
Guide your
price limits.

Note: Notice in the upper left corner of the screen in Figures 8-13 and 8-14 the Number of Cars statistics. Each time that you enter additional profile data, the In Your List value is likely to decrease. Merely by specifying year-2000 models and Sedans in Step 2, I reduce the number of matching vehicles from 1,648 in Figure 8-13 down to 221 in Figure 8-14.

4. **Move the money slider in the middle of the screen by clicking and dragging it with the mouse until it indicates the maximum amount of money you're willing to pay and then click the Next button.**

   You now go to the Size page, as shown in Figure 8-15.

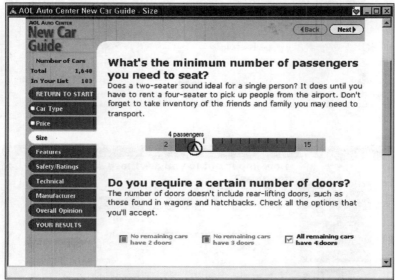

Figure 8-15: Use the Size page to specify the minimum number of passengers you need to carry and other space issues (such as headroom, cargo capacity, and legroom).

5. **Define the size options that matter to you and then click Next.**

   You now see the Features page, where you can decide which options are essential, desirable, or relatively unimportant to you, as shown in Figure 8-16.

6. **Select the appropriate radio buttons for each feature and then click the Next button.**

   You're now at the Safety/Ratings page, as shown in Figure 8-17.

7. **Select the appropriate radio buttons for how much each safety feature matters to you and then click Next.**

   The Technical page appears, as shown in Figure 8-18.

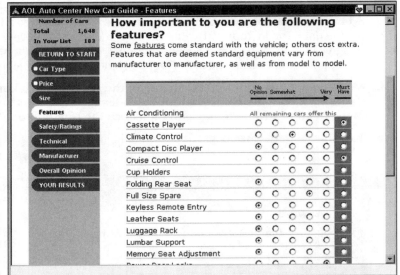

Figure 8-16:
All the options and features you may need (or could care less about) in a vehicle appear on the Decision Guide's Features page.

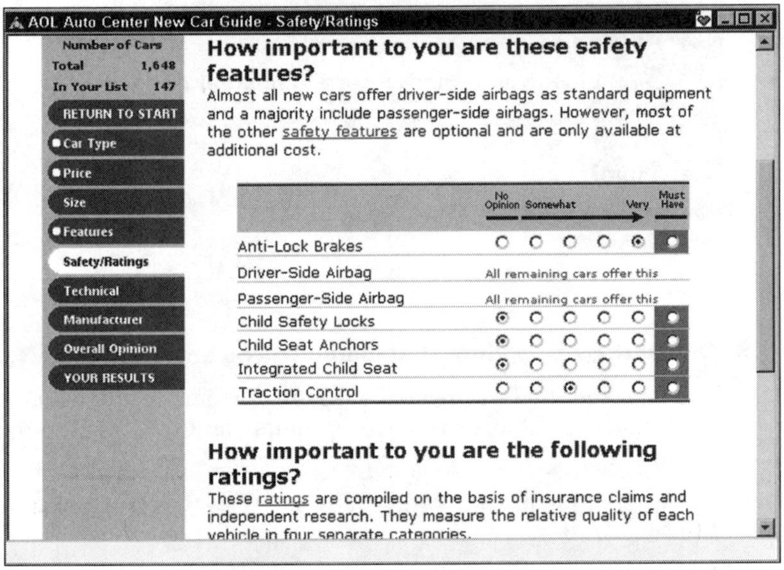

Figure 8-17:
Decide which vehicle safety features matter most to you on this page of the AOL Decision Guide.

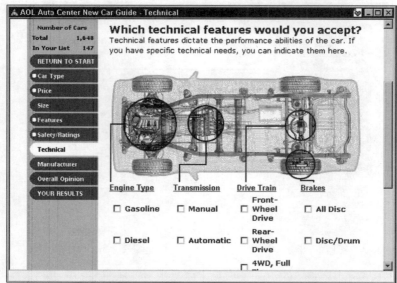

Figure 8-18:
Click any of the blue links (<u>Engine Type</u>, <u>Transmission</u>, and so on) for a definition of the various technical features that the Decision Guide's Technical page lists.

8. Indicate any specific technical requirements that you have by clicking the check boxes for those features you require and then click Next.

Must you have four-wheel drive? An automatic transmission? Click the check boxes wherever something in the list is essential to you. If a feature doesn't matter to you, leave its check box clear. If you need additional information, click the blue links (<u>Engine Type</u>, <u>Transmission</u>, <u>Drive Train</u>, and <u>Brakes</u>) for definitions of these technical features.

You next access the Manufacturer page, as shown in Figure 8-19.

9. Click radio buttons on the Manufacturer page to indicate how much you favor (or to eliminate from consideration) the various auto makes and then click Next.

The Overall Opinion page appears, as shown in Figure 8-20.

10. Click the appropriate radio buttons to spell out how much weight you give to each of the major categories on this page and then click Next.

You now see a list of cars that match your criteria, as shown in Figure 8-21.

Figure 8-19:
If you prefer a certain auto manufacturer — or several of them — click the appropriate radio buttons to tell the Decision Guide your preferences.

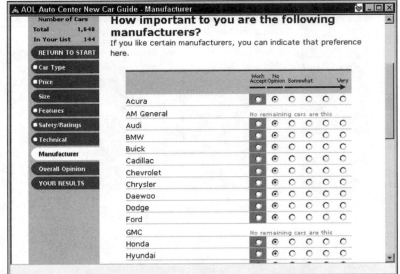

Figure 8-20:
On the Decision Guide's Overall Opinion page, you define the relative importance to your choice of vehicle of several overall categories.

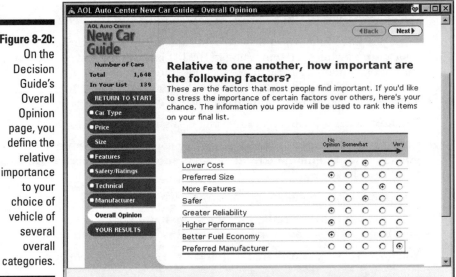

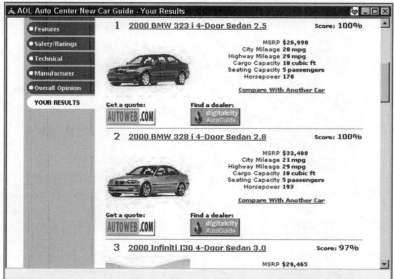

Figure 8-21:
According
to the AOL
Decision
Guide, two
cars, both
BMWs,
match my
lifestyle 100
percent.

Vehicles that survive your paring-down process appear on the Decision Guide's Results page in order of how well they match your needs and wants. In my case, I have 139 cars left after my own exercise with the AOL Decision Guide. Two BMWs match my lifestyle 100 percent. (The 139th car on the list, however, gets a compatibility score of only 64 percent.)

Chapter 9

Safety First: Checking Your Car's Record Online

A major question for many of you concerns the safety of any car you're considering purchasing (and of the one you're actually *driving*, for that matter). Online research can quiet your fears in this area . . . or frighten you out of your ever-lovin' wits.

But honestly, you don't want a car with a whacked safety record, do you?

You want to protect your friends, family, and yourself. After all, anyone riding with you (including you) deserves to feel safe. And don't forget that a car with a good safety record can lower your insurance costs as well as your anxiety level.

This chapter is all about safety and how you can factor that issue into your online car-buying decision.

Considering Safety

Incidents! Cars, like people, vary greatly in the number of suspicious — or downright disastrous — incidents they get involved with. If your girlfriend breaks a video game once, it may simply be a mishap. Forgive her. If she hurls your PlayStation against the wall on a regular basis, you're facing a real anger-management problem here. My advice? Find a different girlfriend.

Similarly, with cars, where you see smoke, you may also find fire. According to Terry Miller, spokesperson for the National Safety Council, "About 20 million drivers are involved in vehicle accidents each year. That works out to about one accident per driver every eight or nine years."

Safety is obviously an issue for most of us. CarPoint, among other sites, can be of great help in assessing safety issues.

Taking all things into consideration, the single most important safety factor is the bulk of the vehicle. The more metal mass around you, the safer you are. In fact, on average, fatality statistics are quite a bit higher for compact and subcompact cars compared with large cars or SUVs. (See the National Highway Traffic Safety Administration's statistics that I offer later in this chapter.)

Sure, a massive SUV pumps more than its share of pollution into the air and sucks more than its share of oil out of the ground. Sure, SUVs are often hazardous to drivers of other cars (because an SUV blocks car drivers' views of the other traffic around them). I saw a great cartoon in the *The New Yorker* dealing with this subject: A man is getting ready to buy a giant SUV in a dealer's showroom. This vehicle looks like a cross between a semi and a Hum-Vee — high off the ground, colossal spotlights, mean-looking bumpers. The salesman, however, says to the hopeful buyer, "I need to see some justification."

We should mention that the same protection a Ford Expedition affords its passengers is also the weapon that, insurers are starting to believe, causes more damage and more serious injury to others than smaller vehicles ever could cause. At the least, this may soon translate to higher insurance costs for the Expedition owner. Safety works both ways.

The justification for buying any large vehicle — SUV or otherwise — is the increase in safety such a vehicle offers you (ignoring the increase in danger you pose to other people). You just can't get around it: If you're hit, you want as much metal around you as possible, as the CarPoint report shown in Figure 9-1 indicates.

Visit CarPoint's safety pages (at `www.carpoint.msn.com` on the Web) for additional pointers.

If seeing the results of crash tests that NHTSA (the National Highway Traffic Safety Administration) conducts interests you, you can also access that information from CarPoint. Click the Table of Contents button on the CarPoint home page, and then click the following links: Shopping for Safety ☞ Crash Testing ☞ Frontal Crash Tests. You then see a page similar to the one shown in Figure 9-2.

Figure 9-1:
CarPoint makes a valid point about the relationship between car size and safety.

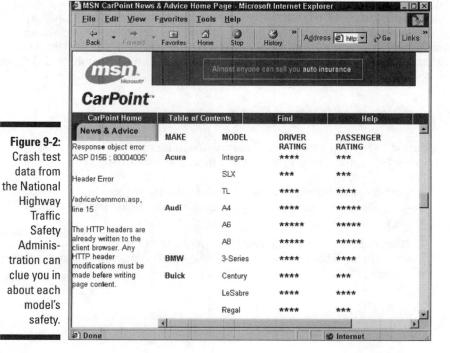

Figure 9-2:
Crash test data from the National Highway Traffic Safety Administration can clue you in about each model's safety.

NHTSA's statistics rate cars by using a scale of from one to five stars, as you can see on CarPoint's Web site as shown in Figure 9-2. The following list describes what each NHTSA rating indicates:

✔ A rating of five stars means a 10 percent or less chance of serious injury.

✔ A rating of four stars means an 11 to 20 percent chance of serious injury.

✔ A rating of three stars means a 21 to 35 percent chance of serious injury.

✔ A rating of two stars means a 36 to 45 percent chance of serious injury.

✔ A rating of one star means a 46 percent or higher chance of serious injury.

Note: The NHTSA defines "serious injury" as possibly life-threatening damage requiring immediate hospitalization.

Speed matters — so lighten up on that pedal!

Crash tests started with the 1980 models. Testers run cars into fixed barriers at 35 mph. Dummies sit in both the driver and passenger seats for the tests. Testers also run a separate 30 mph test for the federal occupant-protection safety standards. Actually — and especially note this information if you have a lead foot — speed is a very significant factor in crash injury-and-death statistics. The test at 35 mph results in injuries that are, on average, 33 percent more serious than those at 30 mph. Why? Because you realize a rapid, exponential increase in damage as speed increases. (See the section "Insurance Institute for Highway Safety," later in this chapter, for details about the more-realistic "frontal-offset" tests that this organization conducts at 40 mph.)

Other safety features

In addition to driving a large car slowly, you can increase vehicular safety by purchasing an automobile or other vehicle with the following safety features:

✔ Impact-reducing *crumple zones* built into the body (also known as *crush zones*). These features give way during a crash, deflecting the impact energy.

✔ A *safety cage* — engineered reinforcements surrounding the passenger compartment. This cage works together with crush zones to protect the occupants.

  ✔ Air bags. (See the sidebar "Airbags save lives," later in this chapter.)

  ✔ Antilock, ABS brakes.

  ✔ Headrests.

  ✔ Seat belts.

Checking Out New-Car Crash Tests

You don't, of course, find much data about theft or injury for new cars, but you can find collision data deriving from *deliberate* collisions that testers conduct to determine how well cars stand up to such events. Government tests drive a car directly into a concrete barrier at 35 mph. Then the testers see what happens to the vehicle and to the crash-test dummies inside it. (It's not a crash test *for dummies*, by the way, so relax.)

Other, perhaps more realistic tests drive two cars into each other somewhat off center, as if the drivers are swerving to avoid a collision. This second kind of test is probably more true to what happens in the real world. But whatever the kinds of tests that people conduct, you can pick up some good information about the structural stability of the vehicle you're considering by accessing such information online.

To find online information about how various cars test, try the following Web address:

```
http://digitaldealer.com/Consumer_Info/
    NewCarInformation/crashtest.htm
```

Getting online information from the National Highway Traffic Safety Administration

The U.S. government is often an excellent source of certain kinds of objective data about vehicles. Try the following Web site, for example, for vehicle-safety data:

```
www.nhtsa.dot.gov
```

This Web site belongs to the National Highway Traffic Safety Administration (NHTSA), a division of the U.S. Department of Transportation. NHTSA has a variety of responsibilities in the areas of reducing the overall number of motor-vehicle crashes annually and reducing the effects of those crashes that do occur.

The NHTSA Web site is a great source of crash-test data, recall notices, safety alerts, and related information. The site does have one drawback, however: It reports only on cars built after 1995. This 1995 cutoff is fairly typical of most Web sites, as you'll find.

The government purchases new cars every year and crashes them to determine the results of head-on collisions on those vehicles. Those world-famous crash-test dummies — which testers equip with embedded sensors — register the vehicle impacts on their legs, heads, and chests. One test is a pass/fail test that crashes a vehicle moving at 30 mph into a rigid, unmoving barrier. U.S. law requires this test in particular, and no one can sell any vehicle that fails this test in the United States.

After conducting all these tests, NHTSA rates the cars on a scale of from one star (the least safe) up to five stars. In comparing crash-test results, however, you must always compare cars in similar weight classes — you can't, for example, compare tricycles with tanks (to exaggerate *just* a bit).

Why size matters

Recent statistics from the National Highway Traffic Safety Administration also indicate that people are ten percent more likely to die in crashes while riding in subcompact cars than if they're riding in full-sized cars. The difference becomes almost 15 percent if you compare minicompacts with full-sized cars.

Airbags save lives

Recently, some controversy has arisen about potential dangers that air bags pose to children, small people, and the frail elderly. These bags, which are supposed to save people, actually caused a number of highly publicized deaths, making many drivers think twice about their use. But don't think twice — it's all right. (Really.) Air bags, in fact, reduce frontal-crash fatalities by 20 percent and injuries by even larger percentages.

NHTSA statistics do show that air bags killed more than 100 people in the past 10 years. Most such fatalities, however, occurred because people either weren't wearing seat belts or weren't correctly restrained. *(You especially need to keep children in the back seat in a child-safety seat.)*

Automakers first installed air bags in a few models in 1984, but by 1990, the law required all auto manufacturers to include them (or, alternatively, automatic seat belts). Because of the incidents of air-bag deaths, however, the NHTSA has more recently permitted the installation of switches that enable drivers to turn off airbags. (Some pickup trucks, for example, now include airbag defeat switches so that you can use a rear-facing child-safety seat. Mercedes-Benz does, too.)

Total recall

Current figures say that around 42,000 people die each year in the United States from car crashes. (The total was 41,471 in 1998; data for 1999 isn't yet compiled.) Auto accidents, in fact, remain the number-one killer of people younger than age 34. *Recalls*, along with crash tests and other government tactics, force manufacturers to do everything possible to improve the reliability and safety of their vehicles.

After the government first instituted the mandatory pass/fail 30 mph crash-test requirement in 1980, for example, many of those tiny models (mostly hailing from Japan) failed the test. Because failing this test resulted in that model being prohibited from further sales in the U.S., those autos (not surprisingly) were rapidly redesigned.

For information on what cars are currently under recall, you can go to the NHTSA site (`www.nhtsa.dot.gov`) and click the <u>Recalls</u> link. You then see the page shown in Figure 9-3.

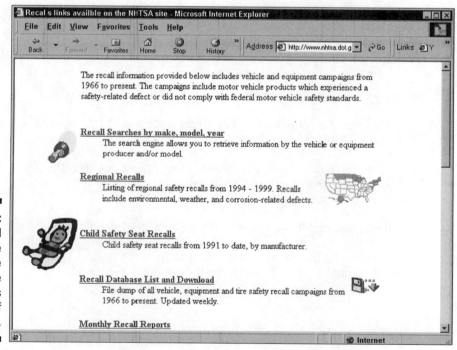

Figure 9-3:
The Recall Links page for the NHTSA site includes quite a bit of useful data.

The NHTSA site lists a surprising number of recalls, so if you own a new car, you may want to check this site from time to time. (Use the Monthly Recall Reports link for the most current information.) In 1998, for example, the NHTSA listed 331 recalls affecting a total of 17,237,716 vehicles. In the past nine years, NHTSA has listed more than 2,100 recalls.

On the NHTSA site's main Recalls Link page, you find a thorough set of links offering the following recall-related information:

- Recall Searches by make, model, year
- Regional Recalls
- Child Safety Seat Recalls
- Recall Database List and Download
- Monthly Recall Reports
- School Buses Recalls
- VOQ (a form enabling you to report a defect)
- Recall Process (a description of FAQs and details about recall campaigns)
- Child Safety Seat Registration Form
- Recall and Quarterly Guide/Form
- Safety Recall Compendium

This site is a good source. You might want to add it to your Favorites (or, if you use Netscape, bookmark it).

Finding recall data on a car you're considering or currently driving is easy. Just click the Recall Searches by make, model, year link. You then see the page shown in Figure 9-4.

If you search for recall information about the 1999 BMW 323I, for example, you discover that recalls affect 34,698 of these cars. The problem stems from overly sensitive side air bags that can blow if you hit a curb or pothole "at substantial speed." You can see the results in Figure 9-5.

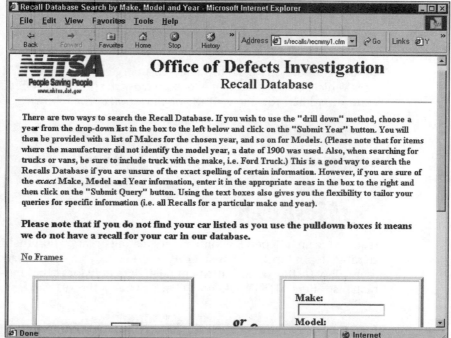

Figure 9-4:
You can use
the search
engine on
this Recall
Database
Web page
to determine
whether
any recall
notices
apply to
your car.

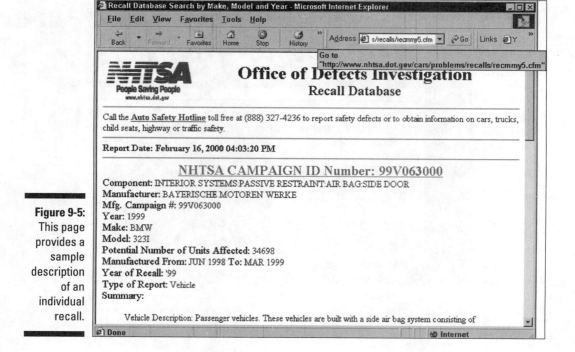

Figure 9-5:
This page
provides a
sample
description
of an
individual
recall.

Using the AAA Foundation for Traffic Safety

The AAA Foundation for Traffic Safety is an organization that studies why motor vehicle crashes happen and endeavors to show everyone how to avoid unsafe situations. You can visit the organization at the following Web address:

```
www.aaafts.org
```

An interesting page in the AAA site is its Progress Report, as shown in Figure 9-6.

CrashTest.com

CrashTest is an independent auto-safety testing organization that boasts considerable depth for those considering a "previously enjoyed" (used) car. Most other safety-testing organizations publish data only for recent models. CrashTest offers NHTSA data going back as far as the 1970s. The CrashTest

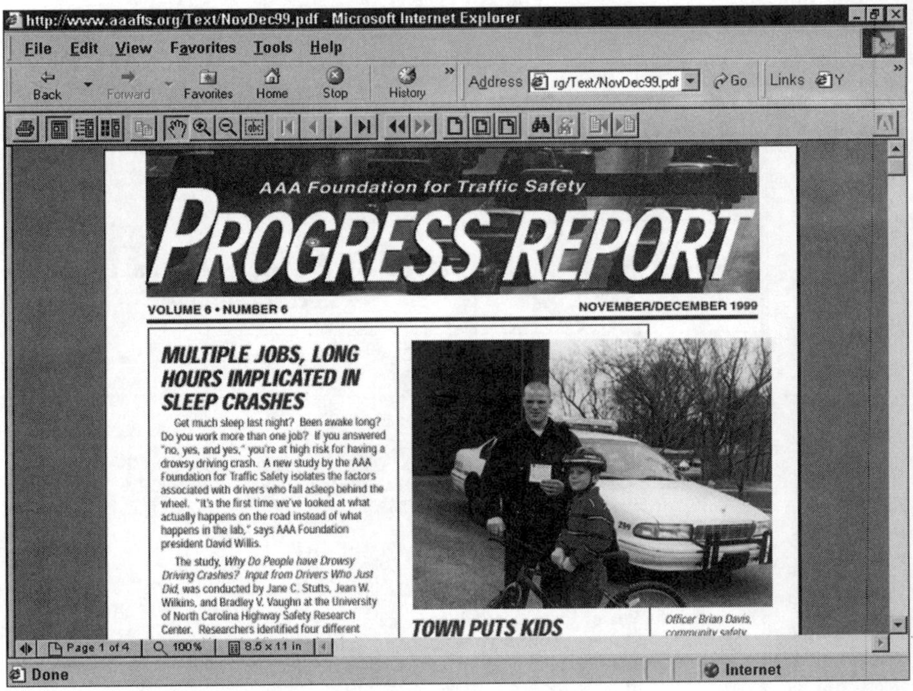

Figure 9-6: The AAA Foundation for Traffic Safety's Progress Report publication covers such issues as sleep crashes, a serious problem only now becoming a target of studies.

Web site also offers a feature enabling you to view the crash stats on two different cars at the same time. Access CrashTest's data at the following Web address:

```
www.crashtest.com
```

Insurance Institute for Highway Safety

The Insurance Institute for Highway Safety (at www.hwysafety.org on the Web) describes itself as "an independent, nonprofit, research and communication organization . . . wholly supported by automobile insurers." Among the information that you can find on the IIHS Web site is vehicle crash-test data on recent models.

If you visit this site, you see a welcome page similar to that shown in Figure 9-7.

Click the Vehicle Ratings link that you see in Figure 9-7, and the page shown in Figure 9-8 appears.

Figure 9-7: Visit the Insurance Institute for Highway Safety Web site for additional information on vehicle safety.

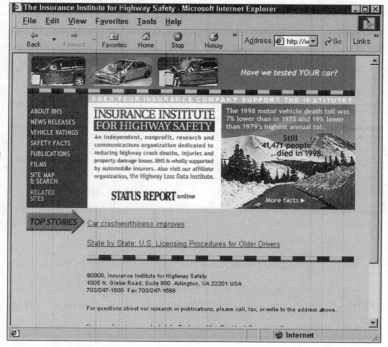

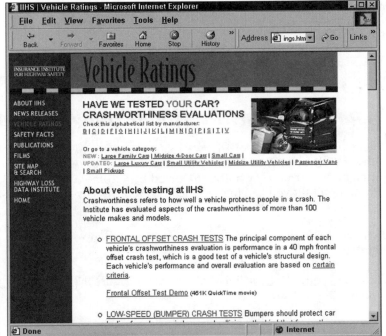

Figure 9-8:
You can look up your car's crashworthiness rating on the IIHS Vehicle Ratings page.

The IIHS uses the realistic frontal-offset crash test (and not the direct-frontal test) for its ratings. (Remember that most people who get into a head-on crash attempt to steer away from it, resulting in an offset.) The IIHS test occurs at 40 mph. As the IIHS describes it, their test reveals "how well each vehicle's front end manages crash energy to limit occupant compartment intrusion, injury risk measured on an average-size male Hybrid III dummy in the driver seat, and how well the belt and air bag perform and interact with the steering column and other vehicle parts to control dummy kinematics (movement)."

Checking the crash-test results for the 1996–99 models of the Mercury Sable, for example, reveals that this car does quite well in a crash situation. (It even gets the Best Pick award from the IIHS.) Figure 9-9 shows part of the detailed IIHS report on the Sable.

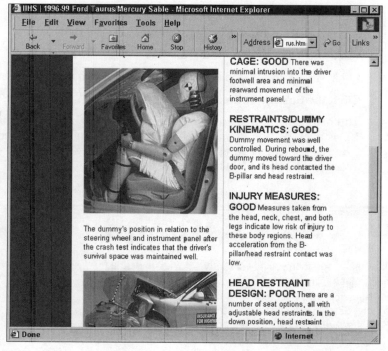

Figure 9-9:
The IIHS
provides
in-depth
reports
about how
various
vehicles —
in this case,
the Mercury
Sable —
fare in its
realistic
crash tests.

Getting Used-Car Stats

One good Web site that can answer your safety questions about recent used cars is that of Liberty Mutual. This site can tell you about your prospective car's theft, injury, and collision statistics. It compares your prospective car against 335 vehicles in seven styles for the years 1995 through 1997.

After you specify the car's make and model, the site displays that car's claim statistics from the Highway Loss Data Insurance.

To use this Web site to determine how the car you're considering compares to other cars, follow these steps:

1. **Open your browser and access the Liberty Mutual Web site by typing** www.libertymutual.com/hldi **in the browser's Address text box.**

   The How Does Your Family Car Measure Up? page appears on-screen.

2. **At the bottom of that page, click the name of your make in the list box to select it.**

   Click BMW, for example, if you're considering a car of that make.

3. **Click the Submit button.**

   A second page appears asking you to select the model.

4. **Click the model name in the list box.**

   Click 318 4D, for example, if that's the model you're considering.

5. **Click the Submit button.**

   The results of your search now appear in three categories. A result of 100 is average (for all makes and models). A result of 200, therefore, is twice as costly as average. (Put another way, it's 100 percent worse than average.) A result of 90 is ten percent better than average.

In case of accident

No matter how much attention you pay to safety features, maintenance, and careful driving, you can still find yourself in an accident. Remember that the National Safety Council statistics indicate that, on the average, each driver can expect involvement in an accident once every eight or nine years. If you have a car or cell phone, consider programming the police, the highway patrol and your insurance agent into it for quick access.

If you're in a car crash, you can take certain steps that increase your odds of getting your car — and possibly your health — successfully restored. Follow these general steps and you get the legal information that you need — and signal to all involved that you know what you're doing and are unlikely to be sloppy or casual on the other end — during the settlement.

Be patient, pleasant, polite, and noncommittal. Don't discuss who's at fault in the accident or any financial issues.

Ask someone to notify the police or make the call yourself. Then exchange registration, insurance-card, and driver's-license information with all the other drivers involved in the accident.

Write down the following information:

✔ The names of any witnesses and their phone numbers.

✔ The names of any people injured and their phone numbers.

✔ The name and badge number of the investigating police officer.

✔ The name, address, phone number, driver's license number, insurance number, registration number, and insurance company for *each driver* involved in this accident.

✔ The other vehicle's license plate number and a description of each vehicle's model, make, year, and color.

Draw a little map showing how the accident occurred (who came from which street, when the other driver(s) arrived at the accident, how the cars were positioned).

As soon as possible, notify your insurance agent.

Part III
Taking the Plunge: Buying a Car Online

The 5th Wave   By Rich Tennant

ORIGINAL VAN-GOGH-OF-THE-MONTH CLUB

"SINCE WE BEGAN ON-LINE SHOPPING, I JUST DON'T KNOW WHERE THE MONEY'S GOING."

In this part . . .

*R*eady to actually shell out some cash on a new set of wheels? If so, you've come to the right part of this book. So put your wallet in gear, and get ready to press the pedal to the metal because in this part, we tell you just how to go all the way to the finish line and actual buy a car online!

First, in Chapter 10, we tell you all you need to know on how to go about securing various financing options online. We give you pointers in Chapter 11 on how to use the Internet to decide whether buying a car is your best bet or if leasing is a better plan for your situation. Chapters 12, 13, and 14 form the nitty-gritty of this part — and of the book itself — by guiding you though the ins and outs of buying a new, a used, or even a collector car on the Internet. (And if you want to know how to negotiate like a pro, we cue you in on all the resources you need for taking on — and running down [metaphorically, of course] — those high-pressure new- and used-car salespeople.) Finally, in Chapter 15, we tell you how to secure the best deal possible for your old trade-in, whether you decide to sell it yourself online or donate it to a needy charity (for a nice tax write-off, of course).

After you cruise through Part III, you're more than ready to roll right on over to the dealer (or roll over the dealer, as you prefer), whether in person or online.

Chapter 10

Finding Financing Online

- -

In This Chapter

▶ Getting quick results when financing online

▶ Looking at Autoweb's financing offers

▶ Securing a loan in 15 seconds

▶ Using CarPoint's various features

- -

*I*f you're a well-prepared car buyer (that is, one who reads this book before buying), you can eliminate all the unnecessary extra charges ("underpainting" or whatever else they try to tack on to a car's price); drive down the actual cost as low as possible; and drive up the trade-in price as high as possible. But even with all those accomplishments and all your preparation, you can still get taken for a ride by a dealer if he sells you an expensive financing package.

Securing Your Financing

Most major online auto sites offer financing features. We explore some of them in this chapter, but you also want to take a look at some of the other general automotive e-commerce sites that we mention in this book. As usual, you want to comparison shop. You're buying a car, but in a very real sense, you're also buying a loan. If you think of the process that way, you may take the time to get the best possible rate, which means obtaining quotes from various sources. (Even interest-rate figures, however, are subject to manipulation. See the sidebar "When accountants get inspired" before you proceed any further.)

All the online auto-financing sites we tested put you under no obligation if you request a loan offer. If you don't like what you find out, you can simply decline the offer. If they've sent you a check, you can simply tear it up. Filling out the application forms takes only a few minutes. The sites affirm that the information is secure. (It usually goes out encrypted via SSL, or secure sockets layer — a popular security measure that encrypts data such as Visa card numbers before they are sent over the Internet.)

When accountants get inspired

Try opening a savings account at a bank. The teller often smiles and tells you, "Now, *this* figure is the interest rate for your savings account... and *this* one is the *other* interest rate for your savings account." They usually make such statements with a secret little grin that adds, "We work with money all the time, so this little paradox is no mystery to *us*."

Accountants, as a class, don't *seem* all that creative, but they aren't always what they seem. You can manipulate financial data in many ways: through write-offs, lease "factors," retroactive payments, double entries, two simultaneous interest rates, and so on.

Anyone who tries to understand the numbers in a typical company's annual report is likely to experience a bit of the old resourceful accounting. Similarly, accountants can figure interest rates *this* way or *that* way — tricky stuff sometimes. (Remember that these people sit around for weeks working out these inventive little formulae.)

We're certainly not going so far as to use the word *hoodwink*, but you get the point. Enter the big voice of government to set the situation right through the APR (Annualized Percentage Rate). The APR is a bottom-line rate — it's the actual cost to you of the loan per year (*annualized* means per year). Whatever else they may (or may not) reveal to you, all lenders now must at least provide you with the APRs of their loan offers. So, if you compare the APRs that various lenders offer, you're now actually comparing apples to apples (instead of, say, to watermelons). You can, therefore, rely on the APR.

What's most surprising is the rapid response — you generally receive an e-mail message offering you the loan (or, if the news is bad, refusing to offer you a loan) within a matter of minutes after you submit your request form. The AAA site that we describe in the section, "AAA's 15-Second Loan (Talk about Rapid!)," later in this chapter even states that most of its decisions take only 15 seconds. You can't reserve a library book online faster than that. Typically, the online lender then sends a check to you (as quickly as the next day), and you fill it in for the amount you want to borrow, up to the limit of the loan for which you receive online approval.

Don't neglect to find out what kind of interest rate the auto dealer can offer you if you finance the vehicle through him. Sometimes dealers use low-interest loans as one of their come-ons. Check with your credit union, too, if you belong to one. These nonprofit organizations can often undercut the current loan rates that other lenders offer.

Some lending institutions use the Internet somewhat differently than we describe in the preceding paragraphs: You can fill out the application form online, but you must later follow up with additional forms or even meet with a human representative to complete the loan. We don't describe these hybrid loan processes in this chapter.

According to statistics, the average new car loan is for $17,000, and buyers use it to purchase a $22,000 car. (The average used car costs $10,000.) Consider your loan with care and check out several of the sites that we mention in this chapter or other promising sites that you may locate as you search the Internet.

As you fill out an application for an online loan, you usually need to provide the following several facts:

- How long you've lived at your current address
- How long you've had your current job
- Your gross income
- Your mortgage or rent payments
- Whether you're requesting the loan by yourself (as an individual) or with someone else (a joint loan)
- The car that you want to buy and how much it's likely to cost
- How much you're likely to get for your trade-in

Remember that these financial institutions make their money by loaning, so they want to offer you a loan. To get a quick, positive answer, however, you generally need a relatively lengthy and relatively strong credit rating.

Fast Financing through eAuto

The eAuto Web site (www.eauto.com/carfinsvc.shtml) offers you financing services (or links to services) that enable you to get your financing in place before you approach the actual purchase (see Figure 10-1). The eAuto site also points out that you get additional benefits if you finance with eAuto online: The rates are low; you make no down payment and pay no fees or closing costs; you get your answer in a few hours and the money, in most cases, the next day; and you can buy from any franchised dealership of your choice.

Go to the eAuto Web site and click the <u>Click here to get a FREE rate and payment quote</u> link. You then go to the CarFinance.com Web site, where you see a page similar to the one shown in Figure 10-2.

Fill in the information that the E-Loan form requests and click the Search button. You then receive a quote of monthly payments that the company bases on several loan periods, as shown in Figure 10-3.

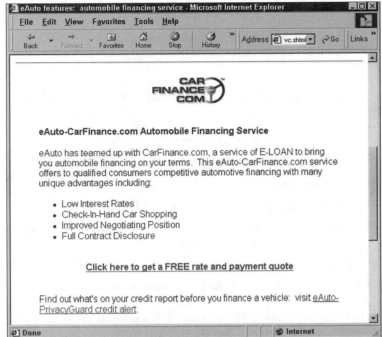

Figure 10-1:
At eAuto, you can expect to find low rates and a rapid response to your loan application.

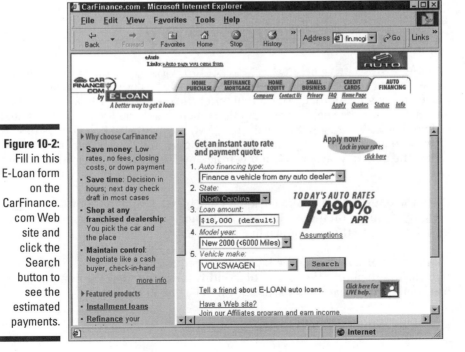

Figure 10-2:
Fill in this E-Loan form on the CarFinance.com Web site and click the Search button to see the estimated payments.

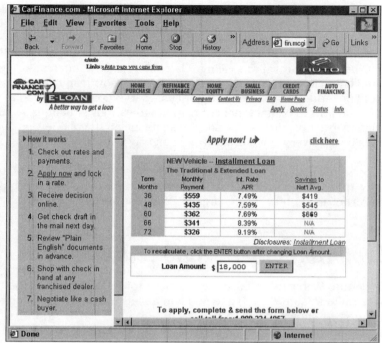

Figure 10-3:
After you
receive
information
on rates for
various loan
periods, you
can scroll
down this
page to fill
in a short
form for
your loan
application.

If you scroll down the page, you find a short form that you can fill in to actually apply for a loan through the company. According to eAuto (and for simplicity, we're just referring to eAuto from here on, although the logo switches to E-Loan), the loan form that you fill out is secure and confidential and puts you under no obligation. The site uses SSL (Secure Socket Layer) to keep your credit and other personal information secure.

SSL is an encryption scheme that Netscape (a company that makes Internet software) developed. SSL facilitates sending encrypted (coded) information over the Internet so that no one except those to whom you're addressing it can actually read it. Internet Explorer and Netscape's Communicator both support SSL, which encrypts data by using a private key scheme. If you ever see a URL that begins with `https` rather than the usual `http`, that's your cue that the page uses SSL.

Seeing results in 15 minutes

We filled in the eAuto loan application — it's brief and takes only a few minutes. A notice appears on-screen telling you that the company has received your application and that you can see the results by clicking the Status link on the eAuto home page or that you're going to receive a confirmation e-mail soon.

Fifteen minutes later, we received an e-mail message containing the loan approval. (Your experience may, of course, differ.) In the e-mail, the company told us the maximum that it was willing to loan (the amount exceeded our request), the name of a personal loan representative we could e-mail or phone, that the loan approval was valid for two months, how much mileage the car could have (if we chose to buy a used car), and how many years old the car could be. Additional information told us what to do if we decided to wait until later and how to contact them or respond to various situations — such as calculating exact payments, speaking to someone on the phone, and so forth. All in all, it was a very fast and very pleasant way to get auto financing.

If you're really in a hurry, you can opt for the overnight service. If the company approves your loan, it sends a check draft to you the next business day via Airborne Express. The charge for this rush service is $12.

Exploring other eAuto features

The eAuto Web site isn't just a good place for financing a loan. Go to its home page (at www.eauto.com) and you find a plethora of links leading to various features, as shown in Figure 10-4.

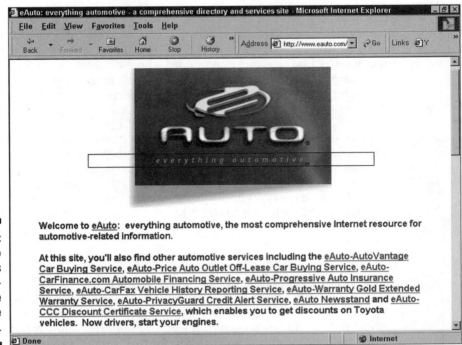

Figure 10-4:
The eAuto Web site is a full-service automobile site.

Among the other elements in the eAuto galaxy of car-related information and features that you can access from its home page (in addition to the financing service that we explore in the preceding section) are the following services:

✔ A car-buying service

✔ An off-lease (returned after the lease was over) car-buying service

✔ An auto-insurance service

✔ A vehicle-history reporting service

✔ An extended-warranty service

Autoweb's Financing Options

The very popular Autoweb site (www.autoweb.com on the Web) also includes a financing feature. Click the <u>Finance</u> link and you go to the PeopleFirst.com page, as shown in Figure 10-5.

Click the <u>Check our low rates and simple terms</u> link at the bottom of the page, and you see a list of rates similar to the one shown in Figure 10-6.

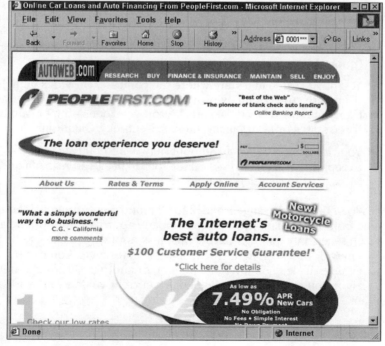

Figure 10-5:
Try Autoweb's PeopleFirst.com page for another rapid-response loan decision.

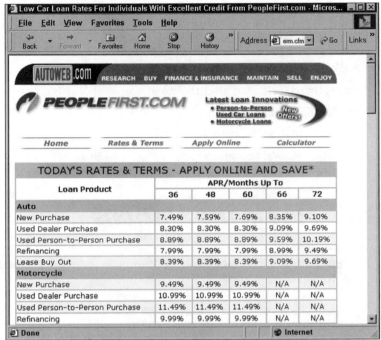

Figure 10-6:
This PeopleFirst.com table of rates tells you what interest rate you can expect from Autoweb for a variety of terms, loans, and vehicles.

Click the <u>Apply Online</u> link to view the Basic Requirements, which include:

- ✔ You must have an "EXCELLENT and SUBSTANTIAL credit record" (quoted from the site).

- ✔ You must reside in a state where the company provides vehicle loans. (Currently, the company provides loans in all states except Hawaii, New Hampshire, and North Dakota. Motorcycle loans aren't available in those three states or in Arkansas, Illinois, Kentucky, Oklahoma, or Wyoming.)

- ✔ Your loan must be for an amount between $7,500 and $75,000 (with the exception of required lower limits of $10,000.01 in Arizona and $15,000.01 in New Jersey and Kentucky).

Auto-loan terms can range from 12 to 72 months; motorcycle-loan terms can range from 12 to 60 months. If the company approves your online application (which takes only minutes during business hours), you can use its check to buy a new or used car, light truck, SUV, or motorcycle. You can buy from a new vehicle dealer, an individual person, or another authorized dealer or broker, or you can choose to refinance a current vehicle loan with a different lender.

AAA's 15-Second Loan (Talk about Rapid!)

If you're really hot to trot about a car — and want an answer instantly — try the Web site of the AAA (American Automobile Association). This company says that its service is available 24 hours a day and that most loans are "rendered in 15 seconds."

Go to the AAA home page at www.aaa.com and enter your ZIP code and click Go. The AAA divides its site into states, so after you provide your ZIP code and click the Go button, you see an entrance page similar to the one shown in Figure 10-7.

If you click the <u>Visitors</u> link, you see a page listing the various options available, which can include travel, a travel agency, insurance, financial services, discounts, safety issues, news, and others. Move your mouse pointer over the <u>Financial services</u> link and a pop-up menu appears. Click the Auto loans and leases option. You see a page similar to the one shown in Figure 10-8.

Click the <u>Click Here</u> portion of the online auto-loan application link.

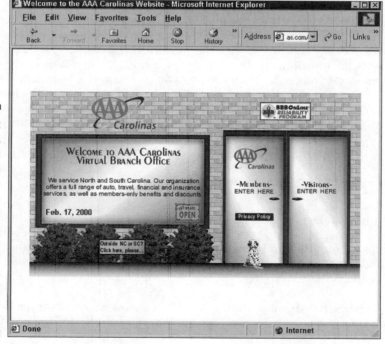

Figure 10-7: The AAA divides its site into state-specific pages; this page services customers in both North and South Carolina.

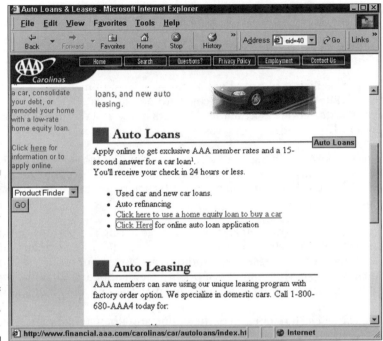

Figure 10-8:
You can
begin your
15-second
loan
application
process on
this page of
the AAA
Web site.

A <u>Click here to use a home equity loan to buy a car</u> link also appears on the AAA Financing page. Some people prefer to borrow against their home because they can save money that way. How? Home-mortgage interest payments are one of the few remaining tax deductions available to the average person. (If you consider refinancing your home in this way, however, make sure that you pay close attention to the fees. In some cases, the fees such a loan involve can erase any savings that you get from possibly lower interest rates and the tax deduction. Do the math, or you may take a bath.)

CarPoint by Microsoft

If you visit the CarPoint MSN Web site (at `www.carpoint.msn.com/finance_insurance`), you find several interesting financial features. Try clicking the <u>Interest Rates</u> link and then selecting your state from the drop-down list box. (You don't need to click a Go button; as soon as you choose a state, you go to the appropriate Web page.)

The page that appears displays the highest, lowest, and average loan rates for your state (for both new and used cars), as shown in Figure 10-9.

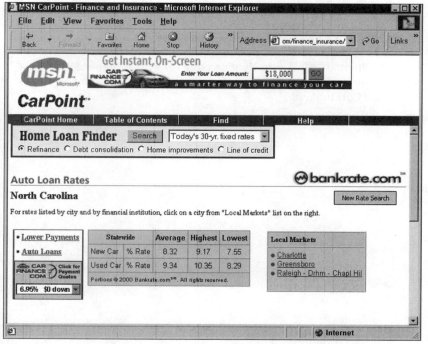

Figure 10-9: This page of the CarPoint MSN Web site shows you the range of available loan rates in your own state; this page shows the rates in North Carolina.

If you can't get approved . . .

If all else fails and the various loan sources that we describe in this chapter turn you down, consider a finance company. The rates that such companies charge are generally higher than those of other sources, but they do consider loans to people whose credit rating is too weak to get quick online approval.

Don't feel too embarrassed if your credit record is less than excellent (or too brief) to qualify you for a loan elsewhere. You're actually in the majority. Research shows that about 60 percent of the adult population falls into this category. Losing a good credit rating isn't all that hard to do, either: It can happen if you get into an unresolved dispute or fail to pay a bill for more than two months. But if you think that your credit rating is good and don't understand why companies are turning you

down, you can take a look at your actual credit rating. The law gives you that right. The credit companies don't need to show it to you for free, unfortunately, but they must show it to you.

You can obtain a free credit report, however, if you sign up for a trial membership in the CreditCheck Monitoring Service. Or you can pay $7.95 for a report from Experian. (You can find this offer at www.freecreditreport.com.) Alternatively, you can obtain a merged, triple-source report from Equifax, Trans Union, and Experian for $29.95 at www.icreditreport.com.

Remember, too, that if you own cash value in a life insurance policy, you can sometimes borrow from it.

Click the various Local Markets links for the rates in your city, as various lending institutions list them, including any fees, the percentage that you must put as a down payment, and other data.

At the main MSN auto-finance page (at `www.carpoint.msn.com/finance_insurance`), you also find direct links to such lenders as PeopleFirst Finance and CarFinance.

Chapter 11

To Buy or to Lease: That Is the Question

Some things in life are 50-50 propositions: leasing versus buying a car, renting versus owning a home, going with the chicken or the fish for your airline meal.

Even professional financial advisors admit that they can't find compelling reasons to recommend buying a car over leasing it and vice versa. Financially, at least, both paths seem pretty much equivalent, with leasing costing just a bit more. So the final decision often becomes more a matter of personal style than a money matter.

Nevertheless, finding out just how many people are leasing these days may surprise you. Research indicates that drivers now lease rather than buy one out of three new cars. And for luxury class vehicles, that figure goes up to more than half!

This chapter attempts to achieve the following two primary goals:

✔ To help you determine whether leasing or purchasing most suits your lifestyle and personality.

✔ To show you, if you do choose to lease, how you can save yourself hundreds of dollars and who knows how many headaches by becoming a prepared customer rather than the opposite. (What's the opposite? People use various names for them: Boiler-room stock pushers call them *whales* (big, rich, and slow); salesmen call them *patsies;* and other names are too vivid to print in a family book.)

So check out the following sections to see just how leasing works, whether it's right for you, and (as this book is all about car buying — or, in this case, leasing — online) where to go to find lease financing on the Internet.

The Pros and Cons of Leasing

If you buy, you own the car. If you lease, you *rent* the car and are paying for its depreciation during the term of your lease.

Leasing is especially attractive to people who don't have the loose cash sitting around for a big down payment, but who want relatively small monthly payments. But always remain alert when getting a car, no matter whether you're buying or leasing. Don't let a salesman lull you into brief, pleasant naps just because the costs — both initial and monthly — are low.

You need always to pay attention to the *overall* cost of a vehicle. Remember that — as in the case of an apartment renter's security and cleaning deposits — you may face some serious costs at the time that the lease ends and you return the car (usually after three years). A lease is normally more expensive than a purchase, if you take all the costs into account. And at the end of the lease comes the day that you give the car back, and you get nothing in return. That, my friends, is a day of reckoning — and it can often result in an expensive shock, as the following section explains.

Your day of reckoning

At the time that your lease is up and you bring in the car, the dealer looks it over very carefully. You usually must pay for any of the following problems:

- Stained upholstery, torn fabric, missing radios, and other damaged or lost components.
- "Excess" mileage.
- Dings, chips, dents, or "unusual" wear.
- Damage to the windows (or pretty much anything else cosmetic).
- And a nice little package of end-of-lease, turn-in fees with imaginative names such as *disposition fee*. (Dealers probably should rename this fee, which is similar to a "market adjustment" and other such fees, to something more along the lines of "get-more-money-for-the-dealer fees.")

I say that you must "usually pay for" these costs, because *you can negotiate them away.* And if you do remove some of these charges, you need to get it in writing that, for example, you're not responsible for any minor damage to the upholstery, dings, and so on. What's more, if words such as *minor, significant damage, unusual,* or *excess* appear in your lease agreement, make sure that the dealer defines those words with specific examples *before* you sign the agreement.

Consider that, at the end of the normal three-year lease, you must look for a new car (and you have no trade-in either). What's more, leases are usually complex documents. Figuring out just what they mean often is quite difficult. You can bet, however, that if your friendly leaser can find a way to wedge in some additional profits here and there, he's sure to do so. Also, many people are so happy when they discover the low initial costs and low monthly payments typical of leases that they simply agree to the lease without giving the overall purchase much thought. They don't realize that you really can *bargain* the terms of a lease, just as you can with a purchase.

On the other hand . . .

Leasing has its good points, too. On the plus side of leasing, consider these:

- ✔ You don't face the hassle of negotiating the value of a trade-in on your next purchase. (You have no trade-in on a lease; you never bought the thing.) This arrangement often works out well because many people use their trade-in to cover the down payment on a new car purchase. But with a lease, you don't usually have a down payment.

- ✔ If the vehicle starts experiencing serious problems, well . . . *you* don't own this clunker.

- ✔ Signing a lease is usually easier and more convenient than buying. (At least it is when you're arranging the lease; the hassles at the time that you return the car are another story altogether.)

- ✔ If the car turns out to be a total lemon, well . . . again, *you* didn't buy it.

- ✔ You get a nice, new car every two or three years.

- ✔ Monthly payments are lower, and remember that often you make no down payment at all. So you can perhaps lease a BMW for the same monthly payment that you may face if you just buy a Honda.

- ✔ If you like the car and want to keep it, they'll probably make you a nice deal for its purchase.

A special kind of lease known as the *open-end lease* may appeal to you. In such an arrangement, you agree up front to pay the difference between the predicted value (known as the *residual value*) of the car at the end of the lease and the actual value (the *realized value*) of the car at lease's end. The leaser writes the predicted value into the lease at the time that you get the car, but he determines the realized value at the end of the lease, after you return the car. In some cases, you may actually get money back if the car is worth more at the end of the lease than the leaser predicted in the residual value.

But, as always, keep your eyes open. Dealers can calculate the realized value several ways: how much money they get after they sell the car to someone; the retail value (as an agreed-on source determines it); the wholesale value; what's known as the *fair-market value;* or even the best *offer* that the dealer gets for the car. You need to know which of these methods of calculation the leaser is using on your lease.

You can find the residual value in the Automotive Leasing Guide. (You can order a sample edition for $11 at www.alg.com on the Web, or you can ask the dealer for one.)

Negotiating a Lease

To facilitate your negotiations when arranging a lease, you first want to find out what the *dealer rebate* is. (You know about consumer rebates — they're generally advertised. But what about money that the manufacturer pays to the dealer?) If you know this amount, you have a really good bargaining chip in your negotiations. You can use your Internet resource to determine the amount of this "secret" dealer rebate.

Always keep in mind that a lease is opposite to a purchase in a key way: If you want to buy this car, or reduce the "damage charges" or other costs, you must engage in some serious negotiations *at the end of a lease*. In a purchase, you establish all the details prior to paying the money, but if you lease, you must return the car back at the end of the lease and can face charges at that time that you may never expect.

Get it in writing

Always get a written *description detailing any permitted wear and tear a vehicle can incur during the period of a lease and what other kinds of damage you must pay for — and get this document* before *you sign the lease.* If you don't, you may face paying for a new set of tires, a new battery, body work for even small nicks, or worse — a little fraying around the edges of the seat covers, for example, and you may even end up forking over the cost of a whole new upholstery job.

Get also a written description of any "disposition fee." And then try to get rid of it. Politely state that you want the leaser to remove this fee from the lease. This fee is similar to its close cousins — ADP (additional dealer profit), ADM (additional dealer markup), "market adjustment," and so on. The "disposition fee" isn't some government requirement, similar to a "disposal fee" if you get an oil change. It has no real meaning at all, other than as yet one more way that car dealers can get their fingers into your wallet.

A dealer usually tells you that this fee covers his cost of getting the vehicle ready for resale or some such argument. Just say to him that you have no interest in his costs of running a business. Paying a "wax fee" to cover the dealer's costs of shining up the car isn't your responsibility. Neither do you want to pay a "restocking fee" to cover the dealer's costs of keeping paper products in the bathroom. Or anything similar. Tell him that you want to merely negotiate the basic costs of the lease and that this process becomes simpler all around if he isn't tucking in extra fees here and there.

But do stay polite. Why? Because you get better results if you're polite. And you're after results — not insults. Maybe working yourself up about these sly little extra fees is more emotionally satisfying, but you're trying to save yourself money here, not vent your righteous anger.

Dealers also usually want to add an "acquisition fee" that's supposed to cover the cost of writing up the lease and managing it during the term. Surprised? It's all kind of a game, really. Car dealers nearly always break down a sale or lease into fragments and then try to hide some of those fragments. It's as if you pick out a new pair of $50 shoes, but after you get to the checkout counter, the cost is actually $60. If you ask about the extra charges, the cashier says, "Well, of course, this amount includes the shoelace fee, the boxing fee, and the sole undercoating fee." Well, of *course* you should realize that the store *always* requires these fees. So what's your problem?

A good negotiator looks at a lease's "acquisition fee" and "disposition fee" and offers to pay the lower of the two but not both. A great negotiator may say, "Why burden ourselves with any of these little tacked on 'fees' and extra charges? Let's haggle over the actual price of this lease and not fog up the negotiation process with unnecessary added factors."

Get in writing, too, the number of miles per year that you can drive without paying a penalty. A typical lease permits 15,000 miles. Find out, too, how much you must pay if you exceed this allotment (and get that in writing as well). A typical cost is $.15 per mile that you drive in excess of the limit, so if you drive 3,000 extra miles, you owe $450. (Some leases, however, specify as much as $.25 per mile.)

Do you usually drive fewer miles than the limit? If so, does your lease give you any credit for *not* using the annual permitted mileage? (If so, make sure that's written into the lease, too.) And if you think that you're likely to use more miles than the default limit, go ahead and negotiate a higher annual-mileage limit and (what else?) make sure the new limit appears in writing on the lease as well.

Questions to answer before leasing

As you're hammering out the terms of your lease, but before finally sitting down to sign it, ask yourself the following questions:

- ✔ What's the APR (the Annualized Percentage Rate, the total interest payment) of your lease, and how does it compare to other leases you've checked out?

- ✔ Does the lease include a premature buyout option, so you can purchase the vehicle before the lease runs out if you wish?

- ✔ How much is the car going to cost you if you decide to buy it at the end of the lease?

- ✔ Can the dealer adjust the length of the lease to something other than the typical two or three years?

- ✔ Does the lease agreement include any odd little charges tucked away inside it? (Read the agreement carefully — doing so may save you hundreds of dollars. Look for things such as an "undercoating charge," "dealer advertising," an AMU, PBS, ABC, NBC or any other creative way the dealer has of saying, "You owe me more money.")

- ✔ What's the security deposit? (Tell the dealer that you're willing to agree to no more than the amount of one month's payment, which is the typical deposit.)

- ✔ Who's responsible if, heaven forbid, an accident totals the car? If someone steals it? If it burns to the ground?

- ✔ What's the penalty if you decide you want to end the lease early and just turn in the car? (Usually, this costs you quite a bit.)

- ✔ What insurance must you purchase? Does it cover all contingencies?

✔ **Is the dealer responsible for repairs and maintenance — *or are you?*** You probably must agree to a maintenance schedule. After all, the dealer can't come over to your place and drive the car in for an oil change every 3,000 miles. But find out who pays if the transmission drops out onto the pavement. In most cases, the ordinary factory warranty for that vehicle covers a leased car. And the warranty usually exceeds the term of the lease (but find out for sure, just to stay on the safe side).

Your bottom line: It's more than dollars and cents

You may think from the information that I give in the preceding sections that leasing is really more trouble than it's worth. But that's not necessarily true. If you're willing to pay a bit more money overall (than you would by purchasing the same vehicle outright) in exchange for the pleasure of driving a new car every three years, go for it.

If renting a car suits your personality and pocketbook, I see no reason for you not to opt for a lease. But do remain aware that, in taking such a course, you face some of the same limitations that you face in renting an apartment. You can hang hairy dice from the mirror (because you can later remove the dice), for example, but you can't replace the radio with a CD changer if the mood strikes you. This car isn't really yours, and if you forget to follow the maintenance schedule or drive too many miles in a given year, you get a sobering reminder that it isn't your car in the additional fees you must pay after you turn it in. And, after the term of the lease is up, you must then immediately find another car to drive (or go ahead and buy the leased car).

If, on the other hand, you like to own the things you use, prefer to avoid car payments that never end, don't care that much about having a new car every few years, or find the necessity of dealing with an annual mileage limit and a regular maintenance schedule annoying, I suggest that you just buy a car instead.

Finding an Online Lease

The process of calculating the costs of a lease online is similar to that of calculating a purchase price. However, not many of the major Internet e-commerce car sites currently feature leasing options. These sites often include features that help you make up your mind about whether to purchase or lease, but they're currently geared mainly toward selling and not leasing. This situation may change, however. The Internet is nothing if not a rapidly evolving medium. I particularly recommend that you visit the site that I describe at the end of this overall section, LeaseSource. But first, the following sections take a look at a few other sources that you can check out for lease opportunities.

Using CarsEverything's lease calculator

Foreknowledge is always valuable. You always want to do your own calculations before agreeing to any lease — and ask for clarification if your figures don't match the dealer's calculations. (This approach is a good way to ferret out those hidden extra "fees" that seem to crop up in every long contract.)

The CarsEverything Web site offers you a handy calculator that can tell you what your monthly payment should be. Just go to the CarsEverything site at `www.carseverything.com` and then click the <u>Lease Calculator</u> link. You then access the calculator, as shown in Figure 11-1. Fill in the selling price, the residual value (see the section "On the Other Hand," earlier in this chapter, for information on determining the residual value), the term of the lease, the tax, and what's known as the *factor*.

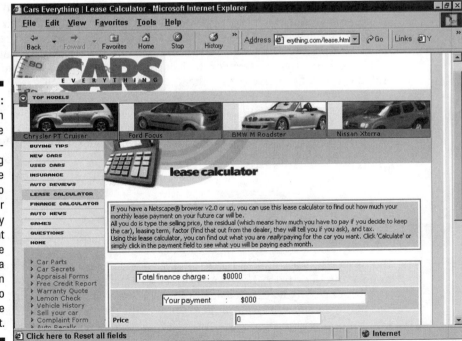

Figure 11-1: You can use the Cars-Everything lease calculator to figure your monthly payment and maybe ferret out a hidden "fee" or two in the lease agreement.

Ask the dealer what their *factor* is. This element is also sometimes known as the *money factor* (and is actually a finance charge that the dealer *could* express as a percentage). But expressing it that way may prove too easy for you to understand, so instead, the leaser expresses it as a number, usually between .0028 and .0042, that he can secretly multiply by a huge amount to translate it into a percentage.

Trying AutoWeb's calculator

Here's another useful calculator. This one shows you what happens if you lease, or buy, the same car. Go to the AutoWeb Web site (at `www.autoweb.com/financecenter.htm`) and then click the <u>Lease Versus Loan</u> link. You then see the calculator shown in Figure 11-2:

If you fill in the numbers for the calculator's questions, as in the example shown in Figure 11-2, and click the Calculate button, you then see the results, as shown in Figure 11-3.

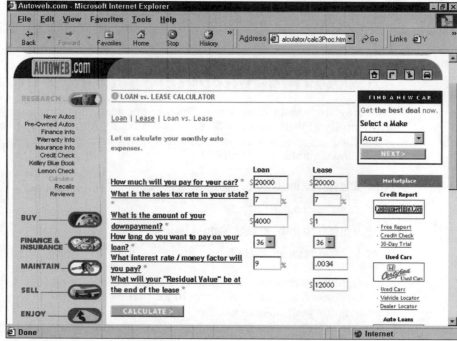

Figure 11-2:
Compare the differences between purchasing versus leasing a vehicle by using AutoWeb's handy online calculator.

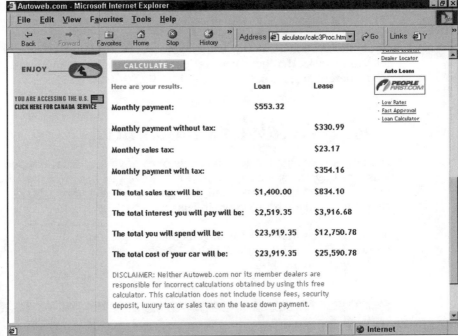

Figure 11-3:
Notice that your overall cost is higher if you lease instead of purchase this car.

Discovering Autobytel's leasing offers

You may also want to check out the lease-application feature that you find at the Autobytel Web site (at `www.autobytel.com`). After you get to the site, click the <u>Financing</u> link under the Activity Centers heading. Then click any of the following links (see Figure 11-4):

- ✓ <u>4 Steps to Individual Loans & Leases</u>
- ✓ <u>2 Steps to a Business Lease</u>
- ✓ <u>6 Steps to Individual Loans & Leases</u>
- ✓ <u>Loan versus lease tool</u>

Autobytel says that you can "simply answer one set of questions, and within two business days, you receive up to four offers from lenders who actually compete for your business." And, best of all, the service is free. This is an excellent site. Spend some time here. That's my advice.

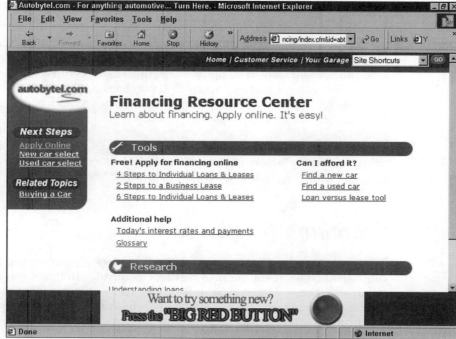

Taking a look at LeaseSource

LeaseSource (at www.leasesource.com on the Web) bills itself as "the Internet's best auto-leasing site." It's certainly worth checking out. As you can see in Figure 11-5, this site offers several interesting features.

The site's Lease Workshop, especially, is most thorough and well worth your time to visit if you're considering leasing a car (see Figure 11-6).

Among the Lease Workshop's handy resources for helping you assess whether to lease are the following tools:

- ✔ The *CarWizard,* offering what LeaseSource calls "the most accurate and comprehensive pricing and data engine on the Internet. CarWizard features residual values, invoice and retail pricing, technical specs, photos, driving reviews and incredible search functionality."

- ✔ The *lease profiler utility,* which offers a seven-question quiz to help you make up your mind.

- ✔ A *Run The Numbers utility* that helps you compare the financial effect of leasing versus buying.

- ✔ A *contract summaries tool* that enables you to check out 38 different lease contracts that the company describes in understandable terms. You'll find it easy to comprehend various aspects of vehicle leases, including wear and tear standards, purchase option fees, insurance, and mileage expenses. This feature gives you a good, solid background to help you understand lease agreements.

Clicking the link to LeaseSource's <u>Leasing Classroom</u> gives you access to definitions of leasing jargon, explanations of residual values, negotiating tips, and more. All in all, LeaseSource lives up to its name and its claims.

Searching for yourself

Because vehicle leasing is such a new and developing topic on the Internet, you should supplement the sites that I recommend with those you find yourself by using a good Internet search engine, such as Google (at `www.google.com`). If you live in Texas, for example, type *auto leasing Texas* into your search engine and you'll get many responses, including `www.wirth-leasing.com`.

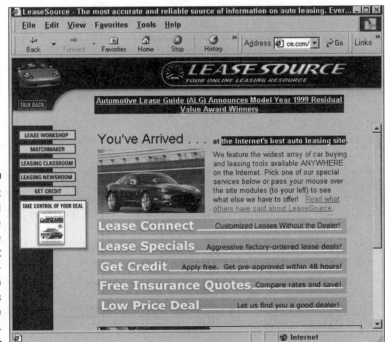

Figure 11-5:
You find some unique features at the Lease-Source Web site, such as the Lease Workshop.

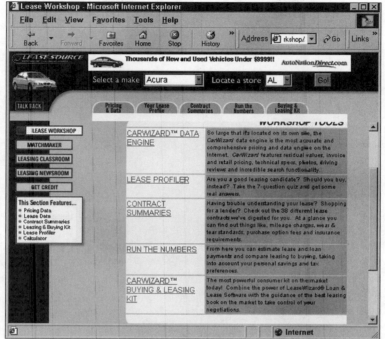

Figure 11-6:
Lease-
Source's
online Lease
Workshop
offers an
excellent
set of tools
for your use
in assessing
whether a
lease is
for you.

Chapter 12

Buying a New Car on the Internet

In This Chapter

▶ Going online to determine which cars are most popular

▶ Negotiating with a dealer on trade-ins and new cars

▶ Buying a vehicle at an online car auction

*B*uying a new car online usually means that you end up getting in touch with a local dealership to finalize the purchase. The online part is where you do research — gather information to prepare yourself for the purchase (and save a good deal of money as a result). The dealership part is where you move from the virtual world of information into the real world of bumpers, tires and salesmen.

You can use the Internet to gather information about vehicles, arrange your financing in advance, and save money on insurance. But you want to actually test-drive the car, see its color for yourself, feel its leg room, examine the trunk space, and otherwise physically engage the machine at a dealership. And you sometimes must negotiate prices — both for the trade-in and the new car — with a real salesperson.

For these reasons, online car-buying services are often mainly referral-services — they put you in touch with a dealer in your area. The difference between the online approach and traditional car buying is that you meet the dealer already prepared. You can, therefore, greatly reduce the amount of time that you spend at the dealership and the amount of negotiation necessary to secure the deal. And above all, you can greatly reduce the price that you pay for a vehicle. Going online to buy a car is really a smart move.

At the time that you first visit the dealer to test drive the car, ask for a blank copy of the dealer's standard contract. Now, however, isn't yet the time for negotiation. You want to go home and, in the peace and quiet of your bubble bath or whatever, read the thing and circle any bad or confusing spots. You're then even better prepared when you return to the dealership for the final negotiations. This tactic is yet another way to do your homework before you get down to the real nitty-gritty of negotiation. You're making *two* trips to the dealer instead of just one, which gives you a significant advantage over just checking things out and making the deal in a single visit.

Sure, a few companies actually do sell cars online, and you never need meet with a real human being to complete the transaction with such online dealers. But these few direct-sales businesses are primarily either credit unions, fleet-sales outfits, or brokers.

Car sales are probably second only to liquor sales in the number of laws governing the transaction. What's more, many of these laws currently rule out auto sales to consumers across state lines.

The companies that people widely use and know on the Internet, such as Autobytel and CarPoint, don't actually sell cars themselves. They merely put you in touch with a dealer. You then finalize the purchase at the dealership.

Several other chapters in this book show you how to do your homework — finding financing, insurance, the car that best suits you, the dealer cost of that car, the value of your trade-in, and so on.

In this chapter, I assume that you've done the homework. You've even gone so far as to take my advice and have already chosen a nearby dealer (for convenient servicing and maintenance) and a dealer large enough to make negotiations as flexible as possible. What's more, you've visited the dealer and taken a test drive — finalizing your selection by actually experiencing the car in the real world (see Chapter 5).

This chapter, therefore, focuses on your actually *buying* a car — the point where you finalize the negotiations with the salesperson and pay some money. Before getting into the details of completing the deal, however, I'm first going to look at some of the cars that other people are choosing. If you've already decided on your dream car, the following lists may reinforce that decision. If you haven't yet decided, however, perhaps checking out a few top-ten lists may inspire you.

Joining the Crowd

If you read some of the other chapters in this book that tell you how to narrow your selection of a new car, but you still can't make up your mind, maybe you just need to go with the crowd.

If you're like most people, you sometimes buy a book or a record simply because it's a bestseller. You figure that sheer numbers of sales must indicate satisfied customers. Popularity, after all, counts. If you can't make up your mind, taking a look at how others made up theirs sometimes helps.

Can the Internet help you determine which new cars are currently selling the best? (The answer is yes.) Which cars are the favorites of GenX buyers or of fat-cat Boomers? Is the Earth round?

To find out which new cars are the most requested at the CarPoint site for the past 12 months, open your Web browser and go to `www.carpoint.msn.com`, CarPoint's home page. Click the Table of Contents link. Then, in the Featured Articles section, click CarPoint User's Top Ten. You see a page similar to the one shown in Figure 12-1.

Also check out `carpoint.msn.com/WindowShopping.asp` to view other interesting top-ten lists.

Figure 12-1: On CarPoint's Top Ten page, you can find current popularity ratings for new cars.

After You Get to the Dealer

After you finish your online research and decide on a vehicle to purchase, you're ready to take up arms and march right in on a dealer — and avoid getting slammed. With the advice that I offer in this book, along with all your online research, you can now give the dealer a few hundred dollars profit on the sale (instead of a few thousand). A few hundred dollars, after all, is plenty of profit for the few hours the dealer spends as you test and then negotiate terms for the new car.

Say that, thanks to your research, you already know what car, what accessories, and what options you want. You've already arranged insurance and financing online. You know the dealer cost of the car you're after, and you're prepared to ask to see the factory invoice. (See, however, the following Warning.) Three steps to a successful purchase remain. The first step is to discuss *and finalize* the money that you're to get for your trade-in. For most of us, the trade-in provides the down payment. That's a very good reason to insist on getting a fair price. Most new car buyers, however, get the shaft during the trade-in negotiation.

I'm repeating this warning from previous chapters so that you're not negotiating in a dreamland. You must get an accurate dealer cost of the car that you're buying. If you get a new-car dealer-price quote from an Internet source, it's merely an estimated dealer cost. This figure can be a low-ball estimate by several hundred dollars. Why? It can exclude extra options, import fees, gas charges, possible extra advertising costs, and so on. At the dealership, ask to see the actual *factory invoice* for the car that you're buying. This figure is usually *higher* than the prices you get on the Internet for the standard models. *Don't* decide your final offer merely on the estimated dealer-invoice price that you find on the Internet.

Don't give away your trade-in

All too many people (most people, in fact) quickly cave in if a dealer offers a really, really low price for their trade-in. In the typical trade-in example that I describe in the following section, if you agree to the salesperson's "considered offer," *you lose money* by being either too timid or too uninformed about auto negotiating. Saving you this ridiculous waste of good money is the topic of this section.

If you're trading in your existing car, your *first step* in negotiating at the dealership is to agree on the trade-in price. The reasons are two: The salesperson is unlikely to start the negotiations with this topic, so you gain immediate control of the negotiation process. More important, most people, after buying a new car, worry that they got too little for their trade-in. Why? Because they *did* get too little.

Most people perhaps spend a couple of hours haggling over the details of the new car they're buying, and then almost everything is set for them to leave the lot in the shiny new car they now love. Only one little detail remains: What do they get for their existing car? At this point, most people cave and accept the (pitiful) offer that the salesperson provides — along with a song-and-dance about how "offering this price is common these days" or "the moon is in the seventh house" or "our mechanic reports rusting on the undercarriage" or whatever.

No goose this year

You can find used car prices in the Blue Book. (See Chapter 4 for the online source.) Three prices are available for used cars. Imagine, for example, that your car lists for a used retail price at $12,000. It's then likely to list for around, say, $9,000 wholesale, with an auction price of about $8,300. A salesperson is likely to offer you around $5,700 and, if you scream and moan, the salesperson may go up to $6,500, weeping all the way about what the sales manager is going to do after this shockingly high price becomes general knowledge. (No Christmas goose for his son Tiny Tim this year. *Thanks to you.*)

Find out the Blue Book value and the Black Book value (the auction value — see Chapter 4) *before* you start negotiations. You want to know what the dealer can sell your car for — and remember that the auction value is a rock-bottom value. If the dealer offers $5,700 (using the examples that I give in the preceding paragraph), you counter with $9,000, the wholesale value. Then you can allow the salesperson to whittle you down to a couple hundred dollars more than the auction price of $8,300.

Just add the word firm

Don't accept any amount lower than the auction price for your trade-in (unless you have a really good reason, such as that the entire undercarriage is *really* rusting). If necessary, extract your current car from the negotiation process. You can almost always easily get the auction price by putting a classified ad in the paper — phoning in the ad and including the word "firm" so that you don't need to haggle with strangers isn't that big of a deal. At the auction price, moreover, you *can* be firm. Someone almost certainly is going to buy it unless you live in some remote Wyoming outback, in which case your negotiation strategies must take geographical extremity into account.

After you save yourself two or three thousand dollars on the trade-in, you can let the sales process move on to Step Two: the cost of the car that you're buying (including all options and accessories — *everything*).

Negotiating the price

Not everyone pays the same price buying the same car at the same dealership. Remember that fact. Unlike most cultures, most Americans simply aren't accustomed to haggling. From lack of practice, they're not good at it. And they tend to think that it makes them look cheap, stubborn, pushy, disagreeable, or impolite — or some combination of these traits.

Unless, however, you're willing to learn the rules of negotiating a low price, you want to pay someone else to negotiate for you (see the section "If You Simply *Can't* Negotiate," later in this chapter), or you really *want* one of those new no-haggle cars (in other words, a Saturn) — expect to lose hundreds and maybe even thousands of dollars on the price of your new car.

People pay different prices

People pay different prices for the same car. You can pay top dollar, or you can pay close to dealer cost — or you can pay somewhere in between. Bad negotiators may give the dealer $3,000 in profit; great negotiators may give the dealer $300 in profit. Obviously, salesmen and dealers prefer to get $3,000 from everyone — but experience shows that they can expect a spectrum of profit depending on how the customer behaves during the process. If you're polite, persistent, and (above all) *prepared* — you can usually drive the price down near the low end of the spectrum.

If you follow the steps that I outline earlier in this chapter, you're likely to get a good price from the dealer for your trade-in (or you do after you sell it yourself through the classifieds). Now to complete the process of buying the new car. This point is where you discuss — *and finalize* — the price of your new car.

The dealer is likely to begin negotiations with the full list price, acting as if that amount's understood as the selling price. I repeat: Remember to proceed with the negotiations at your own pace and remain ready at all times to walk. But always stay friendly and polite. You usually get better results if you don't make an enemy.

Stay polite, yet firm

My favorite tactic is courteous firmness. You do your homework and you know what price you're willing to pay. Respond to the dealer's first offer with whatever price you've *already decided* you're willing to pay (see Chapter 6). One tactic is to simply, politely make your first and final offer. You can sit there and dicker, but make quite plain to the dealer that, no matter what happens, you've already researched the price and you've already made your one and only offer. Other experts suggest making a low offer and then gradually giving in to the salesperson's attempts to bring you up to your final offer. Whatever approach you take, make sure that the dealer's clear that you're a serious buyer and always remain calm and pleasant.

If you feel pressure from the salesperson and become uncomfortable, you can always ask for a different salesperson at that dealership. Or you can leave and take your business elsewhere.

You don't need to explain your personal preferences in a car or describe your lifestyle, your hopes, and your fears. You don't need to make friends with the salesperson or the supervisor. You've arrived at the dealership with a precise idea of what you're willing to pay for a particular car. You know exactly which options and accessories you want (and don't want). You're paying cash — you have a check in hand because you've already arranged the financing (see Chapter 10). You don't need to worry about insurance because that's finalized (see Chapter 16). You've already decided whether you want an extended warranty and what to pay for that. You've reduced all the variables to one: How long does the salesperson take to realize that you're not going to change your offer?

In fact, all you need to tell the salesperson is that you're willing to pay X dollars for X car with X accessories. It's a simple, straightforward few hundred dollars for the dealership to make. Make the dealer aware that he's dealing with an *Internet* buyer. In other words, the dealer has a new kind of customer: someone who knows just what he wants and is already decided on just what he's willing to pay for it. And if you take that advice that I give you earlier in this chapter, you've already studied a copy of the dealer's contract and made a note of any questions that you want the dealer to clear up before you sign the deal.

If you simply can't negotiate

If you absolutely can't stand negotiation but realize that, by avoiding it, you may cost yourself as much as $2,000 or more when purchasing a new car, consider hiring *an auto consultant* (also known as a *buyer's agent*) who can do the dirty work for you. The cost of such a consultant can prove remarkably reasonable, considering the savings that you get in cash and the burden the agent lifts from those who were trained from day one to avoid conflict at all costs. And the operative word here is *costs* if you're overly passive about negotiating.

Can you find such consultants on the Internet? Well, the Internet hosts almost every possible topic. If you can imagine a profession, a service or a topic, you're likely to find it available on the Internet, as the following sections confirm.

Try the National Association of Buyers' Associates

One good resource if you want to hire an agent is the National Association of Buyers' Associates (at `www.naba.com` on the Web), as shown in Figure 12-2.

AutoAdvisor can help you negotiate

Another good online source of auto buyers' agents is AutoAdvisor (at `www.autoadvisor.com` on the Web), as shown in Figure 12-3.

Figure 12-2:
Visit the National Association of Buyers' Agents Web site for leads to people who do your negotiating for you and offer other car-buying services.

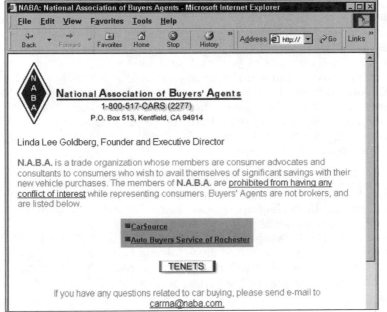

Figure 12-3:
Consider trying the auto buyers' agents at AutoAdvisor if you don't want to negotiate the price yourself for your new car.

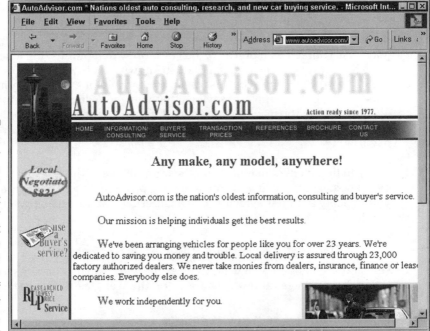

Going, Going, Gone! Using Online Auto Auctions

Although you don't currently find new-car auctions on the Web, you *can* buy a used car via online auctions. And now and then you can find at an online auction a used car that's "almost new" (very low mileage). Some experts claim that if money is your main concern, buying a low-mileage pre-owned car is the greatest bargain going.

Why can't you find new-car auctions online yet? Congressional politicians, or *lawmakers* as they sometimes prefer us to call them, keep on making laws! (No surprise there.) They've made laws governing interstate sales of new autos, and those laws seriously restrict such sales to individuals — and that includes through online auctions. This situation may change in the future, however, as these lawmakers are in the business of making laws, so they sometimes pass new legislation that rescinds their previous legislation.

You, the consumer, face another little problem with buying cars through online auctions: The important test-drive portion of a new-car purchase is usually impossible. Going to eBay to buy a cookbook is fine — if the description of the cookbook fails to mention that the index is torn out and grease splatters cover many of the pages, you're out only a few bucks. But how can you explain yourself if you spend thousands of dollars on a car with serious flaws and then must spend thousands more repairing those flaws? Remember the advice of your grandfather, the farmer: Never buy a pig in a poke. (You can, however, find exceptions to every rule. See the section "New-Vehicle Auctions," later in this chapter, for information about buying new cars online and a special test-drive program that a company known as Rolling Wheels offers.)

Auctions R Us: eBay sells cars

Speaking of eBay, the grand old leader of online auctioning added a special vehicle-auction page to its other auction wares back in August 1999. Some cars were put up for auction at eBay before this official recognition, but now eBay offers this section of its site solely for vehicle auction sales. You can find ordinary vehicles here as well as a special "Showroom" featuring classic cars.

To access eBay's auto zone, first go to eBay's home page (at www.ebay.com on the Web) and then click the <u>Automotive</u> link. You arrive at a page similar to the one shown in Figure 12-4.

The week that I checked, eBay was offering 1,545 cars, 549 trucks, and 139 RVs at auction, as well as hundreds of motorcycles.

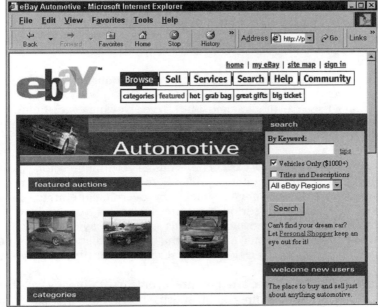

Figure 12-4: eBay now offers a sophisticated, full-featured vehicle-auction section.

If you're not familiar with the eBay auctioning process, you can easily learn about it by connecting to eBay. They offer excellent help and tutorials.

Online auctioning at Microsoft Network

If the possibility of finding a real bargain in a car at an online auction attracts you, in spite of the potential difficulties that I describe in the preceding section, check out the Microsoft Network's auction site (at `www.auctions.msn.com/html/cat17466/page1.htm` on the Web), as shown in Figure 12-5.

If you go to the MSN car auction site, you're probably going to find its features a little familiar if you've ever bought something from eBay or other online auction sites.

New-vehicle auctions

Rolling Wheels, a very interesting online vehicle-auction site, now actually offers new vehicles and also provides for test driving before you buy. The site puts you in touch with one of its "member dealers" in your area so that you can drive the model you want to bid on to see whether it's what you're after. To discover what the Rolling Wheels auction site offers, go to `www.rollingwheels.com` on the Web. You find a page similar to the one shown in Figure 12-6.

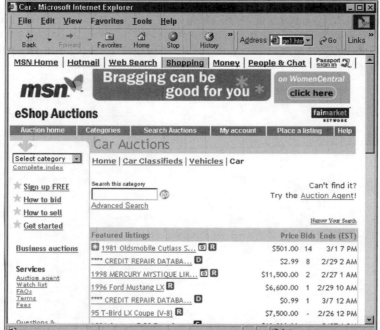

Figure 12-5:
Visit the
Microsoft
Network
eShop
Auctions
site, and
you're in for
an eBay
kind of
experience.

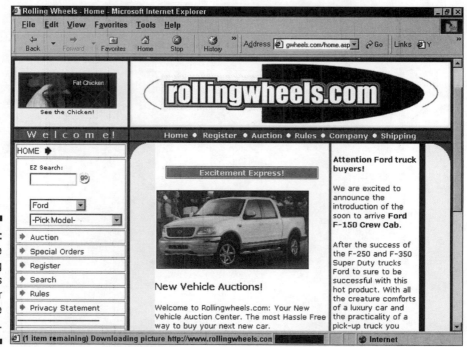

Figure 12-6:
Visit the
Rolling
Wheels
Web site for
new-vehicle
auctions.

This site describes itself in the following manner: "Your new-vehicle auction center. The most hassle-free way to buy your next new car. If you buy a vehicle from Rollingwheels.com, you set your price *and* we guarantee that you're in and out of the dealership in 60 minutes or less. You set your own price because we sell all our vehicles using our exclusive auction format."

Chapter 13

Finding a Used Car on the Internet

*Y*ou can find at least as many good reasons to buy a used car as you can to buy a new one. When buying a used car, all you need is an understanding of what you require in a car, what your budget enables you to afford, and what's available in the marketplace.

Buying a used car can be a wise compromise if you need to replace your old set of wheels but are working with a tight budget. You can often buy, for example, a year-old car with low mileage and warranty protection for thousands of dollars less than it originally sold for new. The reduction in price is because of the vehicle's depreciation, a fact that hits nearly every new car that rolls off a dealer's lot — or Web site for that matter (see Chapter 15).

So although a new car buyer is usually willing to pay what amounts to a premium for the right to be a car's first owner, a savvy used-car buyer saves money by buying the car after it goes through its cycle of depreciation.

In this chapter, we show you why buying a used car may make sense to you. You find out that you can go online to unearth literally thousands of used cars for sale that meet your driving needs and fall within your personal budget allocation. We take you on a tour of the Internet to locate dealers who sell excellent used cars. You receive useful tips on what to look for, and you discover how to save money when you buy. We also point out key online areas that specialize in classified ads for cars — ads similar to those that you see in your local paper. Many more used-car ads are within the reach of your keyboard and modem than you would ever find in a newspaper, plus they're frequently updated and accessible at any time of day.

While the Internet can be a great tool for finding used cars for sale that are not too far from home, you should never buy a used car sight unseen. New cars come with comprehensive warranties and few, if any, defects, so purchasing one online is typically not a risky endeavor. Used cars, on the other hand, usually offer limited or no warranty protection, so you should always take a used car for a test drive before buying it — and have a trusted mechanic look at inside and out if at all possible.

Going on the Internet to Find a Used Car

Tracking down a great used car on the Internet is easy. Your choices abound because you needn't confine your search to any given geographical area. Nor do you face certain time limits, as you may if you physically walk through used car lots. And you can learn a lot about a car by checking out online the info that car makers, dealers, and even ordinary car drivers such as you and me make available.

Using a search engine to find a used car

Many car dealers and newspapers maintain their own Web sites. Some of these sites are better than others, but you can generally find a detailed listing of available used cars — often with pictures and prices — at nearly all such sites. In fact, many dealers generate more income selling used cars than new ones, so it's not surprising that they are willing to invest significant time and resources into marketing their used cars online.

To find these sites, try using any search engine such as those in the following list:

- **AltaVista (at** www.altavista.com**).** This portal claims to offer "the fastest, most comprehensive search service available."

- **Ask Jeeves (at** www.ask.com**).** At Ask Jeeves, you ask a specific question, and the site produces a list of follow-up questions. You select the follow-up question that most closely matches the information you're looking for, and you're then taken to a site that offers that information. For example, submitting the question **Where can I find the nearest Acura dealer?** returns a list of follow-up questions, one of which is **How can I locate the nearest Acura dealer?** Click on that question, and you're immediately taken to a dealer-locator tool at Acura's site.

- **Google (at** www.google.com**).** Here, you won't find all the usual portal bells and whistles, such as the latest headlines and stock market updates, but Google's search engine is quite powerful and efficient. Check it out!

✔ **Northern Light (at** `www.northernlight.com`**).** This search engine offers you the option of searching all of its sources (which includes many newspaper and magazine articles) or just the World Wide Web. If your first search fails to return the information you're seeking, use the drop-down list on the site's home page to select Search The World Wide Web Only and then try your search again.

Search engines enable you to locate Web sites by first entering a keyword or descriptive phrases into a text box. Then you simply click the Search button (or equivalent, as it may be Go or Submit) and wait a moment until the results appear on-screen. If you live in, say, Dallas and are looking for a listing of Acura dealer Web sites, try using the search terms **Acura dealer AND Dallas.** Searching these terms at Google, for example, returns Web addresses for several Acura dealers in the Dallas area.

For additional information on getting the most out of search engines, take a look at Chapter 2.

Checking out what the dealers offer online

All major car manufacturers maintain extensive dealer networks across North America and elsewhere in the world. Most manufacturers, from domestics to imports, also maintain great Web sites to help anchor their far-flung dealer networks. As each new-car dealer takes trade-ins, they immediately become used-car dealers just waiting to make a deal.

The Internet puts you in touch with these "used-car" dealers, enabling you to easily shop at as many car lots as you want, all through the convenience of your computer and modem.

Just follow these steps to check out online what sort of used cars the various dealers offer:

1. **Type the URL of your favorite search engine in your browser's Address box. Then press Enter.**

2. **In the Search box, type the make of the car in which you're interested. Then click the Search button.**

   Suppose that you want to buy a used Acura. Simply type the word **Acura** into the search engine's text box and click the Search (or equivalent) button. At AltaVista, searching the term *Acura* returns the company's Web site as the first listing.

3. **Scroll down, if necessary, until you find a listing for the car maker's Web site. Then click on the car maker's URL (such as** `www.acura.com`**), which should be included with the listing.**

At some sites, it may not be the first listing that you want. Car companies are usually pretty easy to find on the Internet because their Web addresses are often quite simple, using the name of the car maker, such as www.cadillac.com or www.toyota.com or www.jeep.com. However, not all car maker Web sites are so easy to find; Nissan's Web address, for example, is www.nissan-usa.com — visit www.nissan.com and you'll find a site devoted to computers, not cars.

4. **Click on the Pre-Owned link at the car maker's home page.**

    At Acura's Web site, the Pre-Owned link can be found at the bottom of the home page. Other car makers may use different words for their used-car links, such as <u>Certified Used Cars</u> or simply <u>Used Cars</u>. (Notice that, at the Acura site that you visit in this example, you see a number of options after you go to the Pre-Owned section, including links to information about Acura's program benefits and special offers. Such information is good to know if you're buying a used car.)

The Pre-Owned section at Acura's Web site incorporates a dealer lookup and model library, and it even provides a search engine to help you find the exact used model you want in a specific geographical area convenient to you. Notice the brochure request button in case you want to receive it in the mail.

Keep in mind that all new-car dealers also sell used cars, so you're likely to find that an Acura dealer also offers used Acuras for sale. Keep in mind, too, that a new-car dealer who specializes in just one or two particular new car makes probably has a variety of makes and models from other manufacturers on the used-car lot because of trade-ins. You may very well find the perfect used Mazda on an Acura dealer's used-car lot.

Rental-car companies sell their cars, too

You can probably imagine that big rental-car companies buy a lot of brand-new cars each year. But did you know that they're also the biggest sellers of nearly new cars? Rental-car companies like to offer their rental customers as new a car as possible, so they sell their fleets of cars as quickly as possible. And that practice translates into a potential deal for you as a used-car buyer.

Take, for example, Enterprise Rent-A-Car, the biggest rental car company in North America. Check out its Web site (at www.ecars.com) and you find a big pitch by Enterprise to sell a huge selection of slightly used cars to people looking for a great used-car deal.

Enterprise calls its online used-car program "The Perfect Used Car Package: Haggle-Free Buying & Worry-Free Ownership." It's haggle-free because Enterprise offers a one-price system, and it's worry-free because buyers get a great warranty and even a seven-day return policy, which enables them to drive the car for a week and sell it back for the same amount that they're paying for it (minus a small fee to clean the car and check it out to make sure that it's still in good shape).

Rental companies usually offer a huge variety of makes and models in the fleet of vehicles that they rent out. They're definitely worth investigating if you're in the market for a well-maintained, low-mileage, nearly new used car. Here's a list of a few other rental car companies that might have the perfect used car to meet your needs:

- Budget (at www.budgetcarsales.com)
- Hertz (at www.hertz.com)
- Thrifty (at www.thriftycarsales.com)

Combing the classifieds online

A wide variety of used-car classified ads appear on the Internet. Yes, most major newspapers now post their classifieds on the Internet. But so, too, do many e-commerce businesses that have no involvement in the newspaper industry. The selection from which you can choose is abundant, because a car's geographic location doesn't affect in the slightest your ability to find it online. In Chapter 16, I cover a vast selection of places on the Internet where you can go to find automobile classified ads. Many of them include photos of the car and an easy way for you to contact its owner if you have any interest in the vehicle. Make sure that you check out these ads.

Setting Guidelines for Buying a Used Car on the Internet

Knowing how much you can afford to spend on a used car is important. Also important is knowing how you're going to use the car after you own it. Making a checklist that you base on your budget, lifestyle, and motoring needs is always a good idea.

Following are some items that you can use for creating such a checklist:

- **Budget:** Gauging just what you can afford to spend on a car before you set out to buy one is very important. Knowing in advance how much disposable income you have helps you narrow down the kind of car that best fits your budget. Try using online tools that help you track your monthly and yearly costs such as housing and living expenses. By using standard formulas with predetermined percentages that you then apply to various everyday expenses, you can quickly figure out what you can afford to spend on your car. Following are two such online tools that you can use for this purpose:

  - **FinanCenter.Com's Budgeting Center** (at www.financenter.com/budgeting.htm) provides free online calculators that enable you to track how much you're spending, make budget decisions, explore your options, test future scenarios, discover how to decrease your costs, and more. After you get a handle on how much you spend, you then know how much extra cash you have to spend on a car. (Before you leave the FinanCenter.Com site, check out its Auto section for smart car-financing ideas as well.)

  - **Carlist.Com** (at www.carlist.com) is another handy Web site with lots of links to used-car dealers, auto-insurance options, and auto-loan information. Click the <u>Calculate Your Payment</u> link to access the Monthly Payment Calculator, which helps you figure out the monthly financing costs for the car that you want to buy. Simply input the number of payments, interest rate, and loan amount to immediately find out your monthly payment on the financed amount of your car price.

- **Lifestyle:** A wide variety of cars is available in the marketplace — enough to satisfy every human whim possible — so consider the kind of lifestyle that you lead as you narrow your selection to those vehicles that best fit how you live. Consider, for example, the following questions and qualifiers:

  - Do you travel alone, or are you the family chauffeur? If you have, say, four teenage kids at home, that jazzy two-seater BMW convertible may not be right for you.

  - If you're the proud parent of a new baby, you want to make sure that the car you buy has the right safety features and secure moorings for the baby seat.

  - If you travel with cumbersome sporting gear or play the tuba in a local orchestra, you need a car or van that can accommodate all your stuff. The same thing's true for winter skiers.

- Farmers who lug around a lot of tools from one barn to another across muddy pastures need a sturdy chassis and plenty of storage room to carry oversized cargo. The limited usefulness of a second-hand Lincoln Town Car may not impress them much, regardless of what kind of bargain they can negotiate on the price.

- If you live in an area such as Canada or northern Vermont that gets bitter cold and lots of snow, consider something with four-wheel drive, a good passenger-compartment heater, an engine-block heater, and good ground clearance, too. On the other hand, if you live in West Texas, a good air-conditioner is probably worth its weight in gold.

- If you live in a rough and tough neighborhood, think about security. A lock-activated alarm system is a good feature, but a soft-top convertible is easy prey for a bandit with a knife looking to rip you off (literally).

✓ **Motoring needs:** At some point during your online search for the right used car, you may come across a vehicle that stirs the imagination — the car of your dreams. Your heart sings out, "I must buy it!"

Deciding in advance why you need a car adds discipline to your search and helps you avoid the heart pangs that come with finding "the car of your dreams" instead of the car of your *needs*. So make sure that you figure out in advance *why* you need a car and then stick to that objective. Take into consideration, for example, the following questions:

- Do you need transportation simply to get back and forth between home and work? If so, you probably don't want to fall for the medusa of a top-of-the-line 4x4 Ford pickup that's just *perfect* for expeditions across the Baja peninsula.

- Do you plan to trailer a boat or camper? If so, you need a sturdy suspension and a lot of horsepower under the hood for this kind of activity. You also need a trailer hitch.

Saving the Information That You Find Online

By visiting the Web sites that we list in this chapter (and elsewhere in this book), you can find out a lot about what kind of cars are currently available on the market. You can find exactly what you're seeking if you know where to look and you're prepared to focus your search on the Internet sites that are best for your specific purpose.

Saving online information on your computer's hard drive to read in-depth after you're offline is especially useful, because you can then organize that information for future use and access it without connecting to the Internet again. Having such information at hand on your hard drive is also great for quick referrals and comparisons as you get farther into your search.

Follow these steps to save Web pages on your hard drive:

1. **After the information that you want to keep appears on-screen in your Web browser, choose File⇨Save from your browser's menu bar.**

   The Save As dialog box appears on-screen.

2. **Type a file name and choose the folder in which you want to save the file.**

3. **Click the Save button.**

   This action saves the file to your computer's hard drive in the folder that you specify.

4. **Disconnect from the Internet.**

5. **Reduce the size of your browser window or close it altogether.**

6. **Start a word-processing program on your computer.**

7. **Open the file and start reading the information.**

Remember the old adage that "if it looks too good to be true, it probably is"? This adage is especially true about the price of a used car.

Finding Other Used-Car Information Online

The more information that you can gather about a particular make and model, the more easily you can make the right decision about whether to buy it. You can also figure out exactly the right price to pay for the car.

Luckily, you can use the Internet to gather a lot of information from a variety of sources to help you make an informed decision about a car. The following list describes some of the courses of action available to you:

✔ **Use e-mail to talk with people who own the kind of car that you want to buy.** A car's best salesperson (or worst detractor) is usually the person who owns it. If an owner loves her car, she's usually happy to tell you why. If another hates his, he's probably more than willing to supply a list of reasons. Going online to locate people who currently own the kind of car that you want to buy is a great way to get advice, suggestions, and warnings. Chapter 3 helps put you in touch with the car owners with whom you need to talk *before* you buy a used car.

✔ **Check out manufacturer's specs and defects.** You may not find a used brochure to match the used car that you want to buy, but you can find the exact manufacturer's specifications that went into that very same car online.

If you go to the Acura manufacturer's Web site (at www.acura.com) that we mention in the section earlier in this chapter, for example, and click the Pre-Owned link, you find the manufacturer's Pre-Owned Specs Library. That library is a free searchable archive of detailed information covering all Acura models. Checking out what it tells you about the pre-owned Acura that you want to buy is time well spent.

Keep in mind that even the best-engineered cars in the world succumb to manufacturers' defects from time to time. A recall order often follows the discovery of such defects, inviting car owners to take their cars to an authorized dealer who undertakes the necessary repairs at no charge to the customer (other than the inconvenience of bringing the car to the dealer).

By checking a car maker's Web site, you can find out whether the manufacturer has ordered any recalls in the past on the used car that you want to buy. With that information in hand, you can ask the seller to find out whether the necessary work was undertaken at the time of recall.

✔ **Research resale and book-value prices online.** Human nature dictates that sellers are going to try to get the best price possible for their cars. And given the old saying that a sucker is born every day, you can expect the seller to try hard to make you pay as much as possible for your next car. Knowing exactly what a used car is worth in the marketplace, however, helps you to evaluate a seller's asking price and acts as the perfect leverage whenever you're ready to negotiate the final purchase price.

A car's *book value* is the Bible of the used car industry (see Chapter 10). It's the tool that every car dealer and salesperson uses. Finding out your car's book value and researching the car's resale value by studying historical data that's available online helps you understand a car's worth.

You need to remember that the concept of *caveat emptor*, or let the buyer beware, applies whenever you set out to buy a used car, whether you're doing so online or otherwise. You want to make sure that you deal only with reputable people, whether dealers or individuals, and that you have a licensed mechanic properly check out the car that you want *before* you actually fork over your hard-earned money to make the purchase. Organizations such as the Better Business Bureau are only too happy to help out. (See the BBB's listing in the Directory section of this book for details.)

Chapter 14

Buying a Collector Car on the Internet

The term *collector car* covers a lot of territory. It can include antiques, classics, and special-interest cars such as street rods, muscle cars, exotics, kit cars, and replicas. At one time or another, you've probably seen a car on the road, in a showroom, or in a magazine and thought how great it would be if it were only yours.

Maybe you remember that '65 Mustang you wish now that you hadn't sold. Or you recall an afternoon long ago on a winding country road chasing a TR4A in your Spitfire. Or perhaps you just want to be that person turning everyone's head as you drive down the street in your Model A.

Owning a piece of automotive history offers many advantages, not the least of which is the pleasure of rewarding yourself with something you've always wanted. Unlike the situation that occurs with buying a new car, which begins to depreciate as soon as you drive it off the lot, purchasing a collector car can prove a very sound investment. A 1966 Jaguar 3.8S sedan that I bought 20 years ago, for example, has gone up in value by 1,000 percent. (I really wish I hadn't sold that one.)

Owning a collector car can also become a real family affair. Going to cruises or shows, taking the family out for a Sunday afternoon spin, or working on the car with your kids creates memories that can last a lifetime.

Taking Your First Step

The first thing to do if you're considering buying a collector car is to decide on your price range, the type of car that interests you, and whether you want to do any restoration work. Collector cars come in all shapes, sizes, conditions, and price ranges, from a $100 basket case to a $2,000,000 Duesenberg.

If it's love, a buyer needs to know that he's vulnerable and that if he's not willing to pay top dollar for the fully restored car of his dreams, he's likely to spend just as much or more taking a restorable car to that same level of condition. If you can do the work yourself, and it's a labor of love, and you've got the time, that's great; but if you're coming up a little short in any of those categories, you may be in for disillusionment.

You'll never love another MG as much as your first one — trying to recreate the memories with a car that's noisier, slower, and fussier than the one you remember can be rough.

What is a collector car?

There are many categories of collector cars. Antique cars are defined as those that are at least 25 years of age, although most listings are for cars that are much older. The term "classic" is much harder to define. When searching through ads, you will find that a classic car is any car that someone thinks is a classic. I have even seen some new cars described as classics. Maybe the best description is that they are cars with such design, styling, or innovations that they become a valuable and memorable part of automotive history. Some other categories include:

- *Exotics* are cars of limited production, and they are usually very expensive, such as the Lamborghini Contach or the Jaguar XK220.

- *Street rods* are antiques that have been heavily modified for show purposes. I'm sure you remember the hot rods in *American Grafitti,* or you've seen old cars with bright paint jobs and flames painted on the side.

- *Kit cars,* as the name implies, come in pieces and must be assembled. Some, such as the Excaliber, are made to be fitted to a Volkswagen chassis, while some come with their own frame.

- *Replicars* are duplicates of older originals. Like the Excaliber, they can also be kit cars. The best and most expensive replicars are the turn-key packages, the most famous being the Glen Pray Auborn Speedster.

How about a replicar?

Deciding how much you can spend is the easy part. But settling on the kind of car that you want takes a little more thought. Aside from pure aesthetics, you need to consider how you plan on enjoying your new toy. If, for example, you want a car that you can drive every day, an authentic Model T probably isn't a good choice. You may, on the other hand, want to consider the *replicar* market.

Replicars are modern copies of antique (and often very expensive) cars that come with modern drive trains and amenities. Many of them are very hard to tell from the originals. You can drive them on a daily basis. And they cost far less than the originals.

Check the Replicar listing on Hemmings Classified ads to find a wide variety of replicars. If you find something that interests you contact the manufacturer for literature on their products. The quality of replicars can vary a great deal depending on the manufaturer so ask them for a list of purchasers in your area. Contacting owners is the best way to determine the quality of the product. Comparing the current asking price in the classifieds with the original cost will give you an idea of how well a particular replicar holds its value.

The most famous, and the typical example, are Cobras. And don't confuse them with the Zimmers and Excaliburs that were excoriated by enthusiasts and have seen their value evaporate over the years.

The price of a typical collector car can vary a great deal, depending on its condition. In other words, your initial outlay is usually less if you decide to do some restoration yourself — but keep in mind that buying a car in need of restoration doesn't guarantee that the final costs are less than you face if buying one in mint condition. If you're an experienced do-it-yourselfer, you can save labor costs by doing your own restoration. If you don't have the skill, time, or inclination, however, you need to find an experienced professional for the job — and *that* can prove quite expensive.

After you make up your mind on all the issues that concern the purchase of a collector car, you can go ahead and find your own dream car.

Doing Your Research Online

You now need to determine whether you can find the type of car that you want in your price range. Many sites on the Internet list values for new or late-model used cars, but few, unfortunately, give an accurate value for collector cars.

One of the best sources on the Internet for collector-car pricing information is the Hemmings Motor News Web site at www.hmn.com. It's a huge, easy-to-use, and extremely fast site, with more than 30,000 classified ads and many other interesting sections (see Figure 14-1).

If you want a quicker, more enjoyable way to see what all the options are, go out and buy a Hemmings and just thumb through it for a week getting familiar with the turf.

Start your search by assuming that you want to buy a car that you can drive right away (which is usually the case with most collector-car buyers). To find the price range of your car, follow these steps:

1. **Open your browser and access the Hemmings Web site by typing** www.hmn.com **in your browser's Address text box.**

2. **Click the <u>Price Guides</u> link on the Web site's home page.**

3. **Click the <u>Click here for Online.</u>**

Figure 14-1:
The Hemmings Motor News Web site is one of the best on the Internet for classic-car aficionados.

4. Select the <u>Search</u> ☞<u>Click here for ONLINE search of CPI (Cars of Particular Interest) Value Guide</u> links.

The CPI Price Guide Search page appears.

5. Scroll down the page to the list of car manufacturers, as shown in Figure 14-2, and choose the maker of the car you're seeking.

As an example, say that you're considering a Porsche 356B Roadster. Click the Porsche check box to select that automaker.

6. Click the Continue button at the bottom.

You now see a list of all the available cars by the automaker that you selected in Step 5. For the example that I give in that step, it's a list of Porsche models that appears. You can then select the check box for the 356B Roadster (or whatever model you want), as shown in Figure 14-3.

7. Click the Go Search button at the bottom.

Now you see a list of all the years that the 356B Roadster was in production, along with their current values, as shown in Figure 14-4.

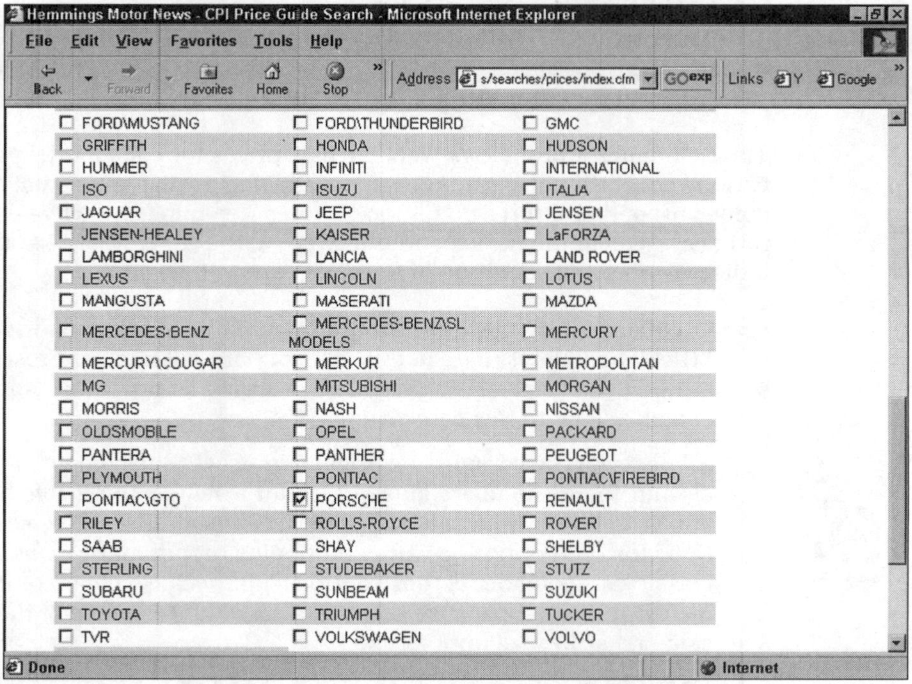

Figure 14-2:
Choose the make of the collector car you're seeking on the CPI Price Guide Search page of the Hemmings Motor News Web site.

Hemmings Motor News - Vehicles For Sale Search - Microsoft Internet Explorer

File   Edit   View   Favorites   Tools   Help

Back   Forward   Favorites   Home   Stop   Address /searches/prices/models.cfm   GOexp   Links Y   Google

☐ 356 Cabriolet	☐ 356 Coupe	☐ 356A Cabriolet
☐ 356A Carrera GS	☐ 356A Carrera GS Cabrio	☐ 356A Coupe
☐ 356A Roadster	☐ 356B Cabriolet	☐ 356B Coupe
☑ 356B Roadster	☐ 356C Cabriolet	☐ 356C Cabriolet SC
☐ 356C Coupe	☐ 356C Coupe SC	☐ 911 American Roadster
☐ 911 Carrera	☐ 911 Carrera 2	☐ 911 Carrera 2 Cabriolet
☐ 911 Carrera 2 Targa	☐ 911 Carrera 4	☐ 911 Carrera 4 Cabriolet
☐ 911 Carrera 4 Targa	☐ 911 Carrera 4S	☐ 911 Carrera Cabriolet
☐ 911 Carrera S	☐ 911 Carrera Targa	☐ 911 Carrera Turbo
☐ 911 Coupe	☐ 911 RS America	☐ 911 Speedster
☐ 911 Targa	☐ 911 Turbo	☐ 911 Turbo 3.6
☐ 911 Turbo Cabriolet	☐ 911 Turbo Coupe	☐ 911 Turbo S
☐ 911 Turbo Targa	☐ 911E Coupe	☐ 911E Targa
☐ 911ES Coupe	☐ 911ES Targa	☐ 911L Coupe
☐ 911L Targa	☐ 911S Coupe	☐ 911S Targa
☐ 911SC Cabriolet	☐ 911SC Coupe	☐ 911SC Targa
☐ 911T Coupe	☐ 911T Targa	☐ 912 Coupe
☐ 912 Targa	☐ 912E Coupe	☐ 912E Targa
☐ 914-4 Roadster 1.7/1.8	☐ 914-4 Roadster 2.0	☐ 914-6 Roadster
☐ 924 Coupe	☐ 924 Turbo Coupe	☐ 924S Coupe
☐ 928 Coupe	☐ 928 GTS	☐ 928GT Coupe
☐ 928S Coupe	☐ 928S-4 Coupe	☐ 930 Turbo
☐ 944 Coupe	☐ 944 Turbo Coupe	☐ 944S Coupe
☐ 944S Turbo Coupe	☐ 944S2 Cabriolet	☐ 944S2 Coupe

Done   Internet

Figure 14-3:
You can specify the exact model that you seek on this page.

The Hemmings Motor News Web site lists prices for each model year of the various collector cars that you can usually find available for sale. Most value guides use either a three-condition, as does Hemmings, or a five-condition rating system. In the three-condition system, the categories — and what they indicate about the condition of the car — are as follows:

✔ **Excellent:** This category indicates a perfect car, which is driven very little, if at all. Most cars in this category are full of recent restorations, although an original with very low mileage and no visible signs of wear can also fall into this category.

All parts on the car must be original or exact replacements and all chassis and engine numbers must match for a vehicle to receive this rating. If you've ever looked at a value guide for newer cars, you've seen additions for such options as air-conditioning or automatic transmissions. A classic-car guide omits these options, not because collector cars never have options but because collectors consider the value of these cars the same regardless of options.

✔ **Good:** This car is of nearly the same condition as excellent, with very little noticeable wear and with low mileage. All parts are original or exact replacements and all numbers match. Most cars in this category are originals that are driven little and well-maintained or are good older restorations.

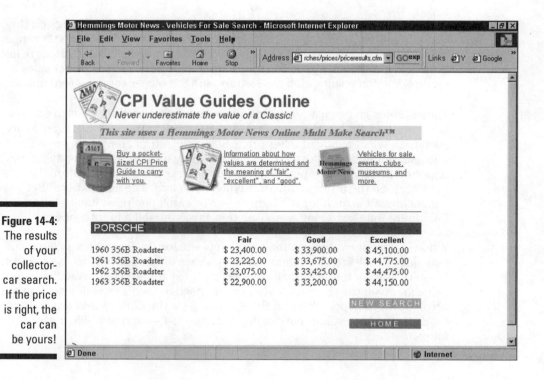

Figure 14-4:
The results
of your
collector-
car search.
If the price
is right, the
car can
be yours!

✔ **Fair:** This category indicates a complete car that's in good driving condition but shows obvious signs of wear and is in need of mechanical and cosmetic restoration.

The five-category system further breaks the Fair category into three separate categories, as the following list describes:

✔ **Excellent:** This category is the same as the Excellent category in the three-category system.

✔ **Fine:** This category corresponds to the Good category in the three-category system.

✔ **Very good:** This category is roughly the same as the Fair category in the three-category system but is closer to the top end. A car in this category may carry the term "easy restoration."

✔ **Good:** This category describes a complete car in need of an extensive mechanical and cosmetic restoration.

✔ **Fair:** This category usually describes a complete car but one that's not drivable and that may also be disassembled.

Price guides never list anything that fails to measure up to even this last category, and collectors usually refer to such a vehicle as a "basket case."

With these valuations in mind, you can look back at the price listings on the Hemmings site. As Figure 14-4 shows, the prices for the 356B Roadster range from $22,900 to $45,100, depending on condition and year. These prices result from data that Hemmings collects from reliable sources such as dealer sales reports, auction results, club newsletters, and CPI-owner survey questionnaires.

These values give you a pretty good idea as to whether your chosen car fits into your budget, but keep in mind that these prices are just averages. Many such cars sell at a much higher price. Some collectors aren't likely to continue searching after they find the car that they want and end up paying a premium price. A corresponding number of buyers (those with more patience), on the other hand, are paying much less. The lesson here? *Be patient* in your search for the right collector car! If you're willing to take a little more time searching, you can often save yourself a lot of money.

While looking for values on the Hemmings site for the Porsche Roadster, you may notice that the CPI Online Guide lists cars only from 1946 to the present. If you're looking for a car that's older than those for which you can find a value guide on the Hemmings site, just go back to the Price Guide section and scroll down the page. You find there a listing for the *Classics and Antiques Gold Book,* which values cars dating back to 1897 — and at $7.95, it's a bargain.

To Restore or Not to Restore

Finding a car in your price range is much less difficult if you're buying a car that's ready to show or just to drive and enjoy. If you buy a car to restore it, however, determining the exact amount of those restoration costs can prove difficult. The upside is that your initial outlay of cash is much less. In other words, you have more time to pay for the finished product.

Restoration offers other advantages, too. Most collector-car owners take a great deal of pride in their cars, but if you restore a car yourself, that feeling of pride becomes even greater. And if you later need to repair the car, you can probably do the work yourself. If you have children who can help with the project, you're introducing them to something that can give them a lot of pride, too.

Of course, the other option is to take the vehicle to a restoration shop. Keep in mind, however, that a typical body-and-fender shop isn't the same as a restoration shop. Even if the shop does great work, the workers there probably don't have the experience for tackling a classic-car project.

Seeing a specialist

You're much better off taking your collector car to a shop that specializes in restoration and performs this kind of work exclusively. Not only does such a shop do a better job, but its mechanics can also give you a far more accurate estimate of the costs than you get elsewhere. You may not find any restoration specialists in your local Yellow Pages, but they're easy to find on the Internet.

To locate a restoration specialist, go back to the Hemmings home page (at www.hmn.com on the Web; refer to Figure 14-1) and follow these steps:

1. **Click the <u>Classified Ads Online</u> link.**

   You arrive in the heart of the Hemmings Motor News Web site.

2. **Scroll down to the bottom half of this Web page to the Other Classifieds section (see Figure 14-5).**

3. **Click the button for Services Offered.**

   You now see a list of all the services that the site describes.

4. **Scroll down the page and select the check box for Restoration.**

Figure 14-5: Choose the Services Offered option on this page of the Hemmings Motor News Web site to determine whether a restoration shop is anywhere near you.

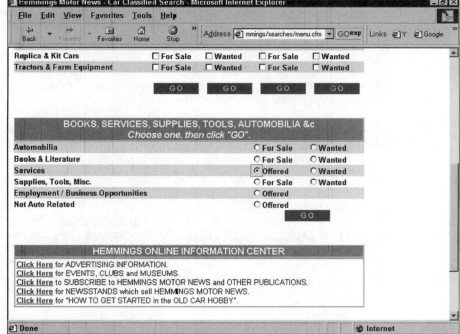

At any given time you find listings for between 120 and 150 shops from all parts of the U.S. and Canada. You may not find one in your hometown but are sure to find one or more in your general area (unless, of course, you live in the wilds of northern Wyoming or something).

If the restoration shop has a Web site of its own, you can find the Web address here and then go to the site to see whether it features photos of cars that the shop's restored. If you visit the shop itself (and you really want to do so before you take your car there), look around. Check out the cars the mechanics there are currently restoring. They're probably proud of the work they do and undoubtedly have photos on display of their past restorations. After you decide to take your car to a particular restoration shop, make sure that you get a written estimate that includes a firm price and a finish date.

Choosing a restorer is also a function of how complete and/or correct you want your restoration to be — a factory Mercedes-Benz 600 window control is still available and costs over $11,000, but you can have it exactly replicated for much less. Which would you do?

Doing it yourself

If you decide to do the restoration yourself, estimating the cost can prove difficult. After you figure out what you need to do, you must then find sources for replacement parts. You may need to take some of the work — such jobs as welding, upholstery, rechroming, or sandblasting — to specialty shops in your area. Go back to the Classified Ads Online page of the Hemmings Motor News Web site and select the Services Offered button. (See the steps in the preceding section for details on accessing this page on the Hemmings site.) Glance through the list and you can find help for any job that you can't do yourself, along with estimates of the costs.

Figuring the cost of parts requires a lot more research. The first place to look is in the Hemmings Classified Ads Online (which you access from the Hemmings home page). Selecting the <u>Collector Cars Parts For Sale</u> link takes you to a screen where you can select your particular make.

Car clubs are another excellent source for parts. Go to the Hemmings Motor News Web site's home page and click the <u>Car Club Central, Events and Museums</u> ☞ <u>Visit Car Club Central</u> links. Scroll down the page that appears, and you can then find your car in the list.

You can find some other good car-club Web sites on the Internet, as the following list shows:

- ✔ Car List (at `http://www.carlist.com/carclub.html`)
- ✔ CC Data (at `www.ccdata.com/browse.Owners`)
- ✔ Car Clubs Worldwide (at `www.carclubs.com`)

Whenever you're on the car club sites, check out their event listings. Car-show flea markets are a great place to find parts, usually at reasonable prices.

After you locate all the parts that you need and after you add up all the costs, add 25 percent to the total. Why? I've never known anyone who restored his own car who didn't underestimate the final cost. Trust me — you're going to run into some surprises and additional expenses before you're through.

Finding That Special Car Online

Unless you're looking for a very rare car, you can search literally hundreds of Web sites to find the machine of your dreams. Consider the following online resources:

- **Online newspapers:** Most newspapers have their own Web pages, and their classified-ad sections are a good place to look online for collector cars for sale. If you start with the papers in your area, you may not need to go far to find your car. People advertising in local papers are expecting to sell their cars locally and may not ask as high a price as those who advertise nationally.

  Note: Buying a car is much like buying a house. You make the best deals buying from a motivated seller, and you find a higher percentage of such sellers by using newspaper ads. (In dealing with classic cars, you usually find that a motivated seller is most often one who started a restoration project and finds himself in over his head. Or perhaps his significant other just told him to get rid of that car . . . or else. Whatever the reason, this is where you find the best bargains.)

- **Online car sites:** Online car sites, such as CarPoint, Autoweb, and Cars.com are good places to look for collector cars for sale. As is the case with most Web sites, they don't often offer a lot of collector cars on sale, so dealing with such sites is mostly a hit-and-miss affair. But remember that you must remain patient in your search — and the more places that you look online, the better are your chances of finding that bargain.

- **Car clubs:** Car clubs usually include a classified-ad section on their Web sites and offer a much more specific search. You're also looking at ads from car lovers, so your chances of finding a car that someone's pampered is much greater at such a site.

- **Online magazines:** Online magazines such as *Car and Driver* (www .caranddriver.com) and *Road & Track* (roadandtrack.com) also feature classifieds that usually offer some very interesting collector cars. *Road & Track* also sells copies of its past road tests on its Web site. I recommend these tests in particular to anyone planning to purchase a collector car. Car enthusiasts conduct these tests, and the reports make for very interesting reading.

- **Collector-car Web sites:** Hemmings Motor News (www.hmn.com) is the granddaddy of all collector-car Web sites. As you can see in the section "Doing Your Research Online," earlier in this chapter, the site offers every conceivable area of interest to the collector-car buff — including the cars. Whatever you're looking for, you can find it on the Hemmings site. Another good site is Classic & Antique Cars (www.antique-auto mobiles.com), which lists ads by the decade from the '20s to the '70s. Almost all sites on the Internet are small and many are companies offering their own cars. None list even one-tenth of what Hemmings has to offer.

Just remember to stay patient as you search online for a collector car. Unless you're looking for a one of a kind or otherwise very rare car, you face plenty of choices. Set your spending limit, determine that you're going to stick to it, and then look for that bargain.

Getting an Appraisal

After you find your dream car, you need to check it out. Most people, including me, wouldn't even consider buying a car without seeing it in person. A few hundred dollars for a round-trip ticket isn't much to pay for the peace of mind that you get from actually seeing the car up close. If you have a good knowledge of cars in general or of that car in particular, an in-person visit may be all that you need to decide to go ahead with the deal. You may also find that you can take the vehicle to a local garage to have a mechanic check it out.

In addition, I recommend that you get an appraisal on the car. An appraisal not only gives you a better idea of the shape that the car's in, but it also gives you a verified value for insurance purposes. Fees for this service aren't that expensive, ranging from $250 to $2,500, depending on the value of the car. And an appraisal provides you with a complete evaluation of the car, including a road test. Several online companies offer this service, as the following list describes:

- **Robert DeMars, Ltd.** (most major U.S. cities): www.robertdemarsltd.com
- **Auto Appraisal Group** (most major U.S. cities): www.autoappraisal.com
- **Sequence ent.** (nationwide): www.sequenceauto.com

After visiting the Web sites, call each company and talk to them in person; then you can choose the company with which you are most comfortable.

Arranging Transportation

Okay. After you find your car, get an appraisal, and actually buy it, you need to get it home. The most obvious solution to that problem is simply to drive it back. If you buy, for example, a Porsche or a Jaguar sedan in good shape, and you're not too far from home, you may want to do just that. Of course, you then must think about insuring and registering your car — and what happens if you break down on the way home? Something as simple as a bad radiator hose may pose a major problem on a rare car out in the middle of nowhere.

Perhaps the safest thing to do is to get someone else to transport the car for you. That way, the transporter's insurance covers the car, and the transport company delivers it right to your door. The cost of this service runs between $.60 and $1.25 per mile, depending on the type and value of the car. The transporter carries the vehicle in an enclosed hauler for maximum protection. These companies calculate the price of the transport from the point of pickup to the point of delivery. If you have a show car, you can also use these companies to transport it to and from the show. Besides the transportation costs, the company charges you a layover fee of $500 to $850 per day while at the event. The more valuable your car is, the more you may want to consider this service. Following is a list of some notable transport companies that are currently online with their own Web sites:

- Thomas C. Sunday, Inc. (Williamsport, PA): www.thomascsunday.com
- Majestic Auto Transport (Alpha, OR): www.auto-move.com
- Newman International Transport, Inc. (Tampa, FL): www.newmaninternational.com
- Passport Transport (St. Louis, MO): www.passporttransport.com
- Intercity Lines, Inc. (Warren, MA): www.intercitylines.com

Registration and Insurance

Registering your collector car is the same as registering a new car, but with one possible exception. Most states have an antique-car classification that usually calls for an additional one-time registration fee that's good for the entire time that you own the car. In most cases, a car needs to be only 25 years old to qualify.

Insurance fees for such vehicles usually depend on your planned yearly driving mileage. If you plan to drive more than 5,000 miles per year, you must purchase a standard auto policy. To qualify for antique- or collector-car insurance, you must meet several criteria, as the following list describes:

- ✔ You must limit your driving to 2,400 miles per year (although at least one company, American Collectors Insurance, offers a 5,000-mile policy).

- ✔ You must garage the vehicle.

- ✔ You must use another car for daily driving.

- ✔ Whenever you drive the car, you can't leave it unattended for long periods of time. You can't drive it to the airport, for example, and leave it in long-term parking while you're on vacation.

The best feature of this type of policy is the price. Because the policy limits your mileage and car collectors generally take very good care of their vehicles, the cost for such policies is very low. Generally, the cost ranges between $7.50 and $15 per $1,000 of value per year. This cost provides full coverage and includes other features that you don't find on standard policies. The policy from American Collectors Insurance, for example, includes a $500 spare-parts coverage. If you purchase spare parts for your car and you lose them or they suffer damage for any reason, the policy covers them.

These policies are also *agreed-value policies*, which automatically increase by two percent every three months with no increase in premiums. If you've ever suffered a loss on a standard auto policy, you know what a hassle getting the insurance company to pay you what you think your car is worth can become. With this kind of policy, however, you agree on a value at the time that you take out the policy and that value, plus the inflation boost, is what the insurance company pays you for a claim.

Check out the following Web sites for information about and to secure antique- or collector-car insurance:

- ✔ American Collectors Insurance, Inc. (Cherry Hills, NJ): www.americancollectorsinc.com

- ✔ Insurance Company.com: www.insurancecompany.com

- ✔ Classic Collectors Insurance Program (Cincinnati, OH): www.classiccollectors.com

You will be able to find all of the information you need on the Web sites, but don't be afraid to call and talk to a real person. You will find them knowledgeable, friendly, and most helpful in helping you decide exactly what coverage is best for you.

Chapter 15

Trade-Ins: Using the Internet to Sell Your Old Car

. . . .

In This Chapter

▶ Finding your car's worth online

▶ Checking out your online options

▶ Investigating online classifieds

▶ Looking at online auctions

▶ Trading your car for something else

▶ Donating your vehicle to charity online

. . . .

*T*hinking about your options for disposing of your existing car is an important step, especially after you decide to buy a new car. After all, the value of your current car may be in the eye of the beholder, but that value has an effect on your buying power.

Fortunately, the Internet opens a world of options to help you maximize the price you get for your car when you dispose of it. Whether you want to sell, trade, donate, or even junk your car, making sure that you get the best value from your automobile is worthwhile.

In this chapter, we show you how to surf the Internet to find dozens of disposal options — and the right one that meets your budget and your tax needs. We drive you around the Web and make pit stops at some of the most innovative disposal opportunities available — ones that you need to know about to maximize the value of your trade-in.

We also show you where to find the best online classified advertising, tell you why Internet auctions may prove the right way for you to find the right buyer, and explore alternative disposal options, including barter sites that enable you to trade your car for something else and bona fide charity organizations that offer tax receipts for your old clunker.

Determining How Much Your Car Is Worth

How much is your car worth? Now, that's a good question — and one that you need to answer before you can think of selling or otherwise disposing of your used car online! Of course, the value of a car fluctuates because of several variables, some of them within your control and some that are out of your control, as the following paragraphs explain. All those variables are worth taking into account as you price your car.

For starters, the way you've maintained your car during the time you've owned it is important. Although the caveat "let the buyer beware" is never more true than when buying a used car, keep in mind that the better you've maintained your car, the more it's worth. The same is true of low mileage. A high-mileage car is simply worth less than one with a smaller number on its odometer. Finally, how you drive a car can affect its value. Although auto technicians can do miraculous repair work these days, a repaired car is still not as desirable as a never-been-wrecked vehicle.

The variables you have little or no control over include what options the car has (power windows, automatic transmission, and so on), what model year the car is, and what type of car you have. We wish we could tell you that you can use the Internet to turn a 1978 Chevette into a 2000 Corvette (what a difference two letters makes!), but that just isn't so.

The Bible of used cars is the *Kelley Blue Book*. You can buy the book itself through an online bookstore, such as Amazon.com, Borders.com, or BarnesandNoble.com, or you can go directly to the Kelley Blue Book Web site (at www.kbb.com) to check out a wealth of information about every car model imaginable (see Figure 15-1). You can use the information that you find online as a base to figure out what your car may be worth.

Edmunds.com (at www.edmunds.com) is a similar service that bases its information on a popular line of books. The Web site does a nice job with its valuation of all used car models, offering detailed evaluations and both trade-in and market prices. A car's *trade-in price* — what a dealer is likely to give you for the car if you trade it in for a newer model — is lower than its *market price*. A car's market price is lingo for the price at which a dealer expects to sell the car to an individual.

CarPrices.com (at www.carprices.com) is another great place to find out how much your car is worth. Click the Used Cars button on the home page of this Web site to access a section that enables you to check a trade-in's value by make and model. This site offers both a wholesale and retail value for the car of your choice.

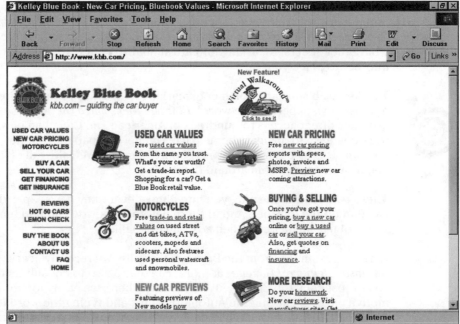

Figure 15-1:
The Kelley
Blue Book is
the industry
Bible for car
valuations.

Taking an Online Tour of Your Disposal Options

Time spent on the Internet is time well spent if you figure out from your online forays how to get the best value out of your existing car. Your choices vary, and you can make your decision easier by thoroughly exploring your online options. If you can discover what kind of market exists for your car, you can tap into it effectively. Some cars are much prized in the used-car market. Others are perfect only for the junkyard — but worth a tax deduction if you donate them to a worthwhile charity. All you need is the knowledge of where to find these resources, and that's what we show you in the following sections.

Online newspaper classifieds

Most newspapers across North America and elsewhere contain classified advertisements. Many newspapers, in fact, rely on the income that classified ads generate to support their news-gathering activities.

As newspapers struggle to find their place in the Internet era, many of them find posting their classified sections online useful. This practice enables you, as a vehicle seller, to consult various classified sections online to compare what other sellers are asking for cars similar to yours. You can also use the Internet to place your ad.

Two key Web sites are worth bookmarking to provide you with direct access to most newspapers in the world. *Bourque Newswatch* (at www.bourque.com) provides direct access to hundreds of American and Canadian newspapers from one easy-to-navigate home page. OnlineNewspapers.com (at www.onlinenewspapers.com) is a more complex Web site full of listings for major newspapers from around the world.

These two URLs alone plug you into almost every key newspaper that you can find on the Internet. And in these newspapers, you can find tens of thousands of newspaper classified ads for cars online.

Here's an example: From the Bourque Web site, we recently accessed the *Arkansas Democrat Gazette* (at www.ardemgaz.com) to consult its classified ads — just click the Classified Ads button. There, we easily found the automotive page by clicking the Automotive link, and typing the word **Chevrolet** into its simple-to-use search engine. In an instant, we received details about hundreds of Chevrolets for sale, including model, year of manufacture, features, and asking price. This method is a terrific way to find out what others are asking for cars similar to yours.

Next, we consulted the paper's Info & E-mail page (just click the Info & E-mail button), which gave us all the information we needed to submit our own classified ad. This section of the site even enables you to use an online form to submit the ad directly to the paper's Classifieds department. Many other newspapers, from *The Miami Herald* (at www.herald.com) to the *Toronto Star* (at www.thestar.com), work along similar lines.

Given the incredible reach of the Internet, visiting several newspapers online within your geographical area to compare both car prices and ad costs is always worthwhile. By finding out what prices people are asking for cars similar to yours, you can make sure that you get a fair price for your old jalopy. And by comparing ad prices, you can make sure that you're not paying too much to place an ad.

Online-only classifieds

A number of independent online used car Web sites have recently set up shop as e-commerce operations. They thrive exclusively online and are well worth considering as a potential place to list your car for sale because they contain many more listings than newspaper classifieds do, and they reach a larger number of prospective buyers.

AutoTrader.com (at `www.autotrader.com`) is one such place. This Web site bills itself as the world's largest selection of used cars with "more than 1.5 million listings, updated daily" (see Figure 15-2).

What we love about AutoTrader.com is that it enables you to list your car for sale for free. Obtaining that free listing is a simple six-step process: Select Your Make, Select Your Model, Enter the Year and Price, Enter the Description, Enhance Your Listing, and Enter Your Personal Information. After your entry is satisfactory to you, submit it and wait for a buyer. (You can modify or remove your listing at any time.)

America Online (at `www.aol.com`) offers its own classifieds: *ClassifiedsPlus*. Users benefit from access to the world's biggest online community. You can access the classifieds section directly off the main AOL home page by clicking the <u>Classifieds</u> link. From there, AOL prompts you to follow a <u>Place Your Ad</u> link to the Place an Ad page. From there, click the <u>Vehicles</u> link; this takes you to a page from which you can choose categories ranging from motorcycles to RVs to parts. The drawback here is that when you click the <u>Used Cars</u> link, you're sent to AutoTrader.com. Still, the combination of an AOL–AutoTrader linkup is a powerful siren call for your ad placement.

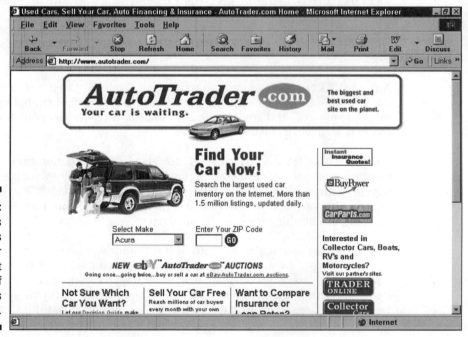

Figure 15-2:
Sites such as AutoTrader.com list millions of used cars for sale.

Trader Online (at www.traderonline.com) is another great classifieds Web site. As a supplement to the *Trader* newspapers that you can buy at newsstands, Trader Online offers for-sale cars, trucks, boats, RVs, and more — just about any mode of motorized travel you can think of. To sell your car for free, click the Autos tab (or whichever of the others best describes the vehicle you have for sale) and then click the FREE classified listing link. This site also offers a link to the Kelley Blue Book site so that you can determine a fair price for your car.

AutoWeb.com (at www.autoweb.com), in affiliation with UsedCar.com (at www.usedcar.com), charges a monthly fee and promises that your ad is going to "reach three million potential car buyers a month." A bonus is that your AutoWeb listing is also posted on Yahoo!'s classifieds page (at automobiles.classifieds.yahoo.com) for additional exposure.

WorldWideWheels.com (at wwwheels.com on the Web) bills itself as the "most comprehensive automobile site on the Net." You can place used car ads here, with or without a photo, for free, and the listing process takes just one or two seconds. All you do is click the Place a Free Ad link, click the ad form link, and fill in the requested information. You must renew the process every three weeks, however, to ensure that the listing continues; this requirement helps Web operators keep track of which cars are still for sale.

CarShoppers.com (at www.carshoppers.com) also offers free classified ads with photos. You must be a member of this site to use it, but membership is free.

AutoNetUSA.com (at www.autonetusa.com/index.htm) is another interesting Web site. It promises the buyer "a faster, easier way of shopping for a new or used vehicle." And anything that enables a buyer to find your car more easily is well worth taking a look at.

CarPrices.com (at www.carprices.com) is also open to members, and its membership is free. During our recent visit, new members were enticed to sign up with an offer of free long-distance telephone service. This Web site offers a simple-to-use ad placement form for the seller, and buyers can enjoy the ease of searching for specific used cars.

On a much smaller scale, the Automotive Database Web site (at www.vaxxine.com/adbase/) lists both vehicles for sale and vehicles that people want. Users not only can browse, but also can post ads in both sections. The listing for each particular car is rudimentary, and interested parties contact the seller directly through e-mail. Although not the vastest archive of vehicles, this site's user-friendliness is attractive.

Online classifieds offer you a great way to get your car out into the open marketplace. But that open marketplace is highly competitive and contains many, many listings from just about everywhere. Consider the key selling points of your particular car and use them in your ad to highlight why a buyer wants to choose your car instead of someone else's similar offering.

Because many locations offer free ad placements, you may want to try posting your ad at several sites to ensure maximum exposure. AutoTrader.com, WorldWideWheels.com, and CarPrices.com are good choices.

Online auctions

Some of the most popular e-commerce operations on the Internet are auction sites. Operations such as eBay.com (www.ebay.com), Bid.com (www.bid.com), and a host of others attract millions of loyal users. Some observers think that online auctions may one day replace classifieds as the medium of choice for the majority in selling and buying between individuals.

You can find many different types of auctions online:

- ✔ Regular auctions, or *English* auctions, are the most popular. Generally, buyers bid on an item until the auction ends, and the item sells to the highest bidder at the end of the auction. If a seller lists an item with a minimum *reserve price,* this ensures that the product doesn't sell for less than a buyer's lowest sale price. Using a reserve bid ensures that you, as a seller, don't need to sell at a price below your comfort level.

- ✔ *Dutch* auctions, on the other hand, are a little trickier. In Dutch auctions, two or more identical items are put up for bid; all winning bidders pay an identical price, which is the lowest successful bid. This form of auction doesn't really suit the sale of your car online, as only one successful bidder can buy your car.

- ✔ Some online sites hold other forms of auctions. Lycos, for example, offers Quick Win auctions. In such an auction, the first bidder to meet your asking price buys the item.

Most online auction houses require that you register as a member or user. Generally, membership is free, and you must agree to a binding agreement with respect to terms of use.

We suggest that you start out at eBay, which is possibly the world's biggest and best-known Internet auction site. This Web site attracts millions of users and offers a vast array of products for auction at any given time of the day. The eBay site boasts a new automotive section, too — one of the slickest we've seen (see Figure 15-3). During a recent visit, the site (at www. ebaymotors.com) featured an auction for Queen Wilhelmina's rare 1946 Daimler limousine. But don't worry if your car is slightly less glitzy. At eBay, you can find room for every kind of car imaginable. (Remember also to check out eBay's tips on how to sell online by clicking the How to sell button.)

CityAuction's Web site (at www.utrade.com) also displays a lot of effervescence. Buyers and sellers meet here to exchange everything from Barbie dolls to BMWs. This site also enables sellers to sign up for FairMatch, a daily e-mail notification service that keeps you up to speed about prospective buyers.

A number of lesser-known auction sites ply their trade exclusively online, and one of these may well prove perfect for your needs:

✔ **AuctionAddict.com** (at www.auctionaddict.com) is an independent Web site that generates a fair amount of action. It thinks of itself as "a huge Internet swap meet" and makes listings available to anyone who registers for a free site membership. The service is free to the buyer, although the site charges a small commission to the seller — but only if the product sells at auction. Whether you're selling a convertible, coupe, hatchback, street rod, or racing vehicle, a buyer may well be lurking at this site just waiting for your auction to begin.

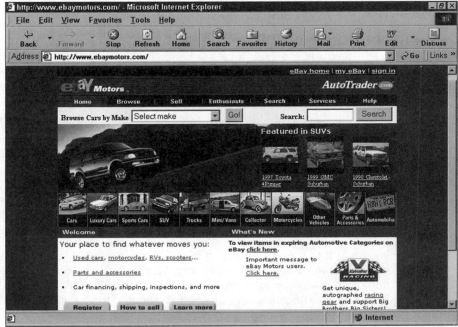

Figure 15-3:
The eBay auction site isn't just the place for finding Beanie Baby auctions. Check it out for auctions of used cars, too.

✔ **ReverseAuction.com** (at www.ra-vehicles.com) presents an intriguing pitch and charges no bidding or buying fees. It offers "online bidding in reverse for old and new cars . . . our prices drop instead of rise, and you can watch this process live on your screen." This site specializes in auctioning antique and classic cars, such as classic Chevrolets and Corvettes (see Figure 15-4). The site collects fees from the seller and is open to members only, although registration is available to everyone except minors.

In their quest to be all things to as many people as possible, several top search engine portals operate popular online auction sites:

✔ **Yahoo! Auctions** (at auctions.yahoo.com) are quite popular. Check out the Seller Guide to discover the rules and what you need to know to register yourself for a Yahoo! ID. Next, click the <u>Automotive</u> link on the main page to access the auctions area, where we recently noted that more than 2,500 car auctions were underway during our one visit. A 1998 Porsche Carrera had two bids, one topping $50,000, while a 1965 Thunderbird had six bids, the highest at just $2,000.

✔ **Lycos' auction site** (at auctions.lycos.com) is one of the biggest in this category. Lycos offers listings for everything from Beanie Babies to gold coins, and the site auctions thousands of vehicles, too. The Lycos auctions require both buyers and sellers to register.

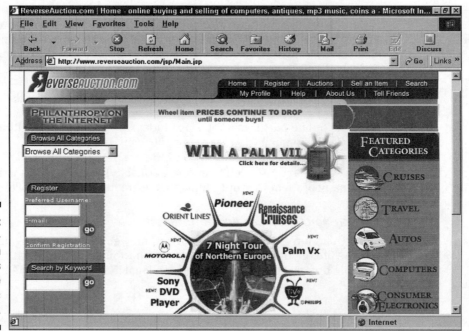

Figure 15-4:
Reverse-Auction.com specializes in antique and classic cars.

✔ **Amazon.com** (at www.amazon.com) is also in the auction game now. Best known as "Earth's Biggest Bookstore," the online monolith is branching out into the sale of a wide variety of goods. Click the Auctions tab on the main page to visit its Auctions page, and then click the Cars & Transportation link to access a page of auctions for cars, parts, and automotive paraphernalia. You need an Amazon.com account to list your car for auction.

For more information about online auctions, check out *Internet Auctions For Dummies* and CliffsNotes *Buying and Selling on eBay,* both published by IDG Books Worldwide, Inc.

Other online disposal options (if you can't get cash)

If you just can't seem to find a buyer who's willing or able to pay cash for your old faithful, you may want to consider other options for disposing of your vehicle online. Two possibilities are to trade — or barter — your car for something else, or simply to donate it to charity, as the following sections describe.

Trading your car for something else by bartering

What are your options if you can't find a buyer for your car with the cash to pay for it? Consider trading it for something else, such as a canoe, a couch, or even a drum set. Trade4It.Net (at www.trade4it.net) is "where one man's junk is another man's treasure." This site is free to buyers, who can wheel and deal and pitch you just about anything imaginable in exchange for your car. Sellers — or those with items for which they want to barter — can set up an account for $9.95 per month to post an unlimited number of listings.

Expect the online barter market to explode over the next year. Other sites, such as CarBarter.com (www.carbarter.com), Barter.com (www.barter.com), Barter.net (www.barter.net), and Barter.ca (www.barter.ca.com), aren't yet operational at the time of this writing. But expect many of them to erupt online this year with their own barter systems.

Donating your used car on the Internet

Hauling that clunker to the local junkyard may end up being the only option left in the life of your car. But wait! Have you thought about donating it to a charitable organization in exchange for a legal IRS tax deduction?

Vehicle Donation Processing Center, Inc. (at `www.donating-a-used-car.com`), as shown in Figure 15-5, acts as a middleman for charities seeking vehicle donations. This service covers many of America's largest urban centers, and it isn't picky about whether the car actually works. Its "main function is to provide a revenue stream for charities in need of funding," which happens if it can sell a car for more than the cost of the towing. Visit the site's list of participating charities, consult the categories of vehicles it's willing to accept, and apply online. (Notice that the service doesn't accept cars that are more than 15 years old.)

Although we demonstrate a wide variety of options open to you online as a car seller in this chapter, you always need to keep in mind whom the buyer is and how he intends to pay you for your car. Never sell merely on the promise of a vague future payment. In other words, make sure that you receive your payment before you hand over the ownership and the keys to your car. There are many scam artists out there, and because of the anonymity a person has through the Web, it's important to be cautious when selling any item online.

Figure 15-5:
If you can't sell your old car, you can always donate it to charity through the Vehicle Donation Processing Center.

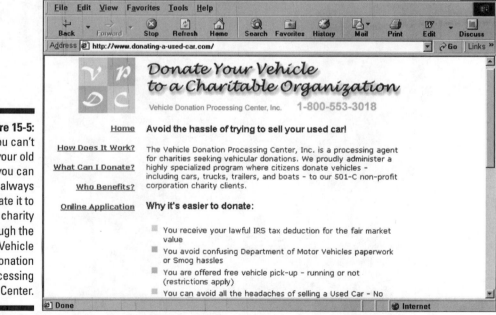

Part IV
After You Buy It

In this part . . .

*I*f the thought of buying insurance sends a cold chill up your spine (or you're thinking, "Insurance? We don't need no steenking insurance! Do we?"), Part IV is ready to answer all your questions. After all, purchasing insurance for your new car is an important way to maintain your investment — and it's more often than not a legal requirement if you live in just about any state of the union. Well, take heart: Chapter 16 tells you how to go online to find the best insurance deals around, as well as how to determine what level of coverage is best for you and your car.

Another aspect of vehicle ownership that can land you in hot water (even if your radiator's not leaking) if you fail to understand the laws of your state involves licensing requirements both for you, the driver, and for your car itself. In Chapter 17, we provide you with several methods for determining the exact driver's- and vehicle-licensing requirements for your home state through your online research.

Make sure that you pay close attention to this part of the book if you intend to take your car out for a spin on the open highway — or even just the streets of your neighborhood — without breaking any laws.

Chapter 16

Insuring Your Car on the Internet

• •

In This Chapter

▶ Saving yourself some money

▶ Understanding the components of auto insurance

▶ Figuring out insurance costs

▶ Choosing a car that you can afford to insure

▶ Trying cars.com

▶ Determining whether the insurance company is safe

▶ Lowering your insurance costs

▶ Answering online insurance questions

• •

*I*nsurance is one of the most fluid and complex economic markets. You can find hundreds of companies (from biggies such as State Farm all the way to Danny's Qwik Klaims) willing to insure your car in many thousands of combinations of ways. The experience can seem daunting. But always remember that, if you need to find an efficient, inexpensive solution to a complex, fluid market question, nothing beats the Internet.

Whatever else it may be, the Internet is surely a great research tool. In this chapter, I show you how to get an insurance quote online and how to get the most for your insurance dollar.

Saving Money on Insurance

The Internet is the perfect place to drive down your costs on everything from travel to TV sets, and insurance is no exception. Fill out a few forms and get quotes from at least three or four online insurance companies. You're likely to find that the annual cost of the same auto coverage can vary by $500 or more.

Money for nothing

Richard Mansfield (one of your authors) recently did the Internet insurance boogie and filled out forms for State Farm, GEICO, and others. He saved $478 off his previous annual auto-coverage costs. Oftentimes, too, when you give the same insurance carrier your auto and homeowner's (or renter's) insurance, you can save even more.

Now that we have this charming little testimonial out of the way, we assume that you have sufficient motivation to read the rest of this chapter. (We know of nothing that matches telling people how they can save money to inspire them to read a few pages in a book.)

What You Need to Know

This chapter can't provide comprehensive coverage of the topic of car insurance. If you want a really thorough discussion, take a look at the book *Buying a Car For Dummies,* by Deanna Sclar (IDG Books Worldwide, Inc.). That book goes into detail about premiums, shopping for insurance, and what you need to know about the policy and its components. It even explains such things as how to file a claim — topics that this book can't cover in detail. Our topic is merely car insurance online.

Nevertheless, the following sections cover some basic points for you to consider whenever you're shopping on the Internet for vehicle insurance.

The big three insurance types

Auto insurance consists of three primary components, and how much you want to purchase of each component is generally up to you. (But we strongly suggest that you purchase a good chunk of liability insurance — unless, of course, you have nothing left to lose.) The following list describes these components of auto insurance:

- **Comprehensive coverage:** This type of insurance provides coverage for all kinds of damages that don't result from an actual crash, up to the value of the car. Your car may or may not be repaired or replaced, depending on the type of claim you have.

- **Collision coverage:** This insurance coverage repairs or gives you the value of your car (in case of a total loss) if you damage it in a collision (either via collision with another vehicle or hitting something stationary, such as a building). This coverage is no-fault — meaning that it doesn't matter if you hit someone or if they hit you — assuming that you haven't violated the terms of your policy. Some policies won't cover your loss if you deliver pizzas, for example, or if you let an unauthorized driver drive your car. The damage to your car will be repaired if you fulfill the terms of your policy. Of course, fault may come in to play in deciding how a claim affects your premiums.

✔ **Liability coverage:** This type of insurance provides coverage if you're at fault in an accident. Hitting somebody after you run a red light may open a can of worms you can't believe. You can face a seemingly endless supply of lawyers and a myriad of complaints from the victims of your carelessness: doctor bills; inability to work; newfound failure to enjoy personal pleasures; lost wages; emotional distress; lack of consortium; pain and suffering; hot flashes; cold flashes; and so on.

We could fill the rest of this book by continuing the sorry list of liability grievances that make lawyers rich and have all too often caused otherwise moral people to exaggerate their problems and whimper, whine, and lie at trials. This nasty factor costs all the rest of us as well in the form of higher insurance premiums.

Fair is fair. Many people actually deserve compensation in liability lawsuits, of course. Others, however, don't. In the final analysis, how deserving someone is simply doesn't matter to you if you're the target of a liability lawsuit. All too often, the sky's the limit in such suits, and you can lose much of what you own as a result. You *do* need liability insurance, Bunky.

How Much Do You Need to Spend?

Hundreds of combinations of auto-insurance options exist. How much coverage do you need? How much money do you have? If your net worth is more than $100,000, you need to think about the potential of being sued. You want to buy liability coverage for your house and your car to protect yourself.

For the car, consider getting at least $500,000 per accident and $200,000 per injured person. Go for $50,000 or more in property damage insurance per accident. That amount may sound like a lot, but a car such as a BMW or Lexus can cost a lot to repair. And even if your current net worth isn't huge, factor in your earning potential. If you expect to prosper, do you want to share it with a stranger just because you forget to get enough liability insurance? Sometimes a judgment can attack your future earnings in a liability case.

As is true of most purchases, you can get a quantity discount on insurance. If you buy both your auto and homeowners insurance from the same company, you can usually get a discount on the rates for those policies.

Lowering your costs

Another way to lower your auto insurance costs is to remove both collision and comprehensive insurance. Don't live in a dream world, though. If you don't carry collision insurance on your car, and then you have an accident that's your fault, chances are good that your auto insurance company won't pay out anything for your damage.

Considering a higher deductible

A *deductible* is the money that you pay for repairs before the insurance kicks in. If, for example, you have an accident that results in $1,000 damage to your vehicle and you have a $500 deductible, you pay $500, and the insurance company pays $500. As is the case with health insurance, you may want to consider boosting the deductible that you must pay in any insurance claim. The usual default deductible is around $500, but you can ask your insurance agent to determine what happens to your rates if you raise the deductible to, say, $1,000.

Can Your Car Choice Boost Insurance Costs?

You can reduce the cost of your insurance in several ways. For starters, you can base your choice of make and model partly on its effect on your insurance payments. How? If a certain model of car is frequently stolen or costs quite a bit to repair, insurance companies jack up the premiums accordingly.

If, on the other hand, you purchase a vehicle that thieves don't seem to want (think station wagon here) or that you can repair for less money, your insurance rates are going to cost you much less.

Checking various car risks

If you want data on how likely your particular car is to attract crooks in your local area, your odds of a drunk smashing into your vehicle, and other risks where you live, you can get some great stats online from Quicken. Quicken is a leading maker of personal finance software and a great source of information about issues that impact your financial situation, such as how likely your car is to get ripped off.

To get information from Quicken, follow these steps:

1. **Go to the Quicken site's Auto Risk Evaluator by typing** `www.insuremarket.com/risks/auto/q.sfa?form=intro` **into your Web browser's Address text box.**

   You see the Evaluator program, as shown in Figure 16-1.

2. **Type your ZIP code in the ZIP Code text box.**

3. **Select your car's make from the drop-down list box.**

4. **Click any (or all) the check boxes next to each of the following categories of risk:**

   • How likely are you to be injured by an uninsured motorist?

   • How well does your car protect you and your family in a crash?

   • How well does your car hold up in a crash?

   • How common are hit and runs in my area?

   • How likely are you to be hit by a drunk driver?

   • Are thieves in love with your car?

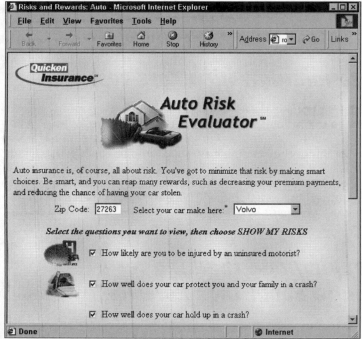

Figure 16-1: This excellent Auto Risk Evaluator can alert you to various kinds of risks, basing its results on such data as where you live and what kind of vehicle you drive.

5. **Click the Show My Risks button.**

   You next see a page asking you to specify which model you drive.

6. **Choose your car model from the drop-down list box.**

7. **Click the Next button.**

   You see the results — a lengthy and highly helpful description of the relative risks in your area, including solid advice on what kind of automobile coverage you need, based on the statistics.

Following is the excellent advice that we received from the Auto Risk Evaluator about what kind of uninsured motorist coverage, for example, makes sense for someone who lives in North Carolina:

   In North Carolina, 7.7 percent of all accidents resulting in injury involved an uninsured motorist.

   North Carolina ranks number 42 in the nation among all states surveyed in injury-related accidents involving an uninsured motorist.

   In North Carolina, your risk of being injured by an uninsured motorist is comparatively LOW. So when you specify your limits and deductibles, you may want to consider no more than an average amount of uninsured/underinsured motorist coverage. (However, if you do a lot of interstate travel, think about obtaining a high level of uninsured/underinsured motorist coverage.)

Determining which cars cost more

For another good place to check out which cars are more expensive to insure, go to CarPoint's finance and insurance page (at `www.carpoint.msn .com/finance_insurance` on the Web) and select your car from the drop-down list under the heading Insurance Ratings, as shown in Figure 16-2.

The results for the Infiniti model we looked up were average on a scale of seven ratings that range from significantly better than average to significantly worse than average.

Stopping and thinking for a minute about that Porsche

Before you purchase that great car you've always dreamed of, determine just how much the insurance premiums are going to cost. Finding out how many people buy a Porsche or some other lovely, ideal car and then must sell it soon after buying it may shock you.

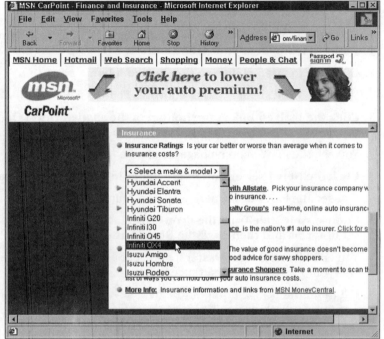

Figure 16-2:
Find out
how your
car's
insurance
costs
compare
with
vehicles of
similar
prices on
CarPoint's
finance and
insurance
page.

Why must such people sell their dream cars? Because they can't keep up the car payments plus the insurance payments. Insurance for fabulous luxury and sports cars is higher than for more everyday vehicles. What you pay for your old clunker isn't what you're going to pay for that Porsche. Taking a big depreciation hit only a short time after buying the car you've always wanted is both costly and embarrassing.

Using Cars.com (It Has the Name!)

One of the most popular automotive sites on the Internet is Cars.com (at www.cars.com). (Now *that* was a good Internet address to register!) As do most other large commercial sites devoted to vehicles, Cars.com includes a section on insurance. Cars.com partners with *InsWeb* to enable you to compare free quotes from several insurers. InsWeb is a good source for such information; it ranks high among more than one online rating service, including a rating as one of the 50 Most Incredibly Useful Sites by *Yahoo! Internet Life*.

To get free insurance quotes from InsWeb, follow these steps:

1. **Go to the Cars.com home page by typing** www.cars.com **into the Address text box of your Web browser.**

2. **Click the <u>Insurance</u> link on the Cars.com home page.**

   You see a page similar to that shown in Figure 16-3.

3. **Click the <u>InsWeb</u> link at the bottom of the shaded Get A Quote area in the middle of the page (refer to Figure 16-3).**

   You see the InsWeb home page, as shown in Figure 16-4.

4. **Click the New User button in the upper left portion of the page.**

   You see the first page, where you start filling in data about yourself.

5. **Choose your state from the drop-down list box on the first page of the set of forms and then click the Begin button.**

   You can fill in the forms faster if you get out your car's registration card and your current auto-insurance policy.

6. **Fill in all the information on the next several pages, clicking the Continue button as you finish each form.**

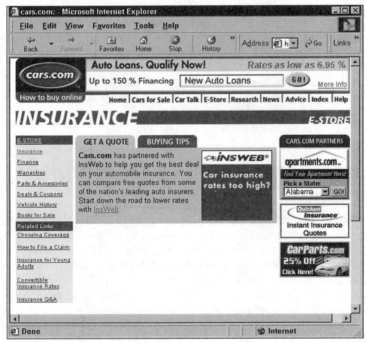

Figure 16-3: Insurance information from Cars.com begins on this page.

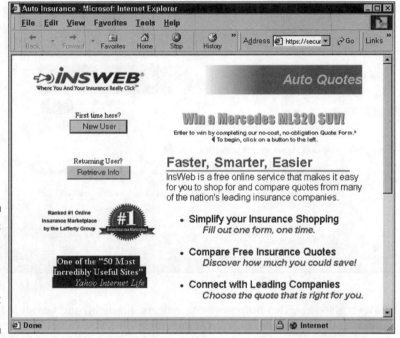

Figure 16-4:
Use the
highly rated
InsWeb
insurance
site to get
free quotes.

This site is well-designed. The thoughtful Save button stores the information you enter up to that point so that if something happens, you don't need to re-enter all the data. (How often "something" can happen may surprise you. All you need to do, for example, is to click your browser's Back button to crash an entire series of forms-entry pages.)

After you finish filling in all the forms (the entire process taking about 15 minutes), you see a list of companies that can provide you with quotes, as shown in Figure 16-5.

7. **Select an insurance agent if you see a list box offering you that option.**

8. **Fill in your address and phone number on the final page and then click the Quote Me button.**

The page that appears tells that you your quote(s) is probably going to arrive within 3–5 days. The page also provides the following information: `Since you've saved your information, you can retrieve it the next time you return to InsWeb. This will make comparison shopping the next time quick and easy.` Now *that's* a nice feature.

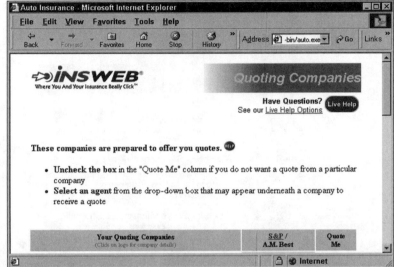

Figure 16-5:
After you
reach this
page of the
InsWeb site,
you can get
your quotes.

InsWeb also provides homeowners, renters, medical, and term life insurance quotes. After you register, you can ask for future quotes without needing to fill in as much information about yourself. InsWeb saves your data for use any time that you want another quote. And the site is very well thought out. After you provide the year, make, and model of your car, for example, it automatically fills in such data as airbags, braking system, and other such information.

Rating the Companies

You want a reliable insurance company, don't you? No government insurance exists for insurance companies the way that FDIC does for bank accounts. You can, however, find insurance company ratings at several Internet sites. Of those we've seen, the one that we recommend is Insure.com (at `www.insure.com/ratings`), which gives you free rankings from the following two sources (see Figure 16-6):

 ✔ Standard & Poor's ratings of a company's financial strength

 ✔ Duff & Phelps' ratings of the company's claims-paying capabilities

Figure 16-6:
Go to the
Insure.com
Web site to
determine
whether
your
insurance
company's
financially
secure.

Getting a Discount

Insurance companies offer many special discounts on auto insurance. If you
have a car alarm, for example, you usually qualify for a discount. The following list describes some of the typical springboards to paying less. Check with
your insurer to see whether they offer the following reductions to determine
whether you're getting as low a rate as you deserve:

✔ **Safe driver:** The biggest discount of all is the one that you get from
simply driving safely. If you had no accidents or tickets (parking tickets
don't matter) in the past three years, your discount can run as high as
40 percent! Some companies (notably GEICO) accept only people who
fall in this category — usually known as *preferred customers*. If you've
had accidents or tickets, you must pay the higher costs until you're
clean for at least three (or more) years. If you've had a very serious
arrest, such as reckless driving or driving under the influence, you're
likely to receive the rating of an *assigned risk* driver, and you can expect
to pay even more.

✔ **Anti-theft devices:** An alarm can reduce your costs by as much as 10 percent.

✔ **Good grades at school:** This measurement correlates with superior reaction times and good impulse control. (And sucking up to teachers is good practice for sucking up to cops.)

✔ **Graduating from special driving courses:** (This discount goes to teenagers who take driver's education or seniors who take defensive driving courses.) This one can give you another 10 percent discount.

✔ **Good citizenship:** Having no misdemeanors in the past three years and no felonies in the past ten years are typical requirements for this deduction.

✔ **Having the right address:** If you live in an urban area, your auto rates are higher than they are if you live in rural areas because of the greater likelihood of theft and accidents in cities. Rural homeowner insurance, however, can run higher than that of urban homeowners because of the less-efficient fire protection that rural areas enjoy.

You may find that this tradeoff is a wash, however, as Richard did after he quit smoking. He called the health insurance lady and she said, "How wonderful! That reduces your premiums with us by 20 percent. Now, uh, have you gained any weight?" "Yes," I answered, "about 35 pounds actually." "Oh dear," she responded, "We need to boost your premiums back up by 20 percent because of that gain . . . sorry."

✔ **Buying the right car:** Ordinary sedans are good. But buying SUVs or luxury cars results in higher repair costs, and sports cars generate more insurance claims on average, also costing you more.

✔ **Buying multiple policies:** Agreeing to consolidate your life, home, and personal liability or other insurance with the same insurer can save you up to 15 percent on the overall costs.

✔ **A strong credit rating:** As does success in school, good credit correlates with low accident rates. People who act responsibly in academia and personal finance are — not surprisingly — also usually responsible behind the wheel. Macho, hot-tempered ex-cons, on the other hand. . . .

✔ **Good personal hygiene, short hair, glasses:** Just kidding. But who knows what the future holds? A correlation's probably in there somewhere.

Further Questions? Contact the DOI

Each state has its own Department of Insurance, and you can likely find answers to questions about such issues as no-fault insurance if you contact them. Use a search engine to look up the Web site for your state's DOI. (If you live in North Carolina, for example, you find through such a search that you can go to www.ncdoi.com for lots of helpful data, as shown in Figure 16-7.)

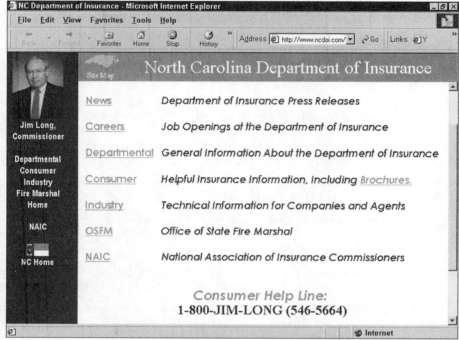

Figure 16-7: State Department of Insurance Web sites, such as this one for North Carolina, can give you helpful information about the insurance laws in your state.

No-fault insurance, by the way, was invented about 30 years ago as a way to, in theory, reduce the costs of insurance by reducing lawsuits. Currently only 13 states still participate in this experiment. (Statistics show that insurance costs generally haven't, as hoped, come down.) The no-fault states, in order of livability, are: Colorado, Florida, Hawaii, Kansas, Kentucky, Massachusetts, Michigan, Minnesota, New Jersey, New York, North Dakota, Pennsylvania, and Utah. (Just kidding; we put them in alphabetical order, not livability. But come to think of it, if you look over this list. . .?)

Your Online Insurance Checklist

So you're all fired up and ready to comparison shop for insurance on the Internet and maybe save yourself a bundle. Before you start serious surfing, however, look over the following checklist as a tool to remind you of some of the important points that we cover in this chapter:

- ✔ If your current insurer raises your rates, use that as an excuse to go cyber-shopping for a better deal.

- ✔ Make sure that you get the kind of coverage that you need: no more, no less.

✔ Always check exclusions. If you're in the media, for example, you may want to find out whether your liability coverage includes lawsuits for libel. Usual exclusions (war and things such as that) are almost always spelled out, but you may want to make sure that you have coverage appropriate to your occupation or location. Sometimes, as is the case with flooding, you may need to apply for separate insurance.

✔ In general, stick with well-known, strong companies such as Allstate or Nationwide — places you've heard of or check out by using the tips in the section "Rating the Companies," earlier in this chapter. You don't want your insurance company going belly-up just as you face a $290,000 lawsuit.

✔ Get enough coverage to protect your net worth and consider also your future earning potential.

✔ Determine whether you want to raise your deductibles to lower your premiums, as we describe in the section "Considering a higher deductible," earlier in this chapter.

✔ If you drive an old car worth less than, say, $3,000, consider dropping your comprehensive and collision coverage to lower your premiums.

✔ If you frequently rent cars, you want to get personal auto insurance that also covers you whenever you're renting. That way, you can refuse the rental agencies' extra-cost insurance.

✔ If you have good, strong medical insurance, make sure that you don't duplicate such coverage in an auto policy.

✔ Be honest when applying for insurance. If you make up any information, the insurance company can deny you benefits if you submit a fraudulent claim. And if a check reveals that's it's a *deliberate* falsification (and the companies *do* check), the company can deny you insurance completely. (Then you need to go to the next insurance company and fill in its form, which asks whether any other company has ever denied you insurance.)

✔ If someone living with you is going to drive your vehicle, but you don't list that person on your policy, you can get in real trouble. By not declaring this driver, you really expose yourself. If that person has an accident with no coverage, guess who pays? You. Remember that the reason you buy insurance is not only because the law requires it, but also because it safeguards your savings, your house, your future income, and your fabulous collection of diamonds and pearls.)

Chapter 17

Looking at Licensing and Other Requirements

After you buy a car, both you and the car need licenses — specifically, a driver's license and a motor vehicle license. The first of these licenses is a card, usually of either plastic or paper, that you must carry with you while driving. The second one is a plate that fits on the car — usually at the back. Depending on the state in which you live, you may need a plate for the front, too. Without these licenses, neither you nor your car can legally go out on the road.

In this chapter, you can find out how the Internet can help you obtain the necessary licenses. We also help you find driver's education assistance in your area through the Internet, show you how to find the details about importing or exporting a vehicle, and show you where to go online to find information about the laws in your area that directly affect how you can drive. So buckle up and prepare yourself for a drive online!

Going Online to Find the Applicable Licensing Laws in Your State

The first thing you need to know to determine which laws apply to your situation is that all motor-transportation licensing, whether for humans or for vehicles, lies in the domain of state law in the United States (or provincial law in Canada). As a driver, you need to get a driver's license from the state (or province) in which you live. Similarly, you must *register* your car (or truck or motorcycle), too. In other words, where you live usually determines which state issues your driver's license and your car's license plate(s). Fortunately, you can discover just what requirements you must meet in your area by going online.

One of our favorite Web sites for quick access to state-government information is FindLaw.com (at `www.findlaw.com`), a monster resource site that's chock full of valuable links to sites in the fields of law, legislation, government services, law firms, and much more. For the purposes of this chapter, we ask you to go straight to FindLaw's section dealing with state government resources (which you can access directly at `www.findlaw.com/11stategov/index.html`), with all the states in a nicely alphabetical listing.

For example, if you live in New York, click the <u>New York</u> link. On the next page, click <u>Government Information</u> and then click <u>State Agencies</u> on the following page. Finally, you arrive at a Web site hosted by the State of New York, containing a complete alphabetical listing of all New York State agencies and departments. You can use a similar approach for all other states in the Union.

Now scroll down the list to click <u>Motor Vehicles, Department of</u>, which accesses that department's official Web site. The whole process we describe here takes only about 30 seconds, give or take half a dozen, depending on the speed of your Internet connection. The following sections tell you how to use the information available on this site (and similar sites of other states) to license both yourself and your vehicle.

Finding out how to get or renew a driver's license online

To demonstrate how to determine the requirements for obtaining (and keeping) a driver's license in your state, we continue with our example of the state of New York. Most states have similar requirements, and although their Web sites may differ somewhat from New York's, the general principles that we describe for finding information for that state usually apply.

First, you need to access the NYS Department of Motor Vehicles — or DMV, as it calls itself (at `www.nydmv.state.ny.us` on the Web) — where you find a series of direct links to key information about driver's license requirements, common questions relating to vehicle registration and titles, DMV forms available online that you can download and print, and even the New York state driver's manual (see Figure 17-1).

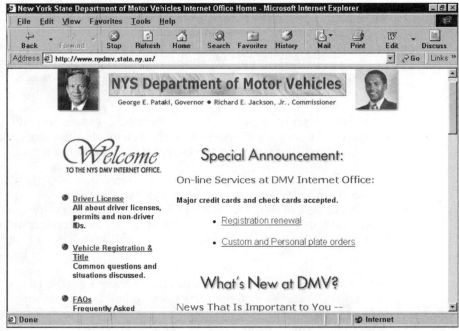

Figure 17-1:
Visit your
state's
department
of motor
vehicles
online for
information
about its
driving
require-
ments.

Click <u>Driver License</u> to find out all about driving in New York State. Here you discover details about how to apply for a new license and how old you must be to hold a license, as well as info about license renewal. You also find out what to do if you're a driver moving to New York or if you lose your license or someone steals it. Look here, too, for identification requirements, the state's point system (you get points if you get a traffic ticket, and if you earn a number of points in a specified period, your license may be suspended), and even stuff that you need to know if you get a traffic ticket.

Your state's online government infobase is also likely to include a listing of all DMV offices, driving statistics (the number of licensed drivers in your state, the number of accidents that occurred in the last year, and so on), and safe-driving tips. New York State, for example, includes on its Web site a section dealing with the consequences of driving while intoxicated.

If you're Canadian, you can follow a similar path through your province's online government resources. Say, for example, that you live in Toronto or Ottawa. You can go to the Province of Ontario's Ministry of Transportation Web site (at www.mto.gov.on.ca/english/) to find an entire section about drivers and vehicles that covers road safety, vehicle licensing, and even emission testing.

Using the Internet to register your car

Registering your newly purchased car is an important step in the ownership process. Until the appropriate government agency in your state approves your vehicle's registration, operating your car on public roads, streets, and highways is illegal.

Although the act of registration may simply be a routine procedure in most cases, it's not always a simple procedure. You must undertake certain steps, assemble the necessary documents, and pay the required fees.

Luckily, you usually find step-by-step checklists online, exactly where you expect them to reside — at your state's department of motor vehicles Web site. In the case of New York state's DMV Web site, for example, you can download Form MV-82 (the Vehicle Registration/Title Application) directly from the Net. You can also consult a list of applicable fees and sales taxes online.

You want to check the category that best suits your needs. The NYS DMV site lists several categories on the same page; to find further information about a category, click its link. On the New York site, you can even find guidance on what to do if you're dead (click the Vehicle Owner Deceased link), information that's perhaps more useful to your next-of-kin than to you at that point. As odd as the fact may seem, the Empire State permits dead people to own vehicles because "the immediate family of the deceased may continue to use the car until the deceased's registration and/or insurance expires."

Most other states offer equally helpful setups on the Internet. You can use the FindLaw.com Web site (www.findlaw.com) that we mention in the section "Going Online to Find the Applicable Licensing Laws in Your State," earlier in this chapter, to access a master list of state government Web sites.

In California, you can visit the Department of Motor Vehicles Web site (at www.dmv.ca.gov) to determine vehicle-registration requirements, new motor-vehicle legislation, the Year 2000 vehicle code, and something known as the "smog impact fee refund," and even find information about the Ronald Reagan Commemorative License Plate, with proceeds going for "educational and historical programs at the Ronald Reagan Presidential Library in Simi Valley." California's Web site is also promising that online vehicle-registration renewal is "coming soon."

The state of Florida's Department of Highway Safety and Motor Vehicles Web site (at www.hsmv.state.fl.us) offers a handy page by the name of Tag & Titles. This area covers everything you need to know about licensing your car in a terrific online Frequently Asked Questions (FAQ) section and provides info regarding disabled-parking permits, specialty license plates, and even some helpful data that you need to know before you buy a used car.

Not all states' departments of transportation handle motor-vehicle licensing. In Missouri, that department seems to focus on road projects and such. (It also provides information about winter road conditions and offers a form that you can use to request a Missouri official highway map.) Instead, Missouri's Department of Revenue (at www.dor.state.mo.us/mvdl/default.htm on the Web) handles the state's motor vehicle licensing, covering similar critical material that you find at the other states' DMV or similar Web sites. Missouri's DOR Web site offers online forms, a nifty registration checklist, a list of vehicle registration offices, and even historical data about the design of the state's license plate.

Exploring Vehicle Import Laws Online

One subject about which you definitely need to know all the necessary laws and requirements is buying a car outside the country (whether in person or through an online dealer or owner). Fortunately, you can find all the information you need to know about the laws and requirements for importing a vehicle on the Internet.

Your car must clear U.S. Customs before you can bring it into the country and register it with the appropriate state authority. So if you're planning to import a car into the United States, you must start your online quest for information with a trip to the U.S. Customs Service Web site (at www.customs.ustreas.gov/imp-exp2/informal/car.htm), shown in Figure 17-2.

Fortunately, the U.S. Customs Service provides an entire section at its site dealing with the requirements for importing a car. In fact, its resources are quite extensive, covering just about everything you need to know: making prior arrangements for shipping; gathering the documentation you need; cleaning the undercarriage to rid it of dangerous pests; paying the applicable taxes and duties; meeting emission standards; and conforming to safety standards. On this last point, Customs states that the importer must sign a contract with a Department of Transport (DOT) Registered Importer (RI), who can modify the vehicle to conform with all applicable safety and bumper standards and who can certify the modifications.

The U.S. Department of Transportation's National Highway Traffic Safety Administration (at www.nhtsa.dot.gov/cars/rules/import on the Web) also wants to know about your car import. The NHTSA's vehicle importation regulations Web site covers Canadian and non-Canadian guidelines, includes a vehicle eligibility list with rules about which vehicles are subject to which importation restrictions, and gives a roster of registered importers. It also offers various newsletters relating to importing vehicles, as well as a booklet listing the Federal Motor Vehicle Safety Standards currently in effect.

After you work your way through both the U.S. Customs and NHTSA Web sites, you want to visit your state's department of motor vehicles home page again for specific requirements that you need to meet to obtain your state's approval to import the vehicle. Go back to the state of New York's Department of Transport Web site, for example, directly accessing the section dealing with car imports on the New York DMV Web site by entering into your browser's Address text box the following URL: www.nydmv.state.ny.us/reg.htm#import. Notice that proof of ownership is high on the list. If you can't prove your ownership of an import, you can't register it in New York.

A great import deal from Volvo

If you fancy a trip to Sweden *and* you're in the market for a new car, you can kill two birds with one stone by purchasing a Volvo. Volvo offers customers a great deal: If you buy the car and agree to come to Sweden to pick it up, Volvo will pay for your trip and put you up in a hotel for one night. The company also offers up to $4,000 in savings if you buy this way. For more information, go to the Volvo Web site at www.volvocars.com, click the ways to buy link, and then click the overseas delivery link. Other European auto makers offer similar deals; check out individual auto makers' Web sites for details.

Finding Driver's Education Online

Most state and provincial governments require you to pass a driver's test before granting you a driver's license. We strongly suggest, however, that you go above and beyond the minimum state or provincial requirements to ensure that you equip yourself as best as you can to deal with various driving challenges. Use the online access to various state governments that we mention in the section "Going Online to Find the Applicable Licensing Laws in Your State," earlier in this chapter, to find direct information about the requirements in your area. Mine the data that you find at automobile club Web sites, too, as we describe in the section "Tips from your friendly automobile associations," later in this chapter.

The State of Florida's Department of Highway Safety, for example, posts its Class E Examination of Florida Traffic Laws online (at www.hsmv.state. fl.us/handbooks/English/exam.html), as well as an entire section about its motorcycle-rider training program (at www.hsmv.state.fl.us/ddl/ motobro.html) and information about parking permits for disabled drivers (at www.hsmv.state.fl.us/dmv/disabled_pkg.html).

Finding driving tips on the Internet

You form great driving habits over time through a mixture of experience, common sense, and road-safety consciousness. Experience comes from driving — and from learning and living through the various incidents on the road that all drivers inevitably encounter, such as hitting an icy patch of road, having to pass a semi, and so on. Fortunately, even if you don't have much experience in various situations, the Internet is a treasure trove of online tips on driving in all types of conditions and getting through all kinds of situations on the road.

The American Automobile Association (AAA) Web site (at www.aaa.com) and the Canadian Automobile Association (CAA) Web site (at www.caa.ca) deserve a spot on your radar screen if you're seeking motoring tips. Both are great places to start your online navigation, offering oodles of links covering just about every category imaginable.

✔ To access the AAA Web site, go to www.aaa.com and key in your home ZIP code. From there, you can access local information for your state or region. By randomly typing in a ZIP code, we accessed the AAA's Southern New England offering, a site that provides info to members only (an online travel agency, maps, directions, and so on) and other areas that are open to any visitor. The Car Doctor, for instance, covers car reviews, car-care tips, info about gas prices, and much more.

✔ The CAA Web site features a great section on traffic safety, which offers valuable information touching on child restraints, school safety patrols, impaired driving, aggressive driving, truck safety, traveler's advice, and winter driving.

(continued)

(continued)

Winter driving can serve as a good skill test for even the most seasoned driver. Fortunately, several Web sites provide excellent tips well worth heeding. Insure.com (at `www.insure.com/auto/winterdrivingtips.html`) offers a list of things for you to check on your vehicle before driving it in wintry weather, plus a number of good points for you to remember while out and about. Icepack.org (at `www.icepack.org/cartips.htm` on the Web) is another online haven for winter-driving advice. Icepack covers a lot of ground, including how to prepare your car for winter, how to drive safely in normal winter-driving conditions, and tips for dealing with extreme conditions — starting the car in extreme cold, digging out after a blizzard, and so on.

Keep in mind, too, that the Internet enables you to find advice from all around the world. Check out the CarToday.com Web site (at `www.carmag.com/content/4x4/drivingtips.html`) in Zaire, Africa, for some good practical off-road driving tips. The site explains the basic principles of a 4x4 vehicle (such as a Jeep) and how it differs from a normal car. It then provides useful tips for crossing soft ground, driving on rough ground, crossing ditches, navigating tricky ascents and descents, motoring through gullies, and even crossing shallow bodies of water.

Not all driving tips come from official sources. A lot of great driving tips can come from your fellow drivers, wherever they live. CarTalk.com (at `http://cartalk.cars.com`) is one place to find useful tips. On one of CarTalk.com's many pages (at `www-dev.cartalk.com/Mail/Letters/09-20/8.html`), we came across tips for driving on the German Autobahns, which are virtual public speedways given that these freeways have no speed limits at all. (Simply remember to use common sense in gauging the value of such driving tips as they apply to your everyday circumstances.)

California's AAA Web site offers a guide to that state's new graduated driver license (at `www.aaa-calif.com/members/corpinfo/teens.asp`), while the Alberta Motoring Association (AMA) maintains a great Web site covering its driver education program (including sections on "Learning the Right Way the First Time," "Emergency Manoeuvres Course," and "Brush-Up Lessons") and also posts its driver's exam online (at `www.ama.ab.ca/tsdeserv/pages/drivexam.htm`).

In essence, the Internet isn't just about surfing. It's also about driving — with a trunkful of rules, advice, discussion, support, and much more. Above all, use your good judgment while driving and enjoy the experience for what it is — the most enjoyable way to get from point A to point B. And with the online suggestions that we discuss in this chapter, we're hoping that you make your next trip a safe and happy one.

Car Buying Online For Dummies Internet Directory

"Look, I've already launched a search for 'reanimated babe cadavers' three times and nothing came up!"

In this directory . . .

*T*hroughout this book, you can find references to many
locations on the Internet where you can locate information, gather resources, plan, plot and organize. In
addition, the Internet is growing daily — existing sites are
revised and new ones are coming online. The Internet is
nothing if not vibrant and bustling. It's a global marketplace like no other in history.

The following pages include many of the sites that we consider the best of their kind. You'll also find lists of other
sites to check out if you don't find what you're looking for
in the primary sites. No list, though, can possibly be comprehensive — or remain comprehensive for long — when it
attempts to cover something as alive and changeable as
the Internet. So be sure to check out the tips in Chapter 2
on how to conduct your own online searches for all the
latest features and information available on that amazing
resource, the World Wide Web.

About This Directory

To use the directory, all you need to do is browse through it, read the descriptions that appeal to you, and then visit those sites.

To help you judge at a glance whether a site may be useful for you, this directory includes some handy miniature icons (otherwise known as *micons*). Here's an explanation of what each micon means:

$ You have to pay a fee to access some services at this site.

▢ This site requires you to register.

▢ This site may require you to use a credit card.

Barter Sites

Why not trade your car for something else, such as a canoe, a couch, or even a drum set?

Barter Board Xchange
www.bbx.com
The BBX Barter Board Xchange is "where one man's junk is another man's treasure." This site is free to buyers who can wheel and deal and pitch you just about anything imaginable in exchange for your car.

Ubarter
www.ubarter.com
Ubarter.Com claims to be "where the world trades." This is a business-to-business barter site, but it features a complete section devoted to automotive, boats, and motorcycles.

Car Safety Information

A vehicle's safety record — even if the data is few and new — can be very interesting. Even brand-new cars must take safety crash tests, and that data is available online.

AAA Foundation for Traffic Safety
www.aaafts.org
The AAA Foundation for Traffic Safety studies why motor vehicle crashes happen and endeavors to show everyone how to avoid unsafe situations.

CarPoint
www.carpoint.msn.com
If you're interested in seeing the results of crash tests (conducted by NHTSA, the National Highway Traffic Safety Administration), click the Table of Contents button, and then click <u>Shopping for Safety</u> ☞ <u>Crash Testing</u> ☞ <u>Frontal Crash Tests</u>.

CrashTest.com
www.crashtest.com
CrashTest.com is an independent auto safety testing organization that boasts considerable depth for those interested in previously enjoyed (used) cars. Most other safety testing organizations publish data only for recent models. CrashTest.com offers NHTSA data going back as far as the 1970s. There's also a feature allowing you to see the crash statistics on two different cars at the same time.

Insurance Institute for Highway Safety

www.hwysafety.org

The Insurance Institute for Highway Safety describes itself as "an independent, non-profit research and communication organization . . . wholly supported by automobile insurers." It also offers vehicle crash test data on recent models.

Liberty Mutual's Used Car Stats

www.libertymutual.com/hldi

Here's another good site that can answer your questions about recent used cars. Liberty Mutual's site can tell you about your prospective car's theft, injury, and collision statistics. It compares your prospective car against 335 vehicles in seven styles from the years 1995 through 1997. After you specify the car's make and model, that car's claim statistics from the Highway Loss Data Insurance are displayed.

National Highway Traffic Safety Administration

www.nhtsa.dot.gov

The U.S. Government is often an excellent source of certain kinds of objective data about vehicles. This is the Web site of the National Highway Traffic Safety Administration (NHTSA), a division of the U.S. Department of Transportation. NHTSA has a variety of responsibilities under the general heading of reducing the number of crashes and reducing the effects of crashes that do occur.

Quicken Insurance

www.insuremarket.com/risks/auto/
    q.sfa?form=intro

If you want data on how likely it is that your particular car will attract crooks in your local area, how likely you are to be smashed into by a drunk driver, and other risks based on where you live, you can get great statistics from Quicken's Auto Risk Evaluator.

Car Talk

Nothing helps you make decisions about purchases like candid comments from experienced people.

Consumer Democracy

www.consumerdemocracy.com/cars.htm

If you want a good place to find out the experiences and opinions of others who have tried and tested the vehicle you're thinking of buying, try the Consumer Democracy site. You'll find all kinds of opinions on all kinds of topics relating to cars and many other consumer items. (Consumer Democracy isn't focused only on cars. You'll find information on printers, toys, golf, and much else.) You'll see statistics, reviews, acclaim, criticism, ratings, comparisons, warnings, and other kinds of discussions and reports.

Talk City

www.talkcity.com

Talk City offers quite a bit of online activity. You can find chat rooms, famous people leading discussions, polls, photo galleries, and much more at this venerable, active site.

Woman Motorist

www.womanmotorist.com

It may not be PC, but there are sites devoted to women only. But even if you're not a woman, you may still find some information of use at the Woman Motorist site. The site isn't chauvinistic — there are reviews by both men and women.

Other Sites to Check Out

Buy Cars Online Car Chat

www.auctioncarsonline.com/chat.htm

Car Talk (featuring Click and Clack)

www.cartalk.cars.com

Classicar.com Chat

www.classicar.com/chatsforums/chat/

Live Corvette Chat

www.c5-corvette.com/C5_Chat.htm

YoCar.com Shop Talk

www.yocar.com/chat/chatmain.tpl

Classic Cars

Just as some people scour the world looking for items to add to their rare camera collection, cars are collected, too. And some car collectors are just as fanatical as the enthusiasts for any other collectable. Get together with others who share your passion at the sites described here.

Hemmings Motor News Online

www.hmn.com

Many sites on the Internet list values for new or late-model used cars, but few give an accurate value for collector cars. One of the best is the Hemmings Motor News Web site. It's a huge, easy to use, and extremely fast site with more than 30,000 classified ads and many other interesting sections.

Car Values Plus

www. hvaa.com/hmn.com

Car Values Plus offers respected evaluations, including an online appraisal service. They can also assist with additional options including pre-purchase condition reports, an escrow service, and shipping.

Other Sites to Check Out

Car List

www.carlist.com

Car Clubs Worldwide

www.carclubs.com

CC Data

www.ccdata.com

Appraisals

When you own precious things, you sometimes want to know what *other* people think those cherished possessions are worth. Think about the huge popularity of the "Antiques Roadshow" television series where people drag in their Aunt Tillie's two-ton armoire to get an appraisal. Owners of classic cars are no exception. And if you're considering buying a classic car, you'll probably want to know how an objective, independent expert values it.

We recommend having any classic car appraised before you plunk down cold, hard-earned cash for it. The appraisal will not only give you a better idea of what kind of shape the car is in, but it will also give you a verified value for insurance purposes. Fees for this service are not that expensive, ranging from $250 to $2,500, depending on the value of the car. (This represents a complete evaluation, including a road test.)

Robert DeMars Ltd.

www.robertdemarsltd.com

This California- and Florida-based appraiser claims to have appraisers in most major cities and has served as expert witnesses in California and Florida litigation.

Auto Appraisal

www.autoappraisal.com

 $

For a minimum $20 fee, this site will provide you with a range of values that fits your automobile. You can also schedule an on-site appraisal for a substantial fee. For $25, the site will search for a particular vehicle that you're trying to buy.

Sequence

www.sequenceauto.com

$

Sequence auto charges $119 for an e-mail appraisal of your automobile and $189 for an on-site inspection. Sequence also does damage and insurance estimates.

USAPPRAISAL

www.usappraisal.com

$

USAPPRAISAL performs appraisals on autos for a variety of purposes, specializing in antique autos. Fees can be based on a per-hour or per-vehicle basis. USAPPRAISAL asks that you contact them for pricing information.

Arranging transport

After you buy your classic car, probably the safest way to have it delivered is to have it transported. The car is covered by the transporter's insurance and is delivered right to your door. The cost of this service is between $.60 and $1.25 per mile, depending on the type and value of the car. Most of the time, transport is via enclosed hauler for maximum protection. The cost is calculated from the point of pickup to the point of delivery.

The more valuable your car is, the more you may want to consider this service. Here is a list of some online transport services that might suit your needs:

Auto-Move

www.auto-move.com

Auto-Move is the Web site of Majestic Auto Transport, which says it's fully insured in 48 states, has 30 years experience, and uses an enclosed three-car hauler with no double decking. They also say that their rates are reasonable, so see if you agree.

Intercity Lines, Inc.

www. intercitylines.com

Intercity Lines, Inc. boasts state of the art 53-foot, fully enclosed air ride trailers and has been in business since 1980. They offer free quotes and automobile transportation is their only business.

Passport Transport

www.passporttransport.com

Passport Transport asserts that it *invented* enclosed auto transport in 1970. Passport claims to be the first and still the finest specialized auto carrier in the United States. They're worth a look.

Thomas C. Sunday, Inc.

www. thomascsundayinc.com

This company transports collector cars, antique cars, classic cars, race cars, and specialty cars — all over the nation.

Other Sites to Check Out

American Collectors Insurance

www.americancollectorsins.com

Arranging classic car registration and insurance

Registering your collector car is the same as registering a new car, with one possible exception. Most states have an antique car classification that usually calls for a one-time fee that is good for the entire time you own the car. In most cases a car has to be at least 25 years old to qualify.

Insurancecompany.com

www.insurancecompany.com

Check out this site for what seems to be every kind of insurance known to man, including precious classic cars. They offer the ordinary (earthquake, life, flood) and the extraordinary (ransom and kidnapping, car wash and wedding). I'm not sure if they'll insure your legs, if you're a singer-dancer-star like Betty Grable (she insured her movie-star legs way back when).

Classic Collectors Insurance

www.classiccollectors.com

This company, Great American, has been providing antique and classic auto insurance for more than 15 years. And they say they've done this without a base rate increase. Their motto is "You perfect it, we protect it."

Credit and Financing

Walking into a car dealership with a blank check is very useful. If you pre-arrange the financing for your new (or used) vehicle, half the hassle at the dealership is already eliminated. Here are some sites where you can locate financing and find cost information online.

AAA

www.aaa.com

If you're really hot to trot about a car and want to get an answer instantly, try the AAA (American Automobile Association). They say that their service is available 24 hours a day and that most loans are "rendered in 15 seconds."

AOL Autos Department

www.aol.com/webcenters/autos/home.adp

AOL maintains a set of auto-buying calculators that can help you figure out various loan options, as well as run comparisons. And, being AOL, there are important resources you can tap into, not least of which are the many people whose online opinions — and chat room real-time discussions — can be of special interest to prospective car buyers.

AutoWeb's Financing Options

www.autoweb.com

The very popular AutoWeb site includes a financing feature. Click the Finance link and you're taken to the PeopleFirst page, an excellent place to get "blank check" lending if you qualify.

BELAIRdirect.com

www.belairdirect.com/quebec/engl/ass-auto/carsoncd/intro.html

If you're trading in your present car, or you just want to know an estimate of the resale value of any car, try BELAIR*direct*. After you arrive at their site, click the How Much is Your Car Worth? link. You see a calculator you can use to get your estimate.

CarPoint Finance & Insurance Department

www.carpoint.msn.com/finance_insurance

At the MSN site, you can find several interesting financial features. Try clicking the Interest Rates link and selecting your state in the drop-down list box.

You can generally expect that the more the car you're buying costs, and the better your credit rating, the lower the interest rate you'll get. So you should check your credit rating to ensure that you know what it, in fact, is, and you should also contest any errors you find in the report (surprise, credit ratings can contain errors). If you do find an error, go ahead and contact the credit company whose data contains the error and get it straightened out.

Car Secrets Revealed

www.igs.net/carsecrets

Said to be among the most-visited automotive sites on the Internet, this site raises issues that are rarely covered elsewhere. Do you feel you're getting ripped off on repairs or insurance? Are you worried that the new car you're about to buy might turn out to be a lemon? Automotive consultant Corey Rudl's book may be just what you're looking for. You can get a taste of the book online at this site.

eAuto-CarFinance.com Automobile Financing Service

www.eauto.com/features/fea_carfin.shtml

eAuto offers financing services to help you gain the advantage of having the financing in place when you approach the sale. eAuto also points out that you get additional benefits when financing with them online: the rates are low; you have no down payment and no fees or closing costs; you get your answer in a few hours and the money, in most cases, the next day; and you can buy from any franchised dealership of your choice.

Experian, Equifax, and Trans Union

www.icreditreport.com

$

Pay $7.95 for a report derived from Experian, or $29.95 for a merged, triple-source report from Equifax, Trans Union, and Experian.

Free Report

www.freecreditreport.com

You can get a free credit report (when you sign up for a trial membership in the CreditCheck Monitoring Service) here. You could take this information to a dealer — either by printing it out, or letting the dealer contact CreditCheck directly.

LendingTree.com

www.lendingtree.com

If you want to figure out the final cost of your new car, the interest rate, down payment, any rebate, the likely trade-in value of your existing car, any money still owned on your current car, and the number of months of the loan, try an online calculator, such as the one available at LendingTree.

Donation Sites

For some people, the idea of hauling that clunker to the local junkyard may be the only option left in the life of their car. If you've got a vehicle you think you cannot sell, think about donating it to a charitable organization in exchange for a legal IRS tax deduction.

Car Donation Nationwide

www.cardonation.org

This site features a simple procedure for donating your car to a charitable institution and collecting the full Kelley Blue Book value of the car for a tax deduction. The site promises that all you have to do is fax in the title and Car Donation will take care of the rest, including towing the car.

Vehicle Donation Processing Center

www.donating-a-used-car.com

The Vehicle Donation Processing Center acts as a middleman for charities seeking vehicle donations. This service covers many of America's most largest urban centers and it isn't picky when it comes to whether the car actually works or not. Its "main function is to provide a revenue stream for charities in need of funding" and this happens when it can sell the car for more than the cost of the towing. Visit the site's list of participating charities, consult the category of vehicle it is willing to accept, and apply online.

Driving Tips

Good driving habits are formed over time through a mix of experience, common sense, and road safety consciousness. Fortunately, others' experiences can be found on the Internet in the form of driving tips covering just about every road condition and driving situation.

AAA

www.aaa.com

Driving tips abound on the Internet. The American Automobile Association (AAA) and the Canadian Automobile Association (CAA) (www.caa.ca) should be on everyone's radar screens when it comes to motoring tips. Both are great places to start your online navigation with oodles of links covering just about every category imaginable.

Accident Reconstruction

www.accidentreconstruction.com

This site provides fascinating accounts of car accident and traffic investigations. Accident Reconstruction provides a bookstore, directory of experts, learning center, and discussion area. It's more useful than you may think.

Car Today 4X4 Tips

www.carmag.com/content/4x4/
  drivingtips.html

Keep in mind that the Internet allows you to find advice from all over the world. Check out a Zaire, Africa Web site called CarToday.com for some good practical off-road driving tips. The site explains the basic principles of a 4X4 vehicle (such as a Jeep) and how it differs from a normal car. It then goes on to provide useful tips for crossing soft ground, rough ground, ditches, tricky ascents and descents, motoring through gullies, and even getting past shallow bodies of water.

Icepack Winterizing Tips

www.icepack.org/cartips.htm

Icepack.org is another online haven for winter driving advice. It is maintained by "a group of public and private agencies in Illinois and Indiana." Icepack covers a lot of ground, including How to Prepare Your Car for Winter (Simple Winterizing Tips, Winter Emergency Kit, and so on), Safe Driving in Normal Winter Driving Conditions (Handle Your Car on Snow and Ice, Winter Tips for Young Drivers, and so on), and Dealing With Extreme Conditions (Starting the Car in Extreme Cold, Digging Out After a Blizzard, and more).

MADD

www.madd.org

One sobering Web site well worth visiting, especially if you are a teen driver, or the parent of a teen, is MADD — Mothers Against Drunk Driving. In its own words, MADD "is more than just a bunch of angry moms. We're real people, moms, dads, young people, and other individuals just trying to make a difference. We are determined to stop drunk driving, support the victims of this violent crime, and prevent underage drinking." It goes a long way towards that goal with testimonials, statistics, discussions, programs, and public policy initiatives.

Ohio Department of Transportation

www.dot.state.oh.us/dist11/tips.htm

The State of Ohio's Department of Transportation provides its succinct suggestions, notably "leave early, slow down, and stay off the road when traveler's warnings are issued."

Winter Driving Tips

www.insure.com/auto/winterdrivingtips. html

Winter driving can actually be a good skill test for even the most seasoned driver. Fortunately, several Web sites provide excellent tips well worth heeding. Insure.com covers winter weather well.

Funky and Specialty Sites

Just in case you're one of those who likes to go off the beaten path to supplement your more conventional research, here is a little collection of intriguing locations on the Internet that may be just what you're looking for.

About.com

cars.about.com/autos/cars

This Web site is a good source of links to other sites for all kinds of information, discussions, books, awards, repair histories, museums, parts, dealers, and loads of other topics of interest to car buyers and owners. The information at this site is broader than it is deep, but it's deepening all the time. Give it a try.

Cartalk's Psychological Test

cartalk.cars.com/Survey/Results/Psycho graphics

Are you driving, or considering, a car that harmonizes with your personality? Don't fight your own character by trying to fit into a vehicle that is just plain wrong for you. The Car-O-Scope test promises to "help you determine if you're driving a car that fits your psychographic profile."

Coupon City

www.coolsavings.com.

Various rebates are out there, but you must know about them to get the cash. Many price quote sites alert you about rebates, but you can find other kinds of savings. The Web offers a cool site named CoolSavings — and it's not just for cars. You visit it, find coupons, send them to your printer, and use them. They include vehicle coupons, though, so see what's offered. You may not get a $2,000 rebate offer, but you could get a free pair of binoculars. Binoculars? Sure — if you need a pair, why not get them for free?

Gillet Vertigos, Solectrias, Twikes, and 1000 Others

autopedia.com/html/MfgSites.html

Do you want to visit a less mainstream site than Ford or GM? Interested in something, perhaps, like a Gillet Vertigo, a Solectria, or a Twike?

Find the Web sites and toll-free 800 numbers of everyone from Subaru to Steyr-Daimler-Puch here.

Insurance

Just as having financing or leasing arranged before you even go into the local dealership to purchase a vehicle is useful, having your insurance already means that you have one fewer problem to worry about.

Cars.com

www.cars.com

One of the most popular automotive sites on the Internet is Cars.com. Like most other large commercial sites devoted to vehicles, Cars.com includes a section on insurance. Cars.com has partnered with InsWeb to allow you to compare free quotes from several insurers. On Cars.com you'll find information such as their Insurance Guide (a Q and A format), and explanations of how to decide what coverage you need, how to file a claim, and other useful data.

Insure.com

www.insure.com/ratings

You want your insurance company to be reliable, don't you? There is no government insurance for insurance companies the way there is an FDIC for bank accounts. However, you can find insurance companies rated in several Internet sites. Of those we've seen, the one we recommend is Insure.com, which gives you free rankings from two sources.

Allstate.com

www.allstate.com

Most of the major insurance companies have an online presence. At the Allstate site, you'll find a nice tutorial feature — Insurance 101, as well as safety tips, calculators, and other tools to help you decide how and where to insure your vehicles.

Leasing

For many people, leasing is a better route than buying. Both the down payment and the monthly payments are usually lower — though you do end up having to turn in the car after a few years. If you think leasing might be for you, try these sites for additional information.

CarsEverything

www.carseverything.com

The CarsEverything site offers a handy calculator that can tell you what your monthly payment should be. Click the Lease Calculator link. Enter the selling price, the residual (what you must pay them if you decide to keep the vehicle), the leasing term (how many months the lease lasts), the factor (this is an additional cost you must request the dealer to divulge), and the tax. Then click the Calculate button and you'll find out your monthly payment as well as the total finance charge.

Autobytel

www.autobytel.com

You can check out the lease application feature at Autobytel.com. When you get to their site, click the Financing link under the Activity Centers heading.

AutoWeb Finance Center

www.autoweb.com/financecenter.htm

Another useful calculator lets you compare what happens if you buy or lease the same car. Go to AutoWeb and click the Lease Versus Loan link.

LeaseSource

www.leasesource.com

LeaseSource bills itself as "the Internet's best auto leasing site." It's certainly worth checking out. There are several interesting features at this site, among them the Leasing Classroom and the Leasing Workshop. For instance, in the Classroom, you get negotiation pointers, an "Ask the Expert" tool, an explanation of the "lease's pieces," and discussions of the sometimes baffling wording used in leases, such as *residuals* and *factors*.

Legal Matters

When you talk about automobiles, you have to talk about the various laws that govern them — including licensing, customs, and so on. As you cruise through the sites in this section, remember: It's not just a good idea, it's the law.

Canadian Ministry of Transportation

www.mto.on.ca

If you are a Canadian, follow a similar path through your province's online government resources. Let's say you live in Toronto or Ottawa. Go to the Province of Ontario's Ministry of Transportation to find a whole section about "Drivers & Vehicles" covering road safety, graduated licensing, and even emission testing. If you live in another province, enter that province rather than .on.

FindLaw.com

www.findlaw.com

One of our favorite Web sites for quick access to state government information is FindLaw.com, a monster resource site chock-a-block with valuable links in the fields of law, legislation, government services, law firms, and a lot more. Go to Findlaw's section dealing with State government resources. Click US State Resources and then click on your state. Then click Government Information ☞ State Agencies ☞ Motor Vehicles, Department of, which brings up that department's official Web site. Finally, click Motor Vehicles.

Your state's DMV (Deptartment of Motor Vehicles) will often provide a set of direct links with key information about driver license requirements, common questions related to vehicle registration and title, DMV forms available online that you can download and print out, and even the a Driver's manual to help you pass that driver's license test.

U.S. Customs

www.customs.ustreas.gov/
   imp-exp2/informal/car.htm

Your car has to clear U.S. Customs before it can enter the country and be registered with the appropriate state authority. So, if you are planning to import a car into the United States, start with a trip to the U.S. Customs Service. Fortunately, the U.S. Customs Service has a whole section at its Web site dealing with importing a car. In fact, the resources here are quite extensive, covering just about everything you need to know: Prior Arrangement, Documentation, Cleaning of the Undercarriage, "Duitable Entry" vs "Free Entry," applicable federal tax, emission standards, and even required standards relating to safety, bumper, and theft prevention.

U.S. Department of Transportation

www.nhtsa.gov

If you import a car into the U.S., then you need to inform the U.S. Department of Transportation's National Highway Traffic Safety Administration. The NHTSA's vehicle importation regulations Web site covers U.S. and Canadian guidelines, a vehicle eligibility list, and a roster of registered importers. It also offers various newsletters relating to importing vehicles, as well as a booklet listing the Federal Motor Vehicle Safety Standards currently in effect.

Mechanics and Auto Service

You can't avoid it forever. Sooner or later something is going to go wrong with your Mustang Sally. When it does, you can get help and information from the Internet.

And don't forget that a good place to start is to check out Web sites for local mechanics. Car repair is almost always local. They may have just one or two, or even a half dozen service bays and mechanics on duty. Their reputation rests on their ability to meet the needs of your community. So how can the

World Wide Web figure into this service? Well, some of the better of these shops often hang a shingle out on the Internet, and a good search engine can prove valuable when trying to track down a good repair shop near where you live or work.

ASA

www.asashop.org

The Automotive Service Association (ASA) represents 13,000 members by advancing "the professionalism and excellence in the automotive repair industry through education, representation and member services." Use the ASA's Web site to search for a member in your area and to consult its "Automotive Tips" section where you can find out about its "Consumer Bill of Rights for Motorists" and more. The ASA Web site also features links to a number of legislative resources, including "State Laws and Regulations for Replacement Crash Parts," a "Summary Of State Aftermarket Parts Disclosure Laws," and the ASA's position on a number of legislative issues.

ASE

www.asecert.org

ASE is the Institute for Automotive Service Excellence. It includes more than 420,000 professionals with current ASE certification. According to information at its home page, "They work in every segment of the automotive service industry: car and truck dealerships, independent garages, fleets, service stations, franchises, and more." Its mission is "to improve the quality of vehicle repair and service in the United States through the testing and certification of automotive repair technicians."

AskMe.com

www.askme.com

AskMe.com allows you to ask questions of experts on a variety of subjects, and one section involves auto repair and parts. To access the maintenance area, click Sports & Recreation ☞ Autos & Trucks ☞ Auto Maintenance & Repair. The neat thing about this site is that it links you up to real people who answer your questions. Not only can you view previews questions and answers, but you can also rate the answers already given and even add your own thoughts if you think you can add something useful. But the main thing here is to ask the question you need answered. And you can do it here with as much detail as you think you need.

AutoShop Online Automotive 101

www.autoshop-online.com/auto101.html

Check out AutoShop Online, "the United States' largest independent car and truck repair helpline." Its Automotive 101 is a free tutorial "on the inner workings of the major subsystems of the modern automobile." It's a great archive covering the engine, drive train, suspension, even heating and air conditioning.

AutoShop Online Service Inquiry Form

https://www.medilinks.net/secure/ autoshop/sec_inquiry.html

$

AutoShop Online has a pay-as-you-go Service Department Inquiry Form, promising you "direct access to experts and information for solving your automotive problem." All of it is based on a massive database of "the most frequent repair problems and their solutions for over 10,000 different makes, models and years of vehicles." You can examine a list of sample questions and answers to determine if this kind of online service suits you before you ante up with money. That's a nice feature.

Global4AutoParts.com Car Care Tips

www.global4autoparts.com/
Car%20Care%20Tips.htm

Global4AutoParts.com sells car parts worldwide. But its Web site also offers detailed car care tips. During a recent visit, I found out more than I need to know about shock and strut installation and removal. Impressive, indeed.

Mr. Goodwrench

www.gm.com

Visit General Motors on the Internet and click the GM Goodwrench button to access an excellent array of owner's service resources. GM promises to "take the guess-work out of caring for your vehicle" with auto advice covering everything from cleaning fabric stains to engine overheat-ing. It even has an online driver's log and maintenance scheduler you might well find useful. Sign up for the Driver's Log and you'll receive e-mail reminders when main-tenance is called for on your car!

PepBoys

www.pepboys.com/cartips/list.shtm

PepBoys, the giant chain of automotive parts supplies, offers visitors to its Web site a useful list of Car Care Tips. Here you can find out "How To Know If you Need A/C Maintenance," "How to Wash and Wax," "The Difference Between Conventional And Synthetic Motor Oils," "Battery Service Tips," and even how to be prepared for roadside emergencies.

Subaru Care

www.suburu.com

Over at the Subaru Web site, click on the Subaru Care button to access warranty info, car care tips, and maintenance schedules.

Online Reviews

If you want to get the lowdown on a car, truck, or other vehicle that interests you, few sources are better than narrative reviews. They attempt to describe the feel-ing of driving the vehicle and also cover any other points of interest to the prospec-tive buyer. Here are some of the best sources of online reviews.

1StopAuto

1stopauto.com/review.htm

This general-purpose vehicle site allows you to access in-depth reports on many late-model vehicles.

Autobytel.com

www.auto-reviews.com/reviews/
autobytel.htm

Best known as an online car-buying ser-vice, Autobytel.com is also a good source of automobile and truck reviews. You're likely to be pleased with the accuracy and depth of their coverage.

Black Book

www.blackbook.net

Available since 1955, the Black Book spe-cializes in providing "the latest wholesale prices direct from the auction lanes." Its publishers claim that one of its great strengths is up-to-the-minute pricing. This service is quite similar to the highly respon-sive price shifts available from a stock market where values move virtually hourly.

Consumers Union

www.consumer.org

The publisher of Consumer Reports has its own, distinct Web site. This site appears to specialize in governmental actions, recalls, court cases, environmental issues, and similar topics. For instance, at the time of this writing, a series of interesting articles titled "The Risk of Rollover in Some Sport-utility Vehicles and Consumer Union's Testing for Such Risks" appears there. These reports are free.

Edmunds.com

www.edmunds.com

$

Featuring their three famous magazines — *New Cars Prices & Reviews, Used Cars Prices & Reviews,* and *Used Cars & Trucks Prices & Ratings* — this site also offers a wide variety of information, including road tests, vividly written reviews, Town Hall (online discussion groups on all aspects of vehicle ownership), the "deal of the month," and a useful New Car Buyer's Workbook (specific to the auto you're interested in, $9.95). Many people consider Edmunds' reviews to be among the most reliable and thorough.

IntelliChoice CarCenter

www.intellichoice.com

Since 1987, IntelliChoice has been publishing auto reports in the award-winning *The Complete Car Cost Guide.* You can compare vehicles side-by-side, and the site includes a Spanish language version of this feature. You can also find out about current rebates and incentives, try the finance calculator to plan your purchase intelligently, find out all about pre-owned vehicles, and much more. IntelliChoice, an independent research firm, also announces its IntelliChoice awards annually. These are the vehicles that the firm projects will be the best values — based on factors including price, depreciation (which can vary considerably among makes and models), repairs, financing, and maintenance. The firm uses historical data to create projections for a five-year period.

Pace Buyer's Guides

www.carprice.com

The *Pace Buyer's Guides* have been published since 1974, and you can find free

price information and other auto data there. If pricing is your main interest, this site is extremely comprehensive. However, it also includes a variety of additional information, including calculators, recalls, rebates, insurance, warranty, tips, negotiation suggestions, motorcycle information, and other data.

Online magazines

Throughout this book, we mention the sites of several famous car magazines, but many more are available online. Some sites offer electronic versions of their newsstand paper counterparts. Others are all-electronic — no paper involved. Online-only magazines are often referred to as *zines.* Use your favorite search engine to locate any of these that interest you: Autofacts; The Autonaut; Autopedia; All Auto Online; American Automobile Association; Autoweek On line; CarMag; CarSound Magazine; C.A.R.S. Unlimited; Car Talk with Tom and Ray; Eric Anderson's Car Crazy; Kit Car Buyers Guide; Popular Mechanics Auto; Top Gear Magazine; TURBO Magazine; Turbozine; Vette Vues Magazine; WheelBase; and World of Wheels.

The Automobiles Homepage

www.auho.com/98cars/FordExplorer.html

For discussions, archives, photos, specs, and links to reviews (CarPoint, Edmunds) on a wide variety of makes and models, check out AuHo?.

Car and Driver

www.caranddriver.com

You'll find tests, reports, reviews, buyer's guide, archives, 10 best cars, 100 best roads, concept cars, shows, and various other information at the well-known publisher's site. If you have a favorite magazine, such as *Car and Driver,* whose views and reports you trust, you can visit their online site and keep up to date with the latest information.

Consumer Reports

www.consumerreports.org

$ [CREDIT]

Give Consumer Reports credit for some of the very best car reviews available anywhere. The Consumer Reports (CR) site includes special features, such as Five Tips to (sic) Buying a New Car, a Should You Lease quiz, a description of their testing process and test track, and Used Car Advice. However, CR's main specialty is its famous auto reports. Alas, the site is not free. But in this case, you do get what you pay for.

Consumer Reports charges a $3.95 monthly fee for unlimited online access to its massive, and continuing, consumer research. Also look at the Consumer Reports site for their e-ratings, which provide customer satisfaction ratings for more than 50 of the most popular e-commerce organizations. If you want a specialized 10–15 page New Car Report, it costs $12 for the first one and $10 for each additional new-car quote ordered at the same time.

Microsoft's CarPoint

carpoint.msn.com/home/New.asp

Launched in 1995, CarPoint is one of the oldest, largest, and most comprehensive sources of information about cars on the Internet. The site gets more than three million unique visitors every month. (Uniqueness counts because some Web sites like to inflate their activity by counting every visitor, even repeat connections.)

Motor Trend Online

www.motortrend.com/bl/bl_f.html

You can peruse data from this publisher online: Reviews, news, links, and other features are yours for the clicking.

Road & Track Online

www.auto-reviews.com/reviews/
    road_and_track.htm

Yet another magazine publisher creates a presence online. You'll find MSRP and dealer invoice pricing, as well as reviews of new and used cars, trucks, SUVs and vans.

Online Vehicle Auctions

You may not believe it, but online auctions now feature vehicles as well as the more conventional, predictable online auction items such as collector comics and used books. If you trust yourself not to overbid, check out the following sites.

eBay

www.ebay.com

eBay, the grand old leader of online auctioning, started adding a special vehicle auction page to its other auction wares in August 1999. You can find ordinary vehicles, as well as a special "Showroom" featuring classic cars. Some cars had been put up for auction at eBay before this official recognition, but for some time now eBay has devoted a section of its site to vehicle auction sales.

Microsoft Network Auctions

www.auctions.msn.com/html/cat17466/
    page1.htm

If the possibility of a real bargain attracts you, check out the Microsoft Network's auction site.

RollingWheels.com

www.rollingwheels.com

RollingWheels is a very interesting vehicle auction site that offers new vehicles and also provides for test driving. They put you in touch with one of their "member dealers" in your area so you can drive the model you want to bid on to see if it's what you're after.

Price and Dealer Information

You want to find out the price of your vehicle before you are at the mercy of salespeople. Here are some places online to look for accurate quotes.

AutoAdvisor

www.autoadvisor.com

Those who cannot, simply *cannot*, negotiate may want to consider hiring someone to act as their agent during the car-buying negotiation. Here's a good online source of auto buyer's agents. Also known as an *auto consultant*, a buyer's agent handles the negotiation process for you, generally resulting in a good deal (agents are experienced). And you don't have to face the music yourself.

AutoNationDirect.com

www.autonation.com

AutoNation is the largest automotive retailer chain in the country. It saves you the trouble of doing price research because it posts no-haggle prices online for its entire inventory. AutoNation currently manages 270 Web sites for its various dealerships around the country and has over 400 franchises in 23 states.

AutoWeb

www.autoweb.com

Often the first step when buying a car online is getting an accurate dealer cost for the vehicle you're thinking about. As usual, you should comparison shop — even among online price quote sources. Get a quote from several reliable Internet services. They're (usually) free. They're (generally) objective. And they're well worth your time. AutoWeb is one of the good sites to begin (or even conclude) your online research. It covers the waterfront and is easy to use.

BizRate.com

www.bizrate.com

Is the Better Business Bureau online? Not yet. But there are a couple of other, similar resources. BizRate contacts a sample of shoppers at each e-commerce site and then compiles their responses to questions about their satisfaction. Each site is then rated (up to five stars) and given an on-time index. Some ratings are also provided by BizRate's staff.

carOrder.com

www.carOrder.com

Here's a successful online showroom you can visit to give you an idea of what it's like out there in a virtual salesland. They have a fine research center, and a five-step process for buying a car online that starts with research and ends with free delivery. At this site, you can do everything from choose your options to order the vehicle of your choice.

National Association of Buyer's Associates

www.naba.com

Try the National Association of Buyer's Associates; it's a good resource if you want to hire an agent to help you negotiate a better price for your car.

N.A.D.A.

www.nada.org

To find the Web site of your local dealer, or other information online about them, look at the bottom of their ad in the classifieds of your local paper. As with most other savvy merchants, the ad contains the URL of their Web site. You can also locate local dealers by contacting the National Automobile Dealers Association (N.A.D.A.).

Sam's Club

www.samsclubauto.com/Home.asp

Another good resource for new car purchases is the Sam's Club Auto Program.

You can get quotes there and find dealers who belong to the program, but you must be a member of Sam's Club to use the features. In addition, you can find out the value of your trade-in, read vehicle reviews, find out about warranties and financing, and even get RVs and boats.

Replacement Parts

There is a big difference between saving money on a car part and buying a second-rate car part. Here are some sites where you can buy what you need, get good quality, and yet save money at the same time.

AC Delco

www.acdelco.com

General Motors parts are sold under the AC Delco label. The AC Delco Web site, as far as Big Three manufacturers sites go, may be the best of the lot. The online selection is comprehensive. For instance, you can retrieve the site's air filter catalog, spark plug catalog, and similar listings for oil filters, batteries, and more. We also like the way AC Delco lets you search for the nearest parts retailer near you (whether a dealer, or an independent storefront). It also lets you sign up for the Driver's Log, ACDelco's "easy-to-use online reminder service that helps you plan your automotive maintenance needs." There's more, too. For instance, you can buy owners' manuals for all GM cars (as well as Honda, Isuzu, Hyundai, Isuzu, Suzuki, Kia, and Subaru) right off this Web site. You can also visit the ACDelco "Examinator," an online feature that gives you a close-up look at their parts. Finally, ACDelco also provides a blurb about counterfeit parts; this is advice well worth heeding.

Action Auto Wreckers

www.actionsalvage.com

A trip to the junkyard may be the only way to find that part your car desperately needs, or to find the best price anywhere. Action Auto Wreckers features an online parts catalog covering fenders, headlights, and sheet metal parts for just about every car make imaginable. I clicked on a link for Dodge Daytona and it retrieved over two dozen parts. This site also has a huge list of used engines for sale and note, too, that customers here receive a 5 percent discount on purchases initiated online.

AutoAccessory.com

www.autoaccessory.com

AutoAccessory.com calls itself the "superstore" in its chosen field. You can browse the site's big online catalog by make and model, which covers not only cars and trucks, but also Jeeps and SUVs.

CarParts.com

www.carparts.com

The bricks and mortar crowd have much to learn from CarParts.com, a monster online compilation with over 1.5 million parts listed. This one site is as close to car parts nirvana as you are likely to come across on the Net. We like CarParts.com for a lot of reasons. Obviously, the selection is incredible, but so too are the prices, and the promise of "fast home delivery." This site has the whole realm of replacement parts, along with OEM parts, even recycled parts. A couple of neat features here include the ability to apply any discount coupons that you have against your purchase, the availability of live online parts specialists, and even a car parts auction area where you are likely to find bids for hard-to-find auto manuals on muscle cars. This is one terrific site.

Ford

www.ford.com

The Ford Motor Company has a great section on its Web site for owners. Keep in mind that Ford, like many other manufacturers, represents several car brands these days, thanks to the merger mania of the past years. Ford isn't your father's Ford any more. It's no longer just Ford, Lincoln, and Mercury. Now it's also Volvo, Mazda, Jaguar, and Aston Martin.

Not only does Ford provide great maintenance and safety tips online, but here you will find info about "Genuine Ford Parts," "Motorcraft Parts," "Ford Brand Accessories," "Ford Crash Parts," "Parts Brand Protection," and "Warranty Coverage."

Midas

www.midas.com

This cheerful Web site welcomes you to "The World of Midas." Midas is known to many for its mufflers, but the company offers a lot of other replacement car parts, including brakes, suspension, air conditioning, batteries, and a host of services such as wheel alignment, troubleshooting, and more.

Mopar Parts

www.mopar.com

Mopar is Chrysler's parts site. It's easy to navigate this site. The main categories are devoted to maintenance products, collision repair replacement parts, accessories, performance parts, and even sportswear. On the other hand, the site is short on specific parts info, though it does link up with Chrysler's vast dealer network.

Speedy Muffler

www.speedy.com

Speedy Muffler is a big Canadian outfit that operates in the United States CarX Muffler (www.carx.com). Both have great Web sites with complete listings of replacement services and available discount offers.

Speed shops online

The roar of the engine, the smell of the crowd. If you like to play Mario Andretti or Shirley Muldowney occasionally, then regular car parts just won't do. Check out these Web sites for your specialized needs.

HotRod USA

www.hotrodsusa.com

HotRod USA is a great-looking site, with a rather specialized focus — muscle cars and hot rods. This one offers "over 15,000 parts in our database." The site also warehouses new and used parts for golf cars too.

RaceSearch.com

race-car-parts.com

If you like to race cars or you are simply looking to make your street rod look and feel a little bit more sporty, look no further than RaceSearch.com, billed as "The Ultimate Speed Shop Online," and a tremendous resource for high performance car parts with listings for over 450 brands. From additives and lap belts to shifters and steering wheels, browse this massive catalog or search by part number. This is one to bookmark if you're into speed (or speedy-looking).

Summit Racing

www.summitracing.com

This site allows you to quickly identify parts and accessories and order them online. Or, fill out a quick registration form, and Summit will send you a monthly catalog free of charge. Vrooom!

Tires

This is where the rubber meets the road. If you're very lucky, then tires will be your most expensive repair in the first three years of owning your car.

Michelin

www.michelin.com

Michelin makes and sells tires under its own brand name and under the B.F. Goodrich label, which it bought from B.F. Goodrich back in 1986. It also has a number of online features similar to Goodyear's, including a tire selector. We also liked Michelin's "Essential Tire Guide," with its "lessons" covering buying tips, safety guidelines, tire terminology, and even a lesson in tire "anatomy."

Goodyear

www.goodyear.com

The Goodyear Tire & Rubber Company has an exhaustive Web site. It claims to produce "approximately 230 million tires per year in more than 90 plants located in the United States and 26 other countries." In other words, a lot of replacement tires for a lot of cars, trucks, farm machinery, ATVs, and airplanes around the world.

Other Sites to Check Out

Bridgestone

www.bridgestone.com

Firestone

www.firestone.com

Pirelli

www.pirelli.com

Uniroyal

www.uniroyal.com

Hard-to-find parts

Sure. Parts are a cinch to find if you drive a 1997 Toyota Camry or a Chevy S-10, but what about if you drive a Packard, a Nash, a Studebaker, or an Auburn? Now you're going to have to do a bit of hunting. Check out the sites in this section to get you started?

Cars & Parts Magazine Online

www.carsandparts.com

Some car parts are harder to find than others, especially for older cars. *Cars & Parts* magazine has been in print since 1957. It is one of many publications that bothers to post its classified ads online. This gives greater exposure to hard-to-find parts, such as a listing I came across for Hudson car parts (1935-57). Ditto for gas tanks for 1995 Ford Thunderbirds and a wide variety of other parts.

Car-Part.com

car-part.com

Car-Part.com may be worth a look if you're searching for a special part. It claims to archive "5 million unique auto parts" that you can locate by dealer, or car make and model. This site hosts a link to hundreds of independent parts sellers in Canada and the USA. Car-Part.com can also put you in contact with dozens of "auto recyclers" too.

Franklin Auto Parts

www.franklinautoparts.com

Check out Franklin Auto Parts, a family-owned operation that's been in business since 1933. Granted, the site isn't yet the slickest-looking on the Internet, but Franklin's hasn't been popular this long by ignoring change. It boasts an online endeavor that marries technology with a significant human element. You use a form to describe what part you need, and their staff (real people!) go about locating, pricing, and shipping it to you.

Hemmings

www.hemmings.com

A great place to look for parts is at Hemmings. Hemmings is an institution in print, and online it lives up to its billing as "the world's largest collector vehicle Web site." This place has a terrific search engine to quickly go through a massive listing of parts for hundreds of car makes and models. I tried a casual search for Datsun car emblems and shock absorbers and it returned eleven listings in about a second. Hemmings also hosts an ongoing online auction of car parts (an original 1966 Chevrolet Corvette hood, for instance). Try it out.

Other Sites to Check Out

UsedCarParts.com

www.usedcarparts.com

United Recyclers Group

www.u-r-g.com

Search Engines

The Internet is a huge collection of data, but without any way to extract the pieces of information of specific interest to you, the Internet would be of little use. Understanding how to use search engines can make your efforts to research car buying either effective and enjoyable — or nightmarish. Here are some of the best Internet search engines.

AltaVista

www.altavista.com

For sheer speed and a newsgroup search feature, try AltaVista. For pure newsgroup searching, though, use www.newsgroups.langenberg.com. You'll find information on cars quickly with AltaVista.

AltaVista Discovery

www.discovery.altavista.digital.com

Discovery (from AltaVista) lets you search the Web for everything about vehicles, but it can search your hard drive as well (replacing the Windows Find utility found on the Start button menu). Discovery can also search your e-mail archives, create tree diagrams of Web sites, and highlight hits.

Ask Jeeves

www.askjeeves.com

This site is best if you want a beginner's engine. You can ask it ordinary English questions, such as, "Where can I find out about Buicks?" Very easy to use. If AskJeeves doesn't have an answer to your exact question, it allows you to choose from a number of similar questions that it does have answers to.

Go.com Express Search

express.go.com

One of the best freebies on the Internet — in our view, anyway — is the Go Express Search engine (it's a part of the InfoSeek engine service). Go offers a significant advantage over most other search engines: It allows you to scroll through the hits (so you don't have to keep using the Backspace key or the Back button in your browser to get back to the hit list to click on the next link). In most search engines, you see a list of the hits. You click a likely link. You see that site. If it's not exactly what you're looking for, you must then click the Back button to return to the search engine's list. Go cleverly avoids this wasted time. And when you're preparing to buy a car, you've got better things to do than waste time.

Hotbot

hotbot.lycos.com

For both speed and the sheer number of Web pages covered, few engines can challenge HotBot. It also has a good reputation for accuracy. It uses a modified version of the popularity contest: The more people who visit (and presumably find useful) a particular site, the higher HotBot rates that site. Car buyers can find what they're looking for using engines like this one.

Infoseek

www.infoseek.com

To get the most wide-ranging (and often the most pertinent and useful) list of hits, try

InfoSeek. If you've been trying to find a particular car part, or a specialized truck — you might want to try Infoseek before other search engines. It has a reputation for finding needles in online haystacks.

Langenberg.com

newsgroups.langenberg.com

If you want to search newsgroups for particular information, use the special newsgroup search engine at Langenberg.com. Newsgroups are often the best places to get the buzz on the good, the bad and the really ugly in today's vehicals. People who aren't writing for traditional publications can be highly subjective (in other words, they tell it like they think it is).

Yahoo!

www.yahoo.com

Yahoo! isn't actually so much a search engine as it is a way to drill down for information. It organizes its sites by various categories, the way books in a library are grouped. Yahoo! is very popular, though, and can be a good place for beginners to look around. And Yahoo has a fine specialized auto section, too. Check it out at www.autos.yahoo.com.

Other Sites to Check Out

Google

www.google.com

metacrawler

www.metacrawler.com

Northern Light

www.northernlight.com

Used Cars

Can't see your way to spending $20,000 on a car only to watch the first $3,000 melt away as soon as you drive it off the dealer's lot? Well, you're not alone. Many people these days have made the decision to let some other poor sap absorb the depreciation that occurs when a new car becomes a used car.

Certified pre-owned vehicles

Certified pre-owned vehicles are vehicles that have passed an extensive inspection and appearance test and are being offered through the dealer for resale. These cars usually come with some sort of dealer warranty and lease and financing packages are generally available. Check out the sites listed below or substitute the name of the car you're interested in because their Internet addresses are usually simply the name of the car.

Acura

www.acura.com/pre-owned/
    pre_index.asp

Acura's Web site offers certified vehicles for sale at dealerships around the United States. Limited warranties are available and the site includes an inventory locator in which you enter your price range, location, and year and model information and then the site checks its database of pre-owned vehicles for a car that fits your needs.

Cadillac

www.cadillac.com/preown/index.htm

Cadillac offers a warranty on the vehicles in its certified vehicles, extending the original warranty to 6 years and 70,000 miles of bumper-to-bumper protection.

Unfortunately, the Cadillac Web site doesn't offer a used-car locator database, so you'll have to contact dealerships directly to see what certified pre-owned vehicles they have to offer.

Toyota

www.toyota.com

You can access the Toyota certified vehicle program by going to Toyota's Web page and then clicking vehicles ☞ Toyota Certified Used Vehicles ☞ Inventory Search. You can then search for certified pre-owned Toyota's in your area. Toyota offers whatever balance remains on a 6-year/100,000-mile original warranty for its certified used cars.

Rental car sales

As you can probably imagine, big rental car companies buy a lot of brand new cars each year. But did you know that they are the biggest sellers of nearly-new cars? Rental car companies like to offer their rental customers as new a car as possible. So they renew their fleets of cars as quickly as possible.

Budget Car Sales

www.budgetcarsales.com

The vehicle locator at the Budget Car Sales site is extremely robust. We recommend the detailed search engine that's available by clicking the FIND A VEHICLE link. All you have to do is enter your state into the locator and it can pull up a list of all vehicles available including dealer location, make, mileage, and price. Moreover, you can sort the list by any of these criteria (but we guess that sorting by price probably makes the most sense). Budget offers a wide range of vehicle makes, models, and prices, including pickup trucks and luxury vehicles.

Enterprise Car Sales

www.ecars.com

Enterprise Rent-A-Car is one of the largest sellers of used cars in the U.S., and they are known for the variety and competitive pricing of their cars. Unfortunately, their Web site (as of the time of this writing) lacks a searchable database (at this time anyway extols the virtues of buying a car from Enterprise — mainly their haggle-free pricing and 12-month/12,000-mile warranty. The site then sends you to a toll-free number 1-888-227-7253 for more information. The site promises that it will begin to provide price information on used cars soon, however, so check out the site to see if they have activating the service before calling.

Hertz Car Sales

www.hertzcarsales.com

The Hertz site is well set up and easy to navigate. To locate a used car, just click the FIND YOUR CAR link and then fill in the online form. You can choose your location, the make and model of the car you want, and the price range you're looking into. Hertz offers haggle-free buying, competitive prices, a 12-month/12,000-mile warranty.

Used car finders

If you're in the market for a used car, the Internet can be a great way to find one! Check out these Web sites for finders for used cars.

carlist.com

www.carlist.com

carlist.com is a handy Web site that boasts a searchable database of used cars for sale by their original owners. You can also find a list of dealerships for particular makes of cars.

DealerNet.com

www.dealernet.com

This is a full-service site that supports both new and used cars available through local dealerships. Many of the used cars contain pictures, and you can apply for a quote or to test drive the car online. Also easily available are payment calculators and insurance quotes.

GetAuto.com

www.getauto.com

GetAuto.com enables you to search dealer stock by location.

Trader.com

www.trader.com

This online version of the popular classified newspaper brings together buyers and sellers from around the U.S. and around the world. Search for ads in your neighborhood, or have Trader e-mail you ads that meet your criteria. Also available are links to car dealerships in your area.

Used car evaluation

Before you sign over your title, you'll want to know what you should be paid for it, right? Check out the following sites to figure out how to evaluate your car's value.

CarPrices.com

www.carprices.com

CarPrices.com is another great way to find out how much your car is worth. Click on the "Used Cars" button to pull up a section that lets you check by make and model. It offers both a wholesale and retail value for your car.

Edmunds

www.edmunds.com

Edmunds.com is similar to the Kelly Blue Book service and is based on a popular line of books. The Web site does a nice job with its valuation of all used car models, offering detailed evaluations and both "Trade-In" and "Market" price points.

Kelley Blue Book

www.kbb.com

The bible of used cars is called the Kelley Blue Book. The book itself can be bought through an online bookstore such as Amazon.com, Borders.com, or BarnesAndNoble.com. But you can also go directly to the Blue Book Web site to check out a wealth of information about every car model imaginable. Use the information you find online as a base to figure out what your car may be worth.

Classifieds: Some free, some fee

This whole Internet thing notwithstanding, most people still sell their car by advertising in a classified section of the local newspaper or classified paper. Check this section to find out about using the Internet to search for these sites that allow you to search for the vehicle you want.

AutoNet USA

www.autonetusa.com/index.htm

AutoNetUSA.com is another interesting Web site. It promises the buyer "a faster, easier way of shopping for a new or used vehicle." And anything that makes it easy for the buyer to find your car is well worth taking a look at.

AutoTrader.com

www.autotrader.com

A number of independent online used car Web sites have set shop up as e-commerce operations recently. They thrive exclusively online and are well worth considering as a potential place to list your car for sale. AutoTrader.com is one such place. This site bills itself as the world's largest selection of used cars with "more than 1.5 million listings, updated daily." One great things about this place is that it allows you to list your car for sale for free.

AutoWeb.com

www.usedcar.com

AutoWeb.com, in affiliation with UsedCar.com, charges a monthly fee and promises that your ad will "reach 3 million potential car buyers a month." AutoWeb listings are also posted at Yahoo! classifieds for additional exposure.

CarPrices.com

www.carprices.com

CarPrices.com is open to members and membership is free. During my recent visit, new members were enticed to sign up with an offer of free long distance telephone service. The Web site has a very simple-to-use ad placement form for the seller, while buyers will enjoy the ease at which the site can be searched for specific used cars.

CarShoppers.com

www.carshoppers.com

CarShoppers.com offers free photo classified ads. You've got to be a member of this site to be able to use it, but membership is also free.

ClassifiedPlus at AOL

classifiedplus.aol.com

America Online offers its own classifieds section on the Web. It's called ClassifiedPlus and you can benefit from access to the world's biggest online community and tremendous brand awareness. Access to the classifieds section is directly off the main AOL homepage. The kicker here is that an ad placed in the "Used Car" section defaults to AutoTrader.com. Still, the combination of a one-two AOL-Autotrader link-up is a powerful siren call for your ad placement.

Newspapers.com

www.newspapers.com

Newspapers.com is the place to look to find the sites of all newspapers in America and around the world. And through these newspapers, you can gain access to tens of thousands of newspaper classified ads for cars online.

OnlineNewspapers.com

www.onlinenewspapers.com

OnlineNewspapers.com is a complex Web site full of listings for major newspapers from around the world. This site can also plug you into every key newspaper found on the Net.

WorldWideWheels.com

wwwheels.com/index.htm

WorldWideWheels.com claims to be the most "comprehensive automobile site on the Net." Used car ads here, with or without photo, are free and the listing process takes just a second or two. The process must be renewed every three weeks to ensure continued listing and this way the Web operators can easily keep track of which cars have not yet sold.

Used car auctions

Rare and antique cars are often sold at auction. In fact, you can sell any car at an online auction. If you're worried about getting out of your car what you think that it's worth, then you can declare a *reserve price*, a price below which you won't sell the car.

Amazon.com Auctions

auctions.amazon.com

  $

Amazon.com is also in the auction game. Best known as "Earth's Biggest Bookstore," the online monolith has branched out into the sale of CDs, DVDs, and a wide variety of goods. Visit the auction section off the main page and click on "Cars & Transportation" to access a page dedicated to auctions for cars, parts, and automotive paraphernalia. You'll need an account here to list your car auction.

Auction Addict

www.auctionaddict.com

This independent Web site generates a fair amount of action. It thinks of itself as "a huge Internet swap meet" and listings are available to anyone who registers for a free site membership. The service is free to the buyer, although the site charges a small commission to the seller only if the product sells at auction. Whether convertible, coupe, hatchback, street rod, or racing vehicle, a buyer may well be lurking at this site just waiting for your auction to begin.

City Auction

www.utrade.com

  $

City Auction has a lot of effervescence. Here buyers and sellers meet to swap everything from Barbie Dolls to BMWs.

This site also lets sellers sign up for FairMatch, a daily e-mail notification service that keeps you informed about prospective buyers. You only have to pay a fee at City Auction if your item sells. You don't have to pay a listing fee.

eBay

 $

www.ebay.com

eBay.com is probably the world's biggest and best known Internet auction site. This place has millions of users and a vast array of products on auction at any given time of the day. eBay has a new automotive section, one of the slickest we've seen. During a recent visit, the site featured an auction for Queen Wilhelmina's Rare 1946 Daimler Limousine. It's a bit of a stretch to call that a *used car*. And don't worry if your car is slightly less glitzy. eBay has room for every kind of car imaginable and hopefully the right bidder at the right price for your particular car. And remember to check out eBay's Tips On How To Sell Online.

Lycos Auctions

auctions.lycos.com

  $

Lycos is one of the biggest in the engine-auction category. While it offers listings for everything from Beanie Babies to gold coins, Lycos also auctions thousands of vehicles. Registration for both buyer and seller is required. You can list items for free, but the seller must pay a fee when the item sells.

Reverse Auction

www.ra-vehicles.com

  $

This has an intriguing angle — the price starts out high and winds backward until it gets low enough for someone to want to purchase it. The site has no bidding or buying fees. It offers "online bidding in reverse for old and new cars . . . our prices drop instead of rise and you can watch this live on your screen." This site specializes in antique and classic cars, Chevys, and Corvettes. They collect fees from the seller and the site's open to members-only, although registration is open to everyone but minors.

Yahoo! Auctions

auctions.yahoo.com

Yahoo auctions are quite popular. Check out the Seller Guide to find out the rules and what you need to know to register yourself for a Yahoo ID. Next, click on Cars (or Trucks) off the main page to access the right area where we recently noted that over 2,500 car auctions were underway. A 1998 Porsche Carrera had two bids, with one topping $50,000, while a 1965 Thunderbird had six bids, the highest at just $2,000. One reason to consider using Yahoo! auctions is that they cost no money whatever.

Part V
Keeping Your Car in Good Shape

The 5th Wave — By Rich Tennant

"Oh, that there's just something I picked up as a grab bag special from the 'Curiosities' Web Page."

In this part . . .

*I*f you're like most people, you want to make sure that
your brand-new (or previously broken-in) car runs
smoothly and reliably for many, many years to come. You
need, therefore, to keep up a routine maintenance schedule on your car, as well as make any major repairs that
make become necessary during your ownership.
Fortunately, the Internet can help you in this area, too,
and Part V describes just how you can go online to get the
best advice on keeping your car running — and repairing
it as inexpensively as possible if it's not.

Chapter 18 explains how you can obtain expert service
advice for your car by visiting specific Web sites geared to
your vehicle and its special needs. And if it's a bit too late
for preventive maintenance, you can turn to Chapter 10 to
find out how find replacement parts online for the best
prices going. (The advice in this chapter can prove especially helpful if you decided buy an older used car or a
collector vehicle for which parts are scarce.) Finally, in
Chapter 20, we discuss how you can best exhibit pride in
owning your car through membership in any of a number
of online organizations.

Keeping your car in good shape makes good sense — and
can save you quite a few cents (and dollars) in the long
run. This part can help by getting you hooked up with the
best info available online. Your car is going to love you for
reading these chapters.

Chapter 18

Online Service Advice
for You and Your Car

Some people think of their car as a member of the family. They lavish it with the kind of tender loving care that could blush a newborn baby. Others see their car as an invincible utilitarian appliance on wheels and rarely get around to even dusting off the dashboard.

Either way, your car needs regular maintenance and servicing to ensure that it can continue to provide you with the kind of safe and effective motoring for which it's designed. Regular maintenance means changing the oil regularly, ensuring that tires have adequate air pressure, and replacing wiper blades when they dull. It means that you need to replace parts such as filters, brake pads, and spark plugs as they wear out. It also means that you need to follow a regular service schedule as much as possible — something that every manufacturer recommends.

Fortunately, the Internet can help you understand when, why, and where to undertake car care. It can advise you about how to care for your car on your own and when to get professional mechanics to do it for you.

In this chapter, you can find out how (and where) to tap into expert online service and maintenance advice. You can read about some of the more common service requirements for just about every car, and you can uncover some great Internet resources to help you keep your car in tip-top order.

You also gain a lot of peace of mind by understanding exactly why you need to keep your car in good working order and how simple the task can prove if you just take the necessary time to understand your car's service and repair needs and follow through with timely and quality car care.

Understanding the Importance of Regular Car Maintenance

During your ownership, your car or truck may require a variety of services to keep it in good working order. You may want to perform some of the maintenance yourself, although more complex service and repair activity often requires the help of licensed car-care specialists.

Regular warranty checkups that include oil changes and filter replacements keep your brand-new car in tip-top shape. More important servicing needs arising from breakdowns or accidents may require the repair services of expert automotive technicians and mechanics.

The Internet offers you immediate access to a number of national industry organizations, all eager to foster customer satisfaction and trust by providing members easy access and a promise of a basic, or standard, level of expertise and experience.

The Automotive Service Association (ASA) (at www.asashop.org on the Web) is one such group (see Figure 18-1). It began in 1951 and today represents 13,000 members, advancing "the professionalism and excellence in the automotive-repair industry through education, representation, and member services." Use the ASA's Web site to search for a member in your area and to consult its Automotive Tips section, where you can find out about its Consumer Bill of Rights for Motorists and more. The ASA Web site also carries important links to a number of legislative resources, including State Laws and Regulations for Replacement Crash Parts, a Summary of State Aftermarket Parts Disclosure Laws, and the ASA's formal position on a number of legislative objectives.

ASE is the acronym for the Institute for Automotive Service Excellence (www.asecert.org). ASE has been around since 1972 and boasts more than 420,000 professionals with current ASE certification. According to information at its home page, the organization's professionals work "in every segment of the automotive service industry: car and truck dealerships, independent garages, fleets, service stations, franchises, and more." Its mission is "to improve the quality of vehicle repair and service in the United States through the testing and certification of automotive repair technicians."

The ASE offers Tips to Motorists at its Web site, including a number of car-care "brochures," such as "Choosing the Right Repair Shop," "Getting Your Vehicle Ready for Winter," "Choosing the Right Body Shop," and "How to Communicate for Better Automotive Service." The site also features a number of handy tips for female motorists.

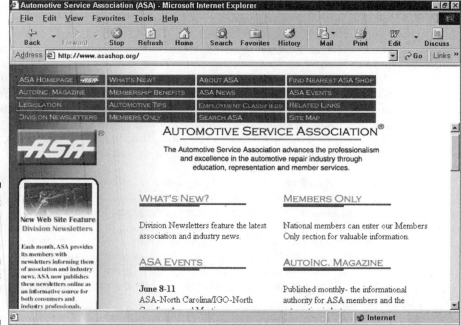

Figure 18-1:
The
Automotive
Service
Association
promotes
professional
excellence.

Check out, too, the International Automotive Technicians Network (at www.iatn.net), which is a group of 26,810 professional automotive technicians from 110 countries. Notice especially the site's Shop Finder, which enables you to locate network members in your area.

We also enjoy I-CAR ONLINE (at www.i-car.com), the Inter-Industry Conference on Auto Collision Repair, which describes itself as a "not-for-profit international training organization dedicated to improving the quality, safety, and efficiency of auto collision repair." Check it out for peace of mind and details about the kind of training a collision repair expert must undergo prior to certification.

After you consult these and other industry groups, you gain a greater appreciation for the professionalism that permeates this sector of the car industry.

Locating Online Service and Repair Information about Your Car

You can find service and repair information all across the Internet, although you do need to sort out the good from the bad. Much of the good, of course, comes from official sources such as the government, automobile agencies, and the car makers themselves. Much of the bad comes from uninformed sources who may have good intentions but not the training or experience to back it up. So make sure that you know your source thoroughly whenever you accept online service advice.

One great source for online car-maintenance information is the United States National Highway Transportation Safety Administration (NHTSA) Web site (at www.nhtsa.dot.gov/cars/problems), which publishes automotive safety notices by make and model. By consulting the NHTSA site, you stay abreast of recalls, technical-service bulletins, defect investigations, consumer complaints, safety studies, and more. It's a great site.

Both the American Automobile Association (at www.aaa.com) and the Canadian Automobile Association (at www.caa.com) offer great information covering automotive and consumer services (and we feature both sites elsewhere in this book). The CAA site, for example, includes a section that it calls Approved Auto Repair Service (AARS), where you can locate automotive repair shops that the CAA approves. It offers another section with the name Driving Costs, where you can calculate how much owning and operating your vehicle costs each year by applying national averages and approximate driving costs.

If your driving costs are out of sync with national averages for your particular car, you probably have a mechanical or electronic problem with your car, and you need to have your service provider check it out as soon as you can.

Checking out service support from car makers

Many of the big car makers offer car-service resources right on their Web sites. Whether big or small, these manufacturers understand the value of appropriate car care, and their online resources point you to valuable service advice.

Visit the General Motors Web site (at www.gm.com) and click the GM Goodwrench button to access an excellent array of owner's service resources. GM promises to take the guesswork out of caring for your vehicle with auto advice that covers everything from cleaning fabric stains to engine overheating. It even provides an online driver's log and maintenance scheduler. Sign up for the driver's log and you receive regular e-mails that remind you when your car needs routine maintenance.

Over at the Subaru Web site (at www.subaru.com), click the Subaru Care button to access warranty information, car-care tips, and maintenance schedules. You can easily find similar information at most of the other big automakers' Web sites, too. Check the Directory section in this book to find the URL for your car's manufacturer.

Car dealers are increasingly using the Net to offer advice and details about the services they're keen to sell you. Most manufacturers' Web sites offer a Dealer Search feature to help you locate the most convenient dealer in your area.

Finding neighborhood repair shops on the Internet

Many car-repair businesses operate on a local basis. They may keep just one or two service bays and mechanics on duty. Their individual reputations rest on their capability to meet the needs of a community rather than on a nation-wide multi-million-dollar advertising campaign.

These shops often hang a shingle out on the Internet, and a good search engine can prove valuable if you're trying to track down a repair shop near where you live or work.

Ask Jeeves (at www.ask.com on the Web) is perfect for this search. Type in its search text box something such as **"Find me car repair on the Internet"** to retrieve dozens of options worth following. One option that we retrieved from this query helps you locate yellow-page listings for automotive repair shops in practically every major city in America.

Another query to Ask Jeeves — **"What are the legal issues regarding car repair?"** — retrieves a Web site from Court TV about car repair. Here you find a primer regarding your obligation to pay for unauthorized car repairs, a cus-tomer's responsibility for paying the difference between a quoted price and the bill, and so on. In fact, Court TV offers on its Web site an entire section of legal resources dealing with automobiles that you may want to check out (at http://consumer.courttv.findlaw.com/topics/autos/index.html).

Sometimes locating online auto service info is all about, well, location. On the Internet, that means dot-com location, and for one business in La Mesa, California, its dot-com location reigns supreme. You see, the domain name CarRepair.com (at www.carrepair.com) belongs to an outfit with the name of Bob Bowen's Auto Service (see Figure 18-2). I can't vouch for Bob Bowen's work, but his location online is dead-on. Another community-based automotive repair business is a Scottsdale, Arizona, shop with the name Car Repair Co., which bills itself as "Your Dealership Alternative." It, too, has a great Web address (at www.carrepairco.com).

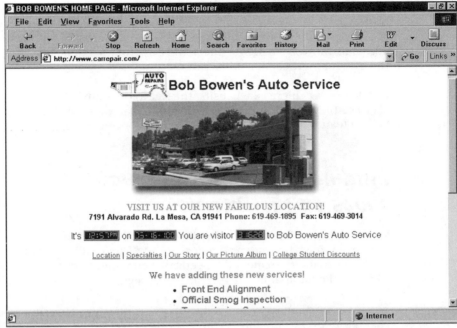

Figure 18-2:
Locating car
repair on
the Net is
often about
dot-com
location.

Seeking friendly neighborhood advice online

If you think of the Internet as your neighborhood (as we do), you may be happy to find out that you can find a lot of neighborly advice online.

Check out the Web site at www.askme.com for the <u>Auto Maintenance & Repair</u> link (see Figure 18-3). The neat thing about this site is that it links you up to real people who can answer your questions. Not only can you view questions and answers, but you can also rate the answers already given and even add your own thoughts if you think that you can offer something useful. But the main thing here is to ask the question for which you need an answer. And you can do so here with as much detail as you think that you require.

PepBoys, the giant chain of automotive parts supplies, offers visitors to its Web site a useful list of car care tips (at www.pepboys.com/cartips/list.shtm). Here you can check out such topics as how to know whether you need A/C maintenance, how to wash and wax, the difference between conventional and synthetic motor oils, battery service tips, and even how to prepare for roadside emergencies.

Figure 18-3:
On the
Internet, you
can find
answers
and advice
about your
auto repair
questions.

Global4autoparts.com sells car parts worldwide, but its Web site (at www.global4autoparts.com/Car%20Care%20Tips.htm) also offers detailed car-care tips. During a recent visit, we found out more than we needed to know about shock and strut installation and removal. Impressive, indeed.

Check out AutoShop Online, too, which considers itself the United States' largest independent car and truck repair help line. Its Automotive 101 (at www.autoshop-online.com/auto101.html) is a free tutorial about the "inner workings of the major subsystems of the modern automobile." It's a great archive covering the engine, drive train, suspension, and even heating and air conditioning.

AutoShop Online also features a pay-as-you-go Service Department Inquiry Form (at www.medilinks.net/secure/autoshop/sec_inquiry.html), promising you direct access to experts and information that can solve your automotive problem. The site bases this feature on a massive database of frequent repair problems and their solutions for more than 10,000 different makes, models, and years of vehicles. You can examine a list of sample questions and answers to determine whether this kind of online service suits you before you ante up with money.

Tapping Into Online Discussions, Lists, and E-Zines

In today's dot-com age, you may need to keep in mind that, not so long ago, the Internet was principally a service teeming with a high level of discussion and debate areas rather than Web-based content and endless sales pitches.

In those innocent days, before the Web existed as we know it today and graphical Web browsers were developed, Usenet and e-mail discussion lists drew people online. Back then, people exchanged ideas and experiences willingly in a general environment where commercial interests were considered inappropriate.

Today, both Usenet discussion forums (or Usenet newsgroups) and e-mail lists continue to grow in numbers and in popularity as they always have, and they continue to do so without the kind of fancy design and high-energy promotion that define the Web. If you're seeking car-service advice, both Usenet and e-mail lists, therefore, may prove well worth your time exploring.

Usenet newsgroups

You can access Usenet newsgroups in a number of ways. If you use AOL, simply type the keywords **Usenet** or **Newsgroups** to access AOL's Internet Newsgroups area. From there, you can search the newsgroups to find one that matches your needs. Other Internet surfers can access Usenet through their Web browsers or e-mail programs.

One simple way for every Internet surfer to access all Usenet newsgroup archives is through Deja.com (at www.deja.com on the Web; refer to Figure 18-4). Although it's recently become a catch-all for e-commerce opportunities, Deja.com was once DejaNews.com, the ultimate repository for Usenet messages both current and historical.

Today, access to Usenet through Deja.com is through a new independent site (at www.deja.com/usenet). From that site, you can use the search function to find specific Usenet groups by typing keywords relevant to your needs and specifying recent or past messages. You're certain to find a wide variety of possible matches, such as rec.autos.makers.chrysler, uk.rec.cars. maintenance, rec.autos.tech, alt.autos.porsche, and alt.autos. antique, to name but a few. A bit of patience links you up to a host of worthwhile discussions perfect for posting your specific car-repair queries.

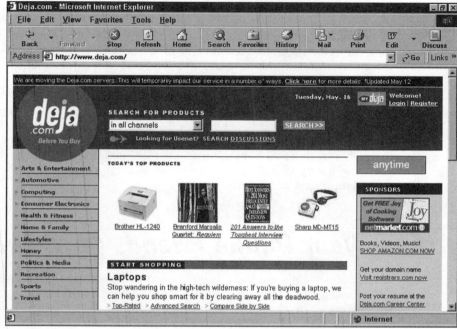

Figure 18-4:
Usenet
remains the
global
repository of
discussions
online.

E-mail lists and e-zines

E-mail lists and e-zines are other possible avenues for you to check out for answers to your questions on car repair and maintenance.

E-mail is, arguably, the backbone of the Internet in terms of use by average people such as you and me. It's the most popular part of the Net, and it keeps each of us in contact with our network of friends online. In fact, more e-mail now goes out online than all the mail that uses the regular postal services around the world.

That's a lot of e-mail — and a lot of people shuttling their messages back and forth across the Net. Numerous e-mail lists have also grown along with the explosive growth in the Net's online population.

People who share a particular interest often share the same e-mail messages. These messages are known as *e-mail lists*, and literally thousands of them exist covering just about every topic imaginable. Some are private and others are by invitation only, but many are open for you to join as both a recipient and participant. *E-zines* are an extension of e-mail lists, and many are also open to join.

ListUniverse.com (at `http://List-Universe.com` on the Web) is the mother list of lists on the Net. It can put you in touch with most e-mail lists and e-zines through a simple keyword search. Type **Chevrolet**, for example, and the search retrieves a listing for the Atlanta F-Body Organization, a group for owners of Pontiac Firebird/Trans Ams and Chevrolet Camaros.

Topica.com (at `www.topica.com`) boasts a huge collection of discussion lists and can help you find people, discussions, and information on virtually any topic. Type **car repair** to access a wide variety of related lists and newsletters. Topica recently acquired TipWorld (a collection of more than 20,000 tips and 140 newsletters) from our publisher IDG and, as a result, boasts that it now has nearly 10 million subscriptions and delivers more than 200 million e-mail messages per month.

Asking Your Online Friends for Advice

Last, but certainly not least, keep in mind that the Internet is a great tool to use if you just want to ask your friends for advice about car repair. If they have e-mail, you can shoot off an e-mail message to them asking for advice about their favorite online sites, no matter where they live — locally or across the world. Tap into their knowledge and use it as best you can. That's part of the fun about being online — sharing what you know.

You need, of course, to weigh all the advice that you get from this chapter, from your friends, and from your own wanderings on the Internet with common sense and practicality. Many aspects of car repair you want to leave to the experts, regardless of how much information, testimonials, and how-to advice you can find elsewhere. These aspects involve the difficult tasks that require special tools and diagnostic components that you mostly find only at professional service businesses, such as car dealers, authorized repair shops, and sometimes even the local gas station. They require a special expertise that comes only from much learning and practice to ensure that the work is done correctly so as to not harm the rest of the car.

But car service and maintenance isn't always about repair. It often means simply keeping your car in routine working order. Much of what you read here can help you achieve that goal.

Most important, as an informed car owner, you need to know how to use the data that you find on the Internet to ensure that you maintain your car sufficiently through the duration of your ownership. What you find through the resources and recommendations in this chapter can help inform you so that you can make the right decisions to enjoy your car to the fullest and then, later, to resell or trade it in at the highest value possible.

Chapter 19

Finding Replacement Parts on the Internet

Cars, both new and used, are the sum of their parts. A car is only as good as its weakest part — which, if you think about it, is pretty surprising considering how much a car costs these days. A defective $3 spark plug, for example, can mean the difference between a $50,000 Porsche that starts and one that doesn't.

Simply put, car parts wear out from time to time, and you need to replace them. Some parts affect the operation of your car, while others can directly affect your safety in a motor vehicle. That's why you always want to keep your car in tip-top condition by replacing parts as they wear out — or even better, *before* they break on you.

To accomplish this goal, you need to follow the car manufacturer's recommended service schedules. A brand-new car carries a warranty that covers standard parts replacement at no cost to you during the lifetime of the warranty (which generally lasts for a year or so, unless you purchase additional coverage — an *extended warranty* — from your dealer when you buy the car). If you're going with a used car, you need to look through the car's service records *before* you buy it. Poor service records may indicate poor service habits and the possible use of inferior replacement parts that may break on you later. Remember that a big gulf lies between a *cheap* car part and an *inferior* car part.

In this chapter, we show you where to go online to buy what parts you need and to save money at the same time. (Your goal, of course, is always to get the best car part at the best price, and we show you exactly how to get the right part at the right price by using the vast resources of the Internet.)

We also take you on a tour of the various car-parts sellers that you can find on the Internet. We visit dealers, wholesalers, parts makers, tire manufacturers, and muffler shops — even junkyard dogs. By the time you finish this chapter, you need never to feel at the mercy of the neighborhood mechanic again.

Getting Authorized Parts from Authorized Online Sources

A modern car is an incredibly complex piece of machinery. Beneath the beguiling styling lines that attract your eye lies an imaginative mixture of mechanical and technological components. Each component is chosen by highly experienced engineers to work well with all others in a way that provides you, the car owner, with pride of ownership and a worry-free driving experience.

Manufacturers recommend that you use only authorized replacement parts that authorized service providers install. They make this recommendation because they know that the overall value of your car relies on its capability to continue to provide you with an excellent motoring service.

The Ford Motor Company (www.ford.com), for example, maintains a great section on its Web site for owners. Keep in mind that Ford represents several car brands, as do many other manufacturers. (Ford isn't just Ford, Lincoln, and Mercury. It's also Volvo, Mazda, Jaguar, and Aston Martin.) To get to the information about parts, as shown in Figure 19-1, click the Service link under the For Owners heading on the Ford home page. For information about parts for other Ford-owned makes, click the make — Volvo, Mazda, and so on — at the Ford home page; then navigate your way to the parts information. (Each make's Web site works differently.)

Not only does Ford provide great maintenance and safety tips online, but you also can find information about Ford parts, Motorcraft parts, Ford-brand accessories, Ford crash parts, parts brand protection, and warranty coverage.

We particularly like the Ford Web site because it features plenty of cross-references and is easy to use. If you're a Ford (or Lincoln, Mercury, Volvo, Mazda, Jaguar, or Aston Martin) owner, all you need to do is to choose a parts section that suits your need — and use it to get the information you need about parts for your vehicle and the warranties that cover them.

Figure 19-1:
A Ford vehicle is the sum of its parts, as you can see on the Our Products area of the Ford Motor Company Web site.

Of course, most of the other big car makers, whether Chrysler, General Motors, or even Ferrari, provide a similar service at their Web sites. Accessing such a site is much like directly accessing an entire library of car parts and advice, although all the manufacturers refer you to their dealer networks if you decide to buy the required part.

Mopar (at www.mopar.com) is Chrysler's parts site. Navigating the site is incredibly simple. Its main categories offer maintenance products, collision-repair replacement parts, accessories, performance parts, and even sportswear. On the other hand, the site is short on specific parts info, although it does link up with Chrysler's vast dealer network.

General Motors parts sell under the ACDelco label. The ACDelco Web site (at www.acdelco.com) may be the best of the lot as far as the Big 3 manufacturers' sites go. The selection online is comprehensive. You can, for example, access the site's air-filter catalog, spark plug catalog, and similar listings for oil filters, batteries, and more. We like the way ACDelco enables you to search for the nearest parts retailer near you, whether it's an actual dealer or an independent storefront. It also enables you to sign up for the *Driver's Log,* ACDelco's easy-to-use online reminder service that helps you plan your automotive maintenance needs.

The site offers much more, too. You can, for example, buy owner's manuals for all GM cars (as well as for Hondas, Hyundais, Isuzus, Suzukis, Kias, and Subarus) right off this Web site. You can also visit the ACDelco FunZone, which offers various puzzles, quizzes, and the ACDelco "Examinator," an online feature that gives you a close-up look at all the parts that the site describes.

ACDelco also provides a blurb about counterfeit parts — advice well worth heeding because counterfeit parts are usually of inferior quality and can compromise your safety.

Purchasing Parts Online from Your Dealer

While researching this chapter, we visited the Ferrari Web site (at www.ferrari.com) and noticed that it was advertising specials on what it calls New Old Stock (or NOS) parts "for vintage Ferraris." NOS parts are available through its authorized North American Ferrari dealer network.

Engine lids, seat linings, window rubber strips, tachometers, and even a black convertible top were touted during our visit, with the express request that we contact our local Ferrari dealer to fill our needs.

But whether you own a Ferrari or Ford, extensive new-car dealer networks ensure a usually adequate supply of auto parts whenever you need them. Your dealer clearly is more than happy to service your car-part needs, and all manufacturers can help you locate a dealer near you through their Web sites.

Buying Parts Online from Automotive-Parts Distributors

With millions of cars on the roads, the market for replacement car parts is, of course, massive. Entire industries now exist to fulfill the needs of car owners and the mechanics who service their vehicles. Among the more frequent parts that require replacement are mufflers and tires. Nowadays, you can buy these most basic of car parts from a variety of sources, including many that offer online services.

For starters, take a look at The World of Midas Web site (at www.midas.com). Midas is known to many for its mufflers, but the company offers tons of other replacement car parts, including brakes, suspension, air conditioning, and batteries, and a host of services such as wheel alignment, troubleshooting, and more (see Figure 19-2).

The Midas Web site details all its products and services and then points you to its network of neighborhood Midas shops. The Web site also promises to list any special promotions that are currently underway at its shops, too.

Speedy Muffler (at www.speedy.com) is a big Canadian outfit that operates in the United States as CarX Muffler (at www.carx.com). Both the Canadian and the U.S. versions boast great Web sites offering complete listings of replacement services and available discount offers. Speedy Muffler, for example, was touting its Cyber-Coupon during my visit, which enables customers who use it to save 15 percent on certain parts.

The Goodyear Tire & Rubber Company (at www.goodyear.com) maintains an exhaustive Web site. Goodyear claims to produce approximately 230 million tires per year in more than 90 plants in the United States and 26 other countries. In other words, Goodyear sells a myriad of replacement tires for thousands of cars, trucks, farm machinery, ATVs, and airplanes around the world.

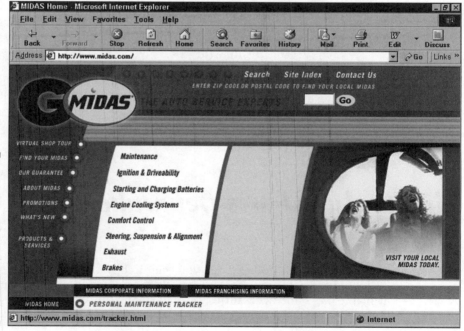

Figure 19-2: Companies such as Midas, known for its mufflers, sell a variety of replacement parts online.

For cars, the Goodyear Web site offers an online catalog, a handy retailer locator, and a listing of current promotions available in your area. It also recommends "the tire best suited for your vehicle" on a page of the site known as the Tire Selector. Simply select your vehicle's year, make, and model (for example, **1993 Mazda MX-6 LS**) from the drop-down list boxes, and the selector recommends the right tire for your car. (In this example, it recommends the P205/55R15 87V as the standard tire size, with a speed rating of 149 mph.) This neat service also enables you to factor in desired handling requirements (such as snow, wet, quiet, long tread life, and so on) and optional tire sizes.

Goodyear's Tire School is a neat addition to its Web site. Check it out to locate tire care and maintenance FAQs, information about common tire-wear problems, and even details about how to make a tire and notes about what ingredients you need to do so.

Michelin (at `www.michelin.com`) makes and sells tires under its own brand name and under the B.F. Goodrich label, which it bought from B.F. Goodrich back in 1986. This Web site offers visitors a number of online features similar to those on Goodyear's site, including a tire selector. In fact, Michelin's site features three tire selectors — one for cars, one for motorcycles, and another one for trucks. Michelin's online catalog not only covers cars, but also bicycles, earthmovers, and more. I like Michelin's Essential Tire Guide because it contains lessons covering buying tips, safety guidelines, tire terminology, and even tire "anatomy."

Most of the other major tire makers, including Bridgestone (at `www.bridgestone.com`), Firestone (at `www.firestone.com`), Uniroyal (at `www.uniroyal.com`), and Pirelli (at `www.pirelli.com`), maintain similar, if less extensive, Web sites, and all are worth visiting if you're in the market for new tires. All these sites provide you with valuable information, direct links to their dealer networks, and timely deals to entice you to buy their products. Uniroyal, for example, was recently offering a $5-per-tire rebate to visitors to its Web site.

Mining Auto-Parts Department Stores Online

Inevitably, the time comes when you want to buy a car part or accessory. With hundreds of car makes and models in production, the wide variety of available parts and accessories, big and small, is as eclectic as the personalities of the people who own and drive the cars. You can find something for just about everyone, from the do-it-at-home amateur mechanic to the Sunday driver looking for a pair of fuzzy dice to hang over the rear-view mirror.

In fact, the selection of available accessories for your car is so huge that it requires a car department store to offer them all. That's what outfits such as NAPA and Canadian Tire are all about: a wide variety of choices at great prices.

✔ **Canadian Tire** (at `www.canadiantire.ca`) is the big auto mart in Canada. This company's Web site also acts more as a corporate brochure than as an online parts bazaar, but it invites visitors to sign up for its free E-Flyer, an e-mail bulletin advisory describing the deals of the week at participating stores in your area.

✔ **Pep Boys** (at `www.pepboys.com`) is a well known auto parts chain with more than 660 stores across the United States. We'd like to see the company pep up its Web site into a first-class online parts catalog, however, instead of serving merely as a plug for its print catalog and network of stores. (Figure 19-3 shows the Pep Boys home page.) Right now, the site showcases only a dozen or so products, ranging from brake pads and air filters to mirror glaze and antifreeze.

Figure 19-3: The Pep Boys site plugs the Pep Boys print catalogs and stores and features a dozen or so common products.

✔ **CarParts.com** (at www.carparts.com) boasts a monster online compilation listing more than 1.5 million parts. This site is as close to car-parts heaven as you're likely to find on the Internet.

We like CarParts.com for many reasons. Obviously, the selection is incredible; so, too, are its prices and promise of fast home delivery. This site offers the entire realm of replacement parts, along with OEM (original equipment manufacturer) parts, and even recycled parts. A few neat features here include the capability to apply any discount coupons that you may possess against your purchase, the availability of live online parts specialists, and even a car-parts auction area, where you're likely to find bids for hard-to-find auto manuals and muscle cars. It's a terrific site for sure.

✔ **Hot Rods USA** (at www.hotrodsusa.com) maintains another great-looking site, albeit one with a more specialized focus. This site offers more than 15,000 parts in its database, all of them online for you to sift through. (Or should we say "shift" through? Hey, in the car-parts business, shift happens!) Hot Rods USA also warehouses new and used parts for golf carts, too, if you do much of your driving on the greens.

If you like to race cars or you're simply looking to make your street rod look and feel a little bit sportier, look no farther than RaceSearch.com (at http://race-car-parts.com), billed as "The Ultimate Speed Shop Online." It's a tremendous resource for high-performance car parts, offering listings for more than 450 brands. The massive catalog includes everything from additives and lap belts to shifters and steering wheels, and you can browse through it or search it by part number. This site's definitely the one to bookmark if you're into the thrill of racing.

Buying Used or Classic Parts Online

Some car parts are harder to find than others, especially for classic cars. *Cars and Parts Magazine* (at www.carsandparts.com) has been in print since 1957. It's one of many publications that posts classified ads online, which gives greater exposure to hard-to-find parts. In the *Cars and Parts* online classifieds, we came across such as a listing for Hudson car parts (circa 1935–57). Ditto for gas tanks for 1995 Ford Thunderbirds and a wide variety of other parts.

Another place to look for parts is at Hemmings (at www.hemmings.com). Hemmings is an institution in print; online, it lives up to its billing as the world's largest collector-vehicle Web site (see Figure 19-4). This place offers a terrific search engine that enables you to search quickly through a massive listing of parts for hundreds of car makes and models. We tried a casual search for Datsun car emblems and shock absorbers, and the search returned 11 listings in about a second. Next, we tried a search for Buick antennas and wiper blades, and that search retrieved more than 100 listings in about the same amount of time. Hemmings also hosts an ongoing online auction of car parts (for such items as an original 1966 Chevrolet Corvette hood, a 6-foot fiberglass truck cap for a 1998–2000 Ford Ranger, and so on).

AutoAccessory.com (at `www.autoaccessory.com`) calls itself a superstore in its chosen field. You can browse its Web site's big online catalog by make and model, not only for cars and trucks, but also for Jeeps and SUVs. You can browse and buy car covers, deerskin driving gloves, mobile entertainment electronics, road-trip gear, and even custom floor mats. You can also buy gift certificates at the site to give to others.

For the heck of it, we typed `www.usedcarparts.com` into a Web browser, and it accessed a cool site hosted by the giant Internet portal About.com. If you access the site, click the <u>Accessories</u> link or the <u>OEM Parts</u> link, and specify what kind of vehicle you have. You access a list of literally dozens of car-parts peddlers, including AAA Rims (selling refurbished alloy rims), Nippon-Motors (hawking used — and warranted — Japanese engines and transmissions), Spoilers4Less (offering all kinds of spoilers), and Warehouse Auto Parts (which specializes in rebuilt replacement parts).

Figure 19-4:
Hemmings boasts the world's largest collector-vehicle Web site.

We also recommend a visit to United Recyclers Group (at www.u-r-g.com), which represents hundreds of automotive parts recyclers in the United States and Canada.

A Canadian site, Global4AutoParts.com (at www.global4autoparts.com) promises good prices because of the currently discounted value of the Canadian dollar. It offers a very good parts catalog and a straightforward search engine.

Car-Part.com (at http://Car-Part.com) may be worth a look-see, too. It claims to archive 5 million "unique auto parts" that you can mine by dealer or car make and model. This site hosts a link to hundreds of independent parts sellers in Canada and the United States. Car-Part.com can put you in contact with dozens of "auto recyclers," too.

And make sure that you check out Franklin Auto Parts (at www.franklinautoparts.com), a family-owned operation in business since 1933. Granted, the site isn't the spiffiest, but part of Franklin's longevity must derive from its capability to move with the times — in this case, with an online endeavor that marries technology with a human aspect that's not worth dismissing. At Franklin's site, you use a form to describe what part you need, and its staff members go about locating, pricing, and shipping it to you.

If all else fails, a trip to the junkyard may prove the only way to find that part your car desperately needs. One dog that barks loudly is Action Auto Wreckers (at www.actionsalvage.com), an online parts catalog covering fenders, headlights, and sheet-metal parts for just about every car make imaginable. We clicked a link for <u>Dodge Daytona</u> and retrieved a list of more than two dozen parts. This site also features a huge list of used engines for sale, and all customers to the site receive a 5 percent discount on purchases that they initiate online.

The beauty about all the choices that we highlight in this chapter is that, on the Internet, you're not stuck dealing with a single source for your replacement car parts. But remember that a car is a complex piece of machinery, and its expert designers invest a lot of time and money into making sure that each part they incorporate into a car is perfect for that particular vehicle. So if you do need to buy replacement parts, whether new, used, or refurbished, always make sure that those parts are meant to go with your car. Your car's going to be glad that you do — and so are you.

Chapter 20

The Pride of Ownership — and Showing It Online

*O*ne of the great things about buying a new car is that "new car smell." You recognize it as soon as you smell it the very first time — and you remember it forever afterward. It's unique in a way that makes aroma companies continually wish that they could bottle and sell it to owners of older cars.

That smell is part of the relative prestige that you get in buying a new car — a prestige that hints at the kind of pride many car owners exhibit for their vehicles. Pride of ownership, of course, isn't just for people who buy themselves a new car; that tangible sense of pride transcends every category of car, whether hot off the lot or antique.

For many car owners, nothing looks better in the driveway than a shiny car. But whether their cars are clean or dirty, new or used, speedy or slow, others much like you — car owners who are proud of their vehicles — lurk somewhere out there in the wide, wide world, and you're bound to find at least some of them online.

In this chapter, we take a look at how proud car owners share their passion with one another on the Internet. We also show you where car fans go to discuss their favorite cars, give you information about how to join car clubs revolving around a specific devotion to your preferred vehicle, and explore the thrill of victory — and the agony of defeat — that's unique to those who pursue the checkered flag.

Above all, you discover how to find others much like you — people who enjoy their cars and enjoy meeting others who do, too.

Our Car-Crazed Society Extends to the Info-Highway, Too

We may forget it these days, but at one time in the not-too-distant past — say, about two years ago — the Internet was known to commentators as the "Information Superhighway," the "Info-Highway," or the "Infobahn," all terms referring to some kind of road of knowledge linking everyone through the vast, interconnecting computer system that makes up the Internet.

Sure, today we call it just "the Internet," a catch-all term that can signify just about any kind of online access that links up to everything else, whether cable, phone, or wireless. But car fans can perhaps more easily characterize the Internet not only as a fantastic info-highway, but also a direct conduit to excellent cars, daring drivers, friendly fans, and others who simply want to share in a good discussion about the automobile.

Elsewhere in this book, you find oodles of links to Web sites for all the car manufacturers and most of the major aftermarket players in the car market. Together, such resources may form the backbone of online automotive content, but they're really only the tip of the iceberg if you're thinking in general terms of how car people hook up online to foster their passions.

Take, for example, Usenet newsgroups. You can go to Deja.com's Usenet Web site (at `www.deja.com/usenet`), type **car** in the Search text box, and watch the varied options fill your browser's window. How about `alt.autos.antique`, `rec.autos.antique`, `alt.autos.ford.focus`, `alt.binaries.pictures.vehicles`, and `rec.autos.sport.nascar`, to name but a handful? In truth, this simple query retrieves 6,391 pages of car-related Usenet discussions — enough to fill your thoughts and tempt your mind for months to come. (See Figure 20-1.)

Next, visit your favorite Search engine — say, AltaVista.com (at `www.altavista.com`) — and type the keyword **auto**. What you see as a result is what you get — in this case, close to 7 *million* pages. One eye-catching site from this vast list is The Auto Channel (at `www.theautochannel.com`); it's not a TV station but a news site that devotes itself to automotive and auto sport news. (See Figure 20-2.) Think of the site as a newspaper centering around nothing but cars. We love it, and we're adding it to our own news site at `www.bourque.com`.

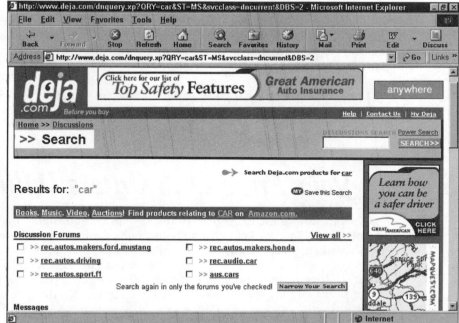

Figure 20-1:
The Usenet
newsgroups
can lead
you to
a wide
variety of
discussions
about cars.

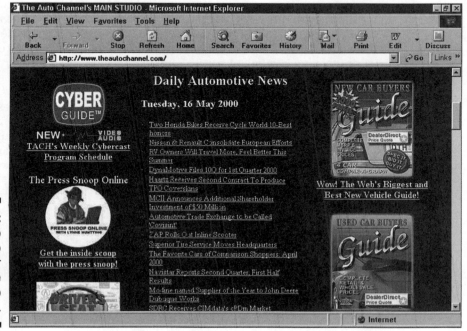

Figure 20-2:
Turn to
The Auto
Channel for
automotive
and auto
sport news.

Another one worth mentioning briefly is Cardealerjobs.com (at `www.Cardealerjobs.com`), a site that exists perhaps for the ultimate car fan: the one who earns a living selling and repairing them. It may not be the fanciest site that we note in this book, but it gets the job done (if you can pardon the pun).

All these sites suggest that you can find on the Net just about everything imaginable relating to cars (or, more appropriately in this case, you find it all on the Info-Highway).

Sharing Your Pride with Others Online

Take a look now at the concept of pride, as in pride of ownership. A friend recently bought a new Acura from my brother's Casino Acura dealership in my hometown. She enthusiastically explained how she visited the dealer's Web site (at `www.casinoacura.com`) to check out the new models, arranged for a test drive online, and then negotiated the purchase price via e-mail. But she beamed with pride as she actually started to explain the features in her new car.

This sense of pride that most car owners show in their wheels underlines a special relationship that people have with cars. For most people, a car is a big investment, perhaps the biggest one they make next to the purchase of a home. But a car represents an extension of one's own individual personality. Whether you're a rugged urban adventurer, a modest family shuttle chauffeur, or a young adrenaline sportster, invariably you choose a car to suit your lifestyle, keeping in mind, of course, the relative limitations of your specific purchasing abilities.

That sense of reflected identity in our cars is what perhaps best describes the reasons behind our sense of pride in them, new or old. And on the Internet, that pride lends itself well to a sharing of experiences — a mutual admiration society revolving around the type and model of your car and the wisdom of keeping in tune with what others are saying and doing with cars similar to yours.

Keep in mind, too, that you don't really need to be an owner to get involved online. After all, you all have your own ideas about what constitutes a dream car, right? And you don't need to own a car to admire it. We have no doubt that you can find a special way to pursue your dreams on the Net without actually needing to buy that practically unattainable dream of yours.

So go online, crawl through the Web, sign up for e-mail lists, and join the discussion groups that best mirror your particular interests to determine what others like you are doing and saying. You're likely to make fast friends with others, both locally and from farther afield, all thanks to the fact that you share an interest in a particular car.

Connecting through Car Clubs on the Net

In many communities around North America and the world, car owners and fans alike get together regularly, perhaps monthly, to share their passions and their pride. These people belong to thriving groups, clubs, and associations with a special devotion to particular car makes and brands.

Enthusiasts of British automobiles in your hometown, for example, are likely to belong to motor clubs. In our area, we know of an MG Club, a Triumph Club, and a Jaguar Club. You don't need to be British or to own a British car to belong. The simple joy of admiring a particular car make is usually enough to qualify you as a member. Hey, everyone needs a fan base, right?

These local clubs, in turn, often belong to national umbrella organizations, which in their turn do much to ensure that enthusiasts from coast to coast derive as much enjoyment out of their local memberships as possible. And given that old saying that strength lies in numbers, many of these national umbrella groups use their strong purchasing power to wrangle deals on parts and services for their membership. So even if you must pay a small fee to join an auto club, the deals that you can realize, not to mention the friendships that you can gain, often more than offset the cost of your membership.

You can now also find many auto clubs, big and small, on the Internet, often with elaborate Web sites featuring monthly newsletters, membership lists, schedules of official events, even classified ads.

Auto aficionados who own similar vehicles often wave or honk at each other to signal "Hello, what great taste you have" as they cross paths on streets, roads, and highways. Online, a somewhat similar effect can occur among people with similar tastes who want to join the BMW Car Club of America (on the Web at www.bmwcca.org — see Figure 20-3). Billed as "The Ultimate Club for The Ultimate Driving Machine," this car club, the biggest BMW club in the world, boasts more than 50,000 members and provides many reasons to join. Sign up online to gain discounts on parts and supplies, access library and video services, tap into valuable help from technical and maintenance experts, and much more. The site itself is free to browse and hosts tech tips, help services, a calendar of activities, info about BMW racing activities, and access to *The Roundel,* the club's official magazine.

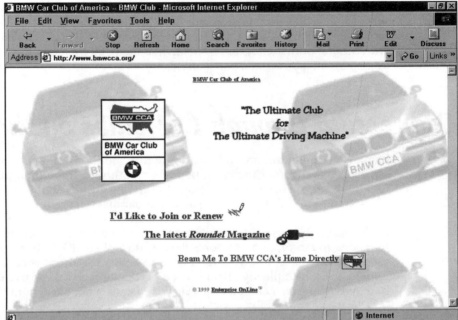

Figure 20-3:
The large
BMW club
enables
fans to
come
together to
celebrate
The Ultimate
Driving
Machine.

Note: Of course, BMWs aren't just cars. The firm also makes some of the best bicycles and motorcycles available anywhere in the world. Fans and owners of motorized two-wheel BMWs alike want to check out the BMW Motorcycle Owners of America (at www.bmwmoa.org on the Web), an excellent source of online material ranging from motorcycle camping and flea markets to member profiles. You can find many other BMW motorcycle resources online, including Internet BMW Riders – The BMW Motorcycle Owners Mailing List (at www.ibmwr.org) and The Chain Gang (at www.f650.com), a group dedicated to the BMW F650.

In all likelihood, a club exists to serve your favorite car brand, too. Using a search engine, we quickly and easily find a variety of motor clubs, notably The Aston Martin Owners Club (at www.amoc.org), the International Toyota MR2 Owners Club (at http://mr2.com), the Rolls-Royce Club of Australia (at www.rroc.org.au), the Dodge Durango Owners Club (at www.durangoclub.com), and the Long Island Corvette Association (at http://members.aol.com/licoa/licoa.htm). All offer information and an open invitation for you to join their virtual communities.

Others we came across include: the Lincoln Car Club (at www.lincoln-club.org); the Honda Owners Club of the United Kingdom (at www.hoc.org.uk); the Alfa-Romeo Owners Club of San Diego (at www.arocsd.org); the Hummer Club (at www.4x44u.com/pub/k2/am4x44u/events/clubs/hummer_club.htm); and the North American Singer Owners Club (at www.singercars.com).

In short, the Internet can put you in touch with a club for just about every car make ever . . . er, well . . . *made.* You can find one that suits your interests, either local or transcontinental, just a click or two away on the Web. Many car clubs belong to global organizations, often with informal links to one another from enthusiasm alone. Others are part of a network that enjoys official sanctions and support from the car manufacturer itself. Still others are more grassroots in nature and operate on a local level independent of somewhat similar activities in other cities. Regardless, most willingly and enthusiastically extend their welcome mats in the hope of fueling their growth with your interest in their particular car brand.

Checking Out Auto Sports Sites Online (Vroom, Vroom!)

Although many car manufacturers produce vehicles specifically known as "sports cars" to great effect in the marketplace, many owners of other types of cars make sport with their own vehicles, notably through time trials, rallies, slaloms, and racing — activities otherwise known collectively as *auto sport.*

In fact, auto sport is a billion-dollar bonanza for car makers and owners alike. For manufacturers, auto sport provides a valuable exposure in a dynamic and exciting setting that mere advertising simply can't buy. It also provides an excellent test bed because a car that you use in auto sport you often push to its ultimate mechanical and electronic limits. Because car parts that tend to break in sport are worrisome for car makers looking to install them in millions of cars, finding out how those parts hold up in extremely competitive conditions is terrific insight to have before making a decision to put a part into your passenger car.

Auto sport — notably car racing — also helps in the evolution of key safety devices, many of which you now find on all new cars on sale in America. Improvements such as seat belts, fuel cells, enhanced ABS braking capabilities, and even stronger transmissions are all a direct result of the types of safety developments that evolve on the race track. Tires, too, enjoy great improvements thanks to the severe wear that they must absorb in sport.

For the car owner and driver, auto sport aids in the development of increasingly safer cars that perform better than their predecessors. The evolution of cars in sport also provides a fair degree of thrills and spills — and a large dose of exciting competition, too.

Today, thousands of people around the world earn a good living catering to a rampant fan base that stretches to just about every country in the world and includes tens of millions of people.

In general, almost all car racing that you find in America operates under sanction from a governing body that ensures adequate technical rules, addresses safety concerns, and develops marketing programs that attract you, the fan, to the race track or the races on TV.

Perhaps the most successful form of motorsport that you find in North America is that of *NASCAR* (at www.nascar.com), known as the home of stock-car racing. The official site of the National Association Stock Car Auto Racing organization, shown in Figure 20-4, is one of the great sports successes on the Internet. It's a great marketing tool for NASCAR because it's now such a popular online destination. The site is full of schedules and links to all teams and drivers. The organization also continually updates the site with all the latest racing news, including race results, standings, schedules, features, frequent chats with series stars, and much more. And because NASCAR fans are known for their exuberance, you can expect a lot of action at all related Web sites.

NHRA Online (at www.nhra.com) is the home of drag racing on the Internet. The National Hot Rod Association boasts the fastest cars driving in a straight line (as opposed to racing on an oval-shaped track, or a road course) that you can find anywhere in the world. NHRA fans can expect a no-nonsense Web site with direct links to teams, drivers, fan clubs, race schedules, series information, national records, classification guides, and even a multimedia center featuring movies and action photos. Make sure that you check out the engine blueprints, too, because NHRA race engines put out more horsepower than a whole corral of Mustangs.

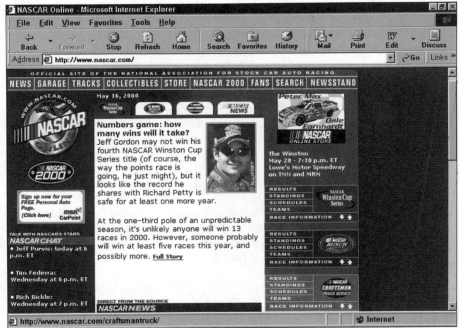

Figure 20-4:
The NASCAR site is the home of stock-car racing.

Fans of open-wheel racing enjoy many other choices in feeding their need for speed. Perhaps the most famous open-wheel race of all is the Indianapolis 500 (at www.indy500.com on the Web), which rightly bills itself as "The Greatest Spectacle in Racing" and runs each spring at the end of May. This fabled race was first held in 1911 and has grown to attract half a million spectators to Indianapolis each year, with millions more glued to their TVs and radios.

IndyCar racing has grown far beyond Indiana. Today, two completely separate championship driving leagues feature top open-wheel racing with sleek vehicles that rocket around oval courses and through city-street courses from coast to coast and internationally. One is the Championship Auto Racing Teams, better known as _CART_ (at www.cart.com on the Web — see Figure 20-5). The other one is the Indy Racing League, or _IRL_ (at www.indyracingleague.com). Both feature top drivers from around the world, with such names as Unser, Andretti, Montoya, Brack, Cheever, and Tracy among them. Although both series feature similar-looking cars, each is technically different from the other. Drivers of one group may not compete with those of the other on the track, but they do compete for fans, TV audience, and media coverage. Luckily for the race fan, that means more races.

Figure 20-5: The CART site boasts news about the top drivers, tells you where you can see the next set of races, and even offers merchadise for sale.

One other major open-wheel racing series worth mentioning here is the *FIA F1 World Championship*, a string of 16 prestigious races held across the globe in a championship that crowns auto racing's "World Champion." *FIA* stands for *I*nternational *A*utomobile *F*ederation (at www.fia.com on the Web), the sport's governing body, which maintains its headquarters in Paris, France. It also governs a number of other auto-sport championships, notably the GT Championship (a series that includes the 24 Hours at LeMans), the World Rally Championship, the European Challenge for Historic Touring Cars, the Inter-Nations Truck Racing Challenge, the European Drag Racing Championship, and the Electro-Solar Cup, among others.

Note: Most important, the FIA is a global body with extensive involvement in the development of safety for the drivers and cars. (Make sure to check out the four points of the "10 seconds" safety campaign — four quick things you can do to greatly increase your chances of a safe ride.) The FIA's Web site features a number of related resources, notably crash-test reports and links to various national automobile organizations such as the American Automobile Association (AAA) and the Canadian Automobile Association (CAA), all members of the FIA.

For direct access to a host of other racing Web sites, visit the Motor Sports area of SportSearch.com (at http://sportsearch.com/Motor_Sports), where you can find direct links to all kinds of auto sport, including demolition derbies, tractor pulling, motorcycle racing, off-road racing, sprint cars, midgets, and enough testosterone-charged horsepower to keep you enthralled through the year.

A word to the wise here: Although watching car races is generally wholesome family fun, the actual act of racing cars isn't for everyone. Yes, it's a passion for those who do it, and it's a sport that's open to just about anyone who wants to learn how to do it. But it's also a sport best left to experienced competitors who conduct their activity within a sanctioned event that motorsport professionals organize. In other words, motorsport doesn't belong on city streets and interstate highways.

Part VI
The Part of Tens

The 5th Wave

By Rich Tennant

"Are you sure it's never been in an accident?"

In this part . . .

Every *For Dummies* book contains a Part of Tens — full of useful and cool little tidbits that don't quite fit anywhere else in the book — and this title is no exception! Although this particular Part of Tens contains only two brief chapters, you don't want to miss it (at any speed)!

Chapter 21 contains ten important things that you need to watch out for in buying a car online (or anywhere else, for that matter). And Chapter 22 offers up ten valuable online tools to help you save money or time while on the road — try out some of these pointers the next time that you head out on the highway. (And you needn't be born to be wild to do so!)

Chapter 21

Ten Things to Watch Out for When Buying a Car Online

● ●

In This Chapter

▶ Avoiding the bait and switch with leases

▶ Understanding price quotes

▶ Getting last-resort financing

▶ Deciding whether to lease or buy

▶ Pricing your trade-in

▶ Preparing yourself psychologically

▶ Getting everything in writing

● ●

*J*ust because using the Internet can help you with fact-finding on pricing, leases, and so forth, you still have to stay on your toes when buying a car online. Here are some pitfalls to beware.

Beware the Lease Switcheroo Trick

You may not believe it, but some dealers hand you a purchase contract to look over only to substitute a *lease* contract later when the time comes to finalize the deal. If you've decided to buy rather than lease, this little switcheroo would likely be very painful and embarrassing.

When you sign something, the law assumes that you've read what you sign. The solution is to be sure to read the entire document when you sign it. Even better, when you go in for your test drive (which should not be the same day that you finalize the purchase) ask them to give you the sales contract to take home and read. Then make a small mark on each page so you can be sure that you're signing the same document that you looked over.

Sounds paranoid, we know. But the lease switch trick is alive and well and living in America. And just because you're paranoid doesn't mean that they *aren't* out to get you.

Don't Take Price Quotes as Written in Stone

Try to get a new car dealer price quote from several sources, such as AutoWeb, Kelly, CarPrices or other online sites (see Chapter 6). Each of the sources provides you with an estimated dealer cost, which is likely to differ in each case. This doesn't mean that the estimates are inaccurate; several variables come into play when quoting car prices such as options, destination charges, sales tax, and new pricing information that may not yet have shown up at a given Web site.

The estimate that you get from the Internet is often low, even by several hundred dollars. Why? The quote may not take account of extra options included on the particular car you're looking at, or extra costs such as import fees, gas charges, advertising costs, and so on. At the dealership, ask to see the actual *factory invoice* for the car you're buying. This figure is usually *higher* than the prices you'll see quoted on the Internet for the "standard" model. Don't decide your final offer merely on the "dealer invoice" price you see estimated on the Internet.

Don't settle for an invoice that the salesman or sales manager tears off the printer. That's not the real invoice price; it's a price guaranteed to make the sales staff a handsome profit. The actual invoice is a separate piece of paper that *looks* like an invoice and has the dealer as the customer and the factory as the distributor.

Don't assume that asking for a price near the invoice price robs the dealer of a fair profit. Dealerships are paid extra for the space on their lot by the factory — this is called *dealer holdback* and if the dealer sells the car quickly (generally within the first three months), he's guaranteed to make a decent profit on it, even if he sells it at $1 over invoice). Of course, if a car is in great demand, they'll reject your offer and wait for the next customer to come along (one who they hope has less information).

If You Have Trouble Getting Financing

If all else fails and you get turned down by the various loan sources I've described in this book, try a finance company. Their rates are generally higher than other sources, but they consider people whose credit ratings are too weak to get quick online approval. Don't be too embarrassed if you have less than excellent (or a too-brief) credit record. You're in the majority. Research shows that about 60 percent of the adult population falls into this not-so-excellent category. It's not that hard to lose a good credit rating either: It can happen if you get into an unresolved dispute, or let a bill go unpaid for more than two months.

If You Have Trouble Getting Financing, Part II

If you think you have a good credit rating and don't understand why you're getting turned down everywhere you apply for a loan — *take a look at your rating*. You can access this information: It's the law. They don't have to let you see your credit rating for free, but they do have to let you see it.

You can get a free credit report when you sign up for a trial membership in the CreditCheck Monitoring Service, or pay $7.95 for a report derived from Experian (www.freecreditreport.com). Alternatively, get a $29.95 merged, triple-source report from Equifax, Trans Union, and Experian (www. icreditreport.com). Also remember that if you have cash value in a life insurance policy, you can sometimes borrow from it.

Should You Lease?

At the end of the normal three-year lease, you'll be forced to look for a new car (what's more, you'll have no trade-in either). Also, leases are generally complex documents and figuring out what they mean isn't always an easy task. You can bet, though, that if your friendly lessor can find a way to wedge in some additional profits here and there, he or she will.

Many people are so pleased when they find out the low initial cost and low monthly payments of the typical lease, they simply agree to it without giving the whole purchase much further thought. Don't fall into this category.

Don't Give Away Your Trade-in

All too many people (most people, in fact) quickly cave in when offered a really, really low price for their trade-in. You're told "our mechanic, unfortunately, found all these flaws with your trade-in." And you end up being either too timid or too uninformed about auto negotiating to argue. If you're trading in your existing car, your *first step* when negotiating at the dealership should be to agree on the trade-in price. You should also try to nail down the price *before* you tell the salesperson which car you're interested in.

After the salesperson knows which car you're interested in, you can't be sure of how much they're actually giving you for your car. They can make you feel really good by saying that they're giving you way more than the car is worth, but they're probably just taking a bit of the top-end profit off the car you want to buy.

Dealers usually want to talk to you in terms of *trade difference* between the car you want to buy and the car you have. The trade difference is the amount of money that you will have to refinance after the dealer pays off your existing loan to buy the new car. Your goal is to get them to quote you the amount they'll give you for your current car *before* they know which new car you want. Then you can bring down the price of the new car to as close to invoice as you can. Then the price should be:

```
(New car price + Options + Extras & incidentals) -
        Trade-in value
```

Suppose that your car lists for used retail at $12,000. It's then likely to list for around, say, $9000 wholesale, with an auction price of about $8,300. A salesperson is likely to offer you around $5,700 and, if you scream and moan, the salesperson may be willing to go up to $6,500, weeping all the way about what the sales manager is going to do when this shockingly high price becomes known. There won't be any Christmas goose for his son Tiny Tim this year. *Thanks to you.*

You have to be realistic about the value of your trade-in, particularly if you financed it for 60 months with little or no down payment and want to trade it in after 36 months. In reality, the payoff on your loan is probably *more* than the value of your trade-in (a condition that car salespeople call being *upside-down*). If you buy a new car under these circumstances, then rest assured that you will be financing the difference between the value of your trade-in and the payoff on the loan in the price of your new car. If you're paying on a loan, then you should go into the negotiation with your eyes open. To do so, do these things:

- Visit www.kelley.com and find out the value of your trade-in (see Chapter 4 for details).
- Call the financial institution that holds your loan for the payoff on your car.
- Expect to have to add any value shortfall to the price of your new car.

If you like to have a new car every three or four years, then you should put as much money down as possible and finance the car for as short a term as your budget allows.

Be Prepared

If you do your homework, as described in this book, you'll enter the negotiation process with a valuable attitude. Don't wander into the car dealership with vague notions about the value of your trade-in, worries about the problems in securing a loan, no idea of the real cost of the new car, and confusion about other factors involved in buying a vehicle. Have the facts already in hand when you first visit the dealership. The Internet is the world's greatest research engine ever — and it can completely and thoroughly prepare you for buying a vehicle. You'll come out a winner if you take a little time to prepare yourself.

Be Aware of Your Wants

Before you enter the showroom, it's important to sit yourself down and make two lists: what you must have, and what you'd merely *like* to have, in your new vehicle. These are two different lists. All too often people come away from the dealer's lot with a CD changer and moon roof (things they wanted), but too little room for their four kids and the dog to fit comfortably for a vacation trip (things they needed). Don't be confused and get a sports car if you need a station wagon.

List the things you must have, then list the things you would like. The second list, your wish list, should be pared down until it fits your budget. It's important to make these lists, and arrive at decisions, before you get into the sales situation where you're likely to either bust your budget, or trade off things you really need for things you merely want.

Be Willing to Walk

In any negotiation, it's highly important that you have a willingness to walk out the door and go somewhere else. Your diction, body language, and other behaviors will all convey whether or not you feel you can drop the haggling process and simply walk out.

If you have the feeling that you *must* get that red beauty sitting out there in the lot, you've been maneuvered psychologically. You've allowed yourself to be manipulated into thinking that there's an emergency, and you feel that you've got to conclude the deal if at all possible. There are many ways to get you to feel this way. They'll tell you they can't get that color again for months, that the model you want is rare and popular, that it's now or never. Don't be pushed into this corner. Be prepared mentally to go to a different dealer (this attitude will show, and it will make all the difference). But you must be mentally strong enough to believe that you can walk, and you must also be prepared to walk if necessary.

Get It in Writing

It's important to take notes during the negotiation process. If you and the dealer agree that you won't be charged for rustproofing, write that down in your notebook (you did bring a notebook, didn't you?). Also nail down all the other "extra" charges, including such items as dealer prep, undercoating, interior protection, paint coating, sealant, "shining," or *any other extra*.

You don't want surprises that can balloon the cost. As you eliminate these unnecessary extras, write each agreement down in your notebook. Then, when the final contract is given to you, *make sure that these items are all in writing*. Take nothing for granted. Check the contract to ensure that all the verbal agreements (the ones you wrote in your notebook) are also spelled out in the contract. Double-check everything for omissions or errors.

Chapter 22

Ten Excellent Tips to Help You Buy a Car Online

*E*ven if you don't have "a friend of a friend in the business," here are some insider tips to help ease your online car-buying experience.

Get a Copy of the Contract

Make at least two personal visits to the dealership. The first visit is merely to allow you to test drive the car you're interested in. And, before you leave the dealership after your test drive, be sure to ask for a blank copy of their contract form. You want to read this over and mark any questions you will want to ask later, or changes you want to make. You want to consider these issues *in the calm of your own home.* Don't put off reading the contract until the last minute when you are at the dealer, negotiating your final price and otherwise distracted by everything that's going on. (You *were* planning to read the contract before signing it, weren't you?)

If You're a Woman

It may not be PC, but there are sites devoted to women car-buyers only. Even if you're not a woman, you may still find some information of use at the Woman Motorist site (www.womanmotorist.com). The site isn't a raving pit of chauvinism — you can find reviews by both men and women.

This site offers a complete panorama of varied topics including reviews, maintenance, tips on buying a used car, safety, a glossary, Q & A, new product features, and a chat feature. It's a good site. Give it a try.

Try Go's Express Search

Anyone who spends any time online must master the art of searching. One of the best freebies on the Internet, in my view anyway, is the Go Express Search engine. Go offers several significant advantages over most other search engines. It allows you to scroll through the hits (so you don't have to keep using the Backspace key or the Back button in your browser to get back to the hit list to click on the next link). A second big advantage is that pages in the hit list are automatically loaded in the background. This means that while you check out one of the links, the links following in the list are loading into your browser. When you click the next link (or Go's Next button), the next site snaps quickly onto your screen.

Search Engines to Try

You can choose from many excellent search engines. Try the following and see if there are a couple that particularly suit you. This is a list of some of the most popular search engines, in no particular order: HotBot; Go2Net (MetaCrawler); AskJeeves; MSN (Microsoft Network); Google; Yahoo!; WebCrawler; AltaVista; DirectHit; Snap; Northern Light; Excite; Infoseek (Go); Netscape; GoTo.

Don't Ignore Any Financing Options

You can get great financing online, and often it's the best deal you'll get. Typically, a blank check is sent to you (as quickly as the next day), and you then fill it in to the limit of the loan you had approved via e-mail online. However, don't neglect seeing what kind of rate the dealer may be able to offer you. Sometimes dealers use super-low-interest loans as one of their come-ons. Also, check with your credit union if you belong to one. These non-profit organizations can often undercut current loan rates. Keep your options open.

Consider an Open-End Lease

A special kind of lease that may appeal to you is called the *open-end lease*. You agree up front to pay for the difference between the predicted value (called the *residual value*) of the car at the end of the lease and the actual value (called the *realized value*) that the car has at the end. The predicted value is written into the lease when you first get the car, but the realized value is determined at the end when you return the car.

In some cases, you may actually get money back if the car is worth more at the end of the lease than was predicted in the residual value. But, as always, keep your eyes open. The realized value can be calculated several ways: how much money they get when they sell it to someone, the retail value (as determined by an agreed upon source), the wholesale value, what's called the "fair market value" or even the best *offer* the dealer gets for the car. You need to know which of these methods of calculation are used in your lease and how to ensure that the car's value will be determined fairly.

Don't Forget that People Pay Different Prices for the Same Car at the Same Dealership

People pay different prices for a new car. You can pay top dollar; you can pay close to dealer cost; or you can pay somewhere in between. If you're a really weak negotiator, you might give the dealer $3,000 in profit; a great negotiator might give the dealer $300 in profit. Obviously, salesmen and dealers would prefer to get $3,000 from everyone — but experience has shown that profit is determined largely by how customers behave during the haggling process. If you're polite, persistent, and above all, *prepared* — you should be able to drive the price down near the low end of the spectrum. You'll find loads of techniques and tips on how to negotiate throughout this book.

Lowering Your Insurance

We all want to save money on insurance, and there are several ways you can. You can usually get a discount on your auto insurance if your insurance carrier also handles your homeowner's or renter's policy. Check, too, to see if you can get a discount if you have more than one auto to insure. Also, if you have a child who's a driver listed on your policy, most insurance companies have "good student" discounts if your school-age student maintains a B grade average. Students who have completed driver's education classes usually get a break, too.

Another option is to ask your agent to see if his company provides a discount for drivers with a good driving record. Many insurance carriers also provide a discount for an annual low mileage (typically 7,500 miles per year), and also if you have a security system (alarm) on your car. Nonsmokers are usually charged (or is that *charred?*) less, too.

One final insurance rates reduction tip is to consider taking a defensive driving class, especially if you're a senior or if you're trying to dig yourself out of a mess of tickets.

Another way to lower your auto insurance costs is to remove both collision and comprehensive insurance. Don't live in a dream world, though. If you don't carry collision insurance on your car, and then you have an accident that's your fault, chances are good that your auto insurance company won't pay out anything for your damage.

You can also consider boosting the deductible. A *deductible* is the money you pay for repairs before the insurance kicks in. The usual default deductible is around $500; if you have an accident with $1,000 damage to your vehicle, you pay $500 and the insurance company pays $500. Ask your agent to see how your rates would change if you raised your deductible to, say, $1,000. Get quotes for various levels of insurance, then make up your own mind about what amounts you really need. And don't forget to make adjustments every couple of years, as the vehicle ages and circumstances change.

Always Have Uninsured/Underinsured Motorist Insurance Coverage

In my state, North Carolina, over 7 percent of all drivers are uninsured. Whoa! And according to statistics, that percentage is likely to be even higher in your state. What do those uninsured drivers mean to you? Consider this: Most people who drive without insurance have few financial resources. That's why they don't have insurance in the first place. That's also why, if they total your car, or hurt you badly, you cannot rely on much, if any, money from them to help you get repaired. In my opinion, it's always worthwhile getting the (relatively inexpensive) addition to your car insurance coverage called *uninsured/underinsured motorist coverage*. See if you have it; if you don't, consider getting it.

Don't Ignore Rental Cars If You're Looking for a Used Car

Did you know that car rental companies are the biggest sellers of nearly-new cars? They like to offer their rental customers as new a car as possible, so they recycle their fleet of cars as often as possible. After all, their rental car customers like the feel of a shiny new-like car. But that means a potential deal for you as a used car buyer. Take, for example, Enterprise Rent-A-Car, the biggest rental car company in North America. Check out their website (www.ecars.com) and you will find a big pitch by Enterprise, or Ecars as it is also known, to sell their huge selection of slightly used cars. Looking for a great used car deal? You might find it there.

Enterprise calls its pitch "The Perfect Used Car Package: Haggle-Free Buying & Worry-Free Ownership". The "Haggle-Free" claim refers to a one-price system that Enterprise offers. The "Worry-Free" claim comes from the great warranty that buyers get, as well as a seven-day return policy that lets you drive the car for a week and sell it back for the very same amount you paid for it, minus a small fee to clean the car. That way, you can check the car out to make sure it is still in great shape. Rental companies usually have a huge variety of makes and models in the fleet of vehicles they rent out. They are definitely worth checking out if you are in the market for a well-maintained, low-mileage, nearly-new used car.

Part VII
Appendix

In this part . . .

All right, so you really do need to buy a new car, but you don't know the Internet from a Raisinet or a camshaft from a Camaro — and when a dealer starts talking about an ADM charge, you're sure that *you're* getting the shaft. Fear not — you're at the part of this book that can help you straighten it all out!

This appendix contains data about using the book's CD-ROM. So if you have questions about any of the terms that we use in this book, about your necessary online requirements, or about the CD, turn here. (We even give you the answers.)

Appendix

About the CD-ROM

• •

*T*he CD that accompanies Car Buying Online For Dummies is full of great car-related programs — enough to drive you wild! For your convenience, the CD's interface is a slick, easy-to-use HTML interface. Here is but a sampling of the cool programs you can find:

- **Car Organizer Deluxe** shareware version that allows you to organize information about car models, dealers, and so on to simplify the process of identifying just the right car.

- **Buy or Lease It** shareware version that can help you make the decision of whether to buy or lease your next car.

- **AutoCare Center** shareware helps simplify the task of auto maintenance.

System Requirements

Make sure that your computer meets the minimum system requirements listed below. If your computer doesn't match up to most of these requirements, you may have problems using the contents of the CD.

- A PC with a Pentium or faster processor, or a Mac OS computer with a 68040 or faster processor.

- Microsoft Windows 95 or later, or Mac OS system software 7.5.5 or later.

- At least 16MB of total RAM installed on your computer. For best performance, we recommend at least 32MB of RAM installed.

- At least 110MB of hard drive space available to install all the software from this CD. (You need less space if you don't install every program.)

- A CD-ROM drive — double-speed (2x) or faster.

- A sound card for PCs. (Mac OS computers have built-in sound support.)

- A monitor capable of displaying at least 256 colors or grayscale.

- A modem with a speed of at least 14,400 bps.

If you need more information on the basics, check out *PCs For Dummies,* 7th Edition, by Dan Gookin; *Macs For Dummies,* 6th Edition, by David Pogue; or *Windows 98 For Dummies* or *Windows 95 For Dummies,* 2nd Edition, by Andy Rathbone (all published by IDG Books Worldwide, Inc.).

Using the CD with Microsoft Windows

To install the items from the CD to your hard drive, follow these steps.

1. **Insert the CD into your computer's CD-ROM drive.**

2. **Open your browser.**

   If you do not have a browser, we have included Microsoft Internet Explorer, as well as Netscape Communicator. They can be found in the Programs folder at the root of the CD.

3. **Click Start⇨Run.**

4. **In the dialog box that appears, type** D:\START.HTM.

   Replace *D* with the proper drive letter if your CD-ROM drive uses a different letter. (If you don't know the letter, see how your CD-ROM drive is listed under My Computer.

5. **Read through the license agreement, nod your head, and then click the Accept button if you want to use the CD — after you click Accept, you'll never be bothered by the License Agreement window again.**

   This action will display the file that will walk you through the content of the CD.

6. **To navigate within the interface, simply click on any topic of interest to take you to an explanation of the files on the CD and how to use or install them.**

7. **To install the software from the CD, simply click on the software name.**

   You'll see two options — the option to run or open the file from the current location or the option to save the file to your hard drive. Choose to run or open the file from its current location and the installation procedure will continue. After you are done with the interface, simply close your browser as usual.

To run some of the programs, you might need to keep the CD inside your CD-ROM drive. This is a Good Thing. Otherwise, the installed program would have required you to install a very large chunk of the program to your hard drive space, which would have kept you from installing other software.

Using the CD with Mac OS

To install the items from the CD to your hard drive, follow these steps.

1. **Insert the CD into your computer's CD-ROM drive.**

   In a moment, an icon representing the CD you just inserted appears on your Mac desktop. Chances are, the icon looks like a CD-ROM.

2. **Double-click the CD icon to show the CD's contents.**

3. **Double-click the Read Me First icon.**

   This text file contains information about the CD's programs and any last-minute instructions you need to know about installing the programs on the CD that we don't cover in this appendix.

4. **Open your browser.**

   If you don't have a browser, we have included the two most popular ones for your convenience — Microsoft Internet Explorer and Netscape Communicator.

5. **Click on File⇨Open and select the CD entitled CarBuy FD. Click the Links.htm file to see an explanation of all files and folders included on the CD.**

6. **Some programs come with installer programs — with those you simply open the program's folder on the CD and double-click the icon with the words "Install" or "Installer".**

After you have installed the programs you want, you can eject the CD. Carefully place it back in the plastic jacket of the book for safekeeping.

What You'll Find

Here's a summary of the software on this CD arranged by category. If you use Windows, the CD interface helps you install software easily. (If you have no idea what I'm talking about when I say "CD interface," flip back a page or two to find the section, "Using the CD with Microsoft Windows.")

If you use a Mac OS computer, you can take advantage of the easy Mac interface to quickly install the programs.

Internet

In case you haven't yet gotten your feet wet on the Infobahn, here are some programs to get you started.

Directory Links Page, by Pierre Bourque and Richard Mansfield.

Freeware. For Windows 95/98 and Mac. URLs? We don't need to type no stinking URLs. At least not when you can click the URLs provided on the handy links page on the CD-ROM. Read through the Internet directory in the book and then click the link on the CD. I love it when a plan comes together!

MindSpring Internet Service Provider, by MindSpring Enterprises, Inc.

Commercial Product. For Windows 95/98 and Mac. In case you don't have an Internet connection, the CD includes sign-on software for MindSpring, an Internet service provider.

For more information and for updates of MindSpring, visit the MindSpring Web site at www.mindspring.com.

You need a credit card to sign up with MindSpring Internet Access.

If you already have an Internet service provider, please note that the MindSpring Internet software makes changes to your computer's current Internet configuration and may replace your current settings. These changes may stop you from being able to access the Internet through your current provider.

Microsoft Internet Explorer 5.0, by Microsoft Corporation, Inc.

Commercial Product. For Windows 95/98 and Mac. Microsoft Internet Explorer is one of two major players in the Web browser market. However, just in case you don't have the latest version (at the time of publication), we include a copy of Microsoft Internet Explorer 5.0 on this CD. You can always find the latest information about Internet Explorer at the Microsoft support site:

www.microsoft.com/ie

If you're running Windows 98 or 2000, you don't need to install this program because it comes with your copy of Windows.

Netscape Communicator 4.7, by Netscape Communications, Inc.

Commercial Software. For Windows 95/98 and Mac. Netscape Communicator is the browser that revolutionized the Internet and is still the best-known browser available. The CD-ROM installs Netscape Communicator version 4.7 and you also have the option of installing RealPlayer G2 (to play streaming audio and video files) and WinAmp (to play MP3 files).

You can always find out more about Netscape Communicator at Netscape's Web site, located, of course, at www.netscape.com.

Before you buy

Buy or Lease It v. 2.0, from KJ Software, Inc.

For Windows 95/98. Shareware. This handy calculator will help you answer the question "Is it better to buy or lease a car?" Part of the answer to this question depends on your own feelings. Do you, for example, like the feeling of owning? Do you have only a little cash to put down? And so on. This program can answer some questions quite astutely, however, such as: Will I have more money at the end of a specified period if I buy, or am I better off leasing? A step-by-step wizard walks you through the information-gathering process.

Car Lease Calculator v. 3.1, from KJ Software, Inc.

For Windows 95/98. Shareware. This program helps you check out your dealer's leasing calculations. Lease calculations are based on six items: manufacturer's suggested retail price (MSRP); best negotiated price; capitalized cost reduction; residual value at lease end (as a percentage of MSRP or in dollars); lease term; and lease interest rate. The Car Lease Calculator lets you enter values for any of these items and for the monthly payment, and it will calculate the unknown value. Keep your dealer on the up and up.

Car Organizer Deluxe 1.3, from PrimaSoft PC, Inc.

For Windows 95 and 98. 30-day trial version. Need to organize information about cars? Well, this program is especially useful when you're collecting information about different car models, car dealers, and any other information that you may want to store in a car catalog.

The program features an unlimited number of records, the ability to add scanned-in images, flexible searching and sorting, powerful reports, label printing, filtering, and more. You can also easily convert your data to HTML format.

For more information, check out www.primasoft.com.

Index

Notes

Notes

Notes

IDG Books Worldwide, Inc., End-User License Agreement

READ THIS. You should carefully read these terms and conditions before opening the software packet(s) included with this book ("Book"). This is a license agreement ("Agreement") between you and IDG Books Worldwide, Inc. ("IDGB"). By opening the accompanying software packet(s), you acknowledge that you have read and accept the following terms and conditions. If you do not agree and do not want to be bound by such terms and conditions, promptly return the Book and the unopened software packet(s) to the place you obtained them for a full refund.

1. **License Grant.** IDGB grants to you (either an individual or entity) a nonexclusive license to use one copy of the enclosed software program(s) (collectively, the "Software") solely for your own personal or business purposes on a single computer (whether a standard computer or a workstation component of a multiuser network). The Software is in use on a computer when it is loaded into temporary memory (RAM) or installed into permanent memory (hard disk, CD-ROM, or other storage device). IDGB reserves all rights not expressly granted herein.

2. **Ownership.** IDGB is the owner of all right, title, and interest, including copyright, in and to the compilation of the Software recorded on the disk(s) or CD-ROM ("Software Media"). Copyright to the individual programs recorded on the Software Media is owned by the author or other authorized copyright owner of each program. Ownership of the Software and all proprietary rights relating thereto remain with IDGB and its licensers.

3. **Restrictions on Use and Transfer.**

   (a) You may only (i) make one copy of the Software for backup or archival purposes, or (ii) transfer the Software to a single hard disk, provided that you keep the original for backup or archival purposes. You may not (i) rent or lease the Software, (ii) copy or reproduce the Software through a LAN or other network system or through any computer subscriber system or bulletin-board system, or (iii) modify, adapt, or create derivative works based on the Software.

   (b) You may not reverse engineer, decompile, or disassemble the Software. You may transfer the Software and user documentation on a permanent basis, provided that the transferee agrees to accept the terms and conditions of this Agreement and you retain no copies. If the Software is an update or has been updated, any transfer must include the most recent update and all prior versions.

4. **Restrictions on Use of Individual Programs.** You must follow the individual requirements and restrictions detailed for each individual program in the "About the CD-ROM" section of this Book. These limitations are also contained in the individual license agreements recorded on the Software Media. These limitations may include a requirement that after using the program for a specified period of time, the user must pay a registration fee or discontinue use. By opening the Software packet(s), you will be agreeing to abide by the licenses and restrictions for these individual programs that are detailed in the "About the CD-ROM" section and on the Software Media. None of the material on this Software Media or listed in this Book may ever be redistributed, in original or modified form, for commercial purposes.

5. **Limited Warranty.**

   (a) IDGB warrants that the Software and Software Media are free from defects in materials and workmanship under normal use for a period of sixty (60) days from the date of purchase of this Book. If IDGB receives notification within the warranty period of defects in materials or workmanship, IDGB will replace the defective Software Media.

   (b) **IDGB AND THE AUTHOR OF THE BOOK DISCLAIM ALL OTHER WARRANTIES, EXPRESS OR IMPLIED, INCLUDING WITHOUT LIMITATION IMPLIED WARRANTIES OF MERCHANTABILITY AND FITNESS FOR A PARTICULAR PURPOSE, WITH RESPECT TO THE SOFTWARE, THE PROGRAMS, THE SOURCE CODE CONTAINED THEREIN, AND/OR THE TECHNIQUES DESCRIBED IN THIS BOOK. IDGB DOES NOT WARRANT THAT THE FUNCTIONS CONTAINED IN THE SOFTWARE WILL MEET YOUR REQUIREMENTS OR THAT THE OPERATION OF THE SOFTWARE WILL BE ERROR FREE.**

   (c) This limited warranty gives you specific legal rights, and you may have other rights that vary from jurisdiction to jurisdiction.

6. **Remedies.**

   (a) IDGB's entire liability and your exclusive remedy for defects in materials and workmanship shall be limited to replacement of the Software Media, which may be returned to IDGB with a copy of your receipt at the following address: Software Media Fulfillment Department, Attn.: *Car Buying Online For Dummies,* IDG Books Worldwide, Inc., 10475 Crosspoint Boulevard, Indianapolis, IN 46256, or call 800-762-2974. Please allow three to four weeks for delivery. This Limited Warranty is void if failure of the Software Media has resulted from accident, abuse, or misapplication. Any replacement Software Media will be warranted for the remainder of the original warranty period or thirty (30) days, whichever is longer.

   (b) In no event shall IDGB or the author be liable for any damages whatsoever (including without limitation damages for loss of business profits, business interruption, loss of business information, or any other pecuniary loss) arising from the use of or inability to use the Book or the Software, even if IDGB has been advised of the possibility of such damages.

   (c) Because some jurisdictions do not allow the exclusion or limitation of liability for consequential or incidental damages, the above limitation or exclusion may not apply to you.

7. **U.S. Government Restricted Rights.** Use, duplication, or disclosure of the Software by the U.S. Government is subject to restrictions stated in paragraph (c)(1)(ii) of the Rights in Technical Data and Computer Software clause of DFARS 252.227-7013, and in subparagraphs (a) through (d) of the Commercial Computer–Restricted Rights clause at FAR 52.227-19, and in similar clauses in the NASA FAR supplement, when applicable.

8. **General.** This Agreement constitutes the entire understanding of the parties and revokes and supersedes all prior agreements, oral or written, between them and may not be modified or amended except in a writing signed by both parties hereto that specifically refers to this Agreement. This Agreement shall take precedence over any other documents that may be in conflict herewith. If any one or more provisions contained in this Agreement are held by any court or tribunal to be invalid, illegal, or otherwise unenforceable, each and every other provision shall remain in full force and effect.

Installation Instructions

To install the items from the CD to your hard drive, follow these steps. If you use a MAC OS computer, see the "About the CD" appendix in this book.

1. **Insert the CD into your computer's CD-ROM drive.**

2. **Choose Start⇨Run.**

3. **In the dialog box that appears, type D:\SETUP.EXE.**

   Replace *D* with the proper drive letter if your CD-ROM drive uses a different letter.

4. **Click OK.**

   A license agreement window appears.

5. **Read through the license agreement, nod your head, and then click the Accept button if you want to use the CD — after you click Accept, you'll never be bothered by the License Agreement window again.**

6. **Click anywhere on the Welcome screen to enter the interface.**

7. **To view the items within a category, just click the category's name.**

8. **For more information about a program, click the program's name.**

9. **If you don't want to install the program, click the Go Back button to return to the previous screen.**

10. **To install a program, click the appropriate Install button.**

11. **To install other items, repeat Steps 7–10.**

12. **When you've finished installing programs, click the Quit button to close the interface.**

13. **You can eject the CD now. Carefully place it back in the plastic jacket of the book for safekeeping.**

IDG BOOKS WORLDWIDE
BOOK REGISTRATION

Register This Book and Win!

We want to hear from you!

Visit **http://my2cents.dummies.com** to register this book and tell us how you liked it!

- ✔ Get entered in our monthly prize giveaway.

- ✔ Give us feedback about this book — tell us what you like best, what you like least, or maybe what you'd like to ask the author and us to change!

- ✔ Let us know any other *For Dummies*® topics that interest you.

Your feedback helps us determine what books to publish, tells us what coverage to add as we revise our books, and lets us know whether we're meeting your needs as a *For Dummies* reader. You're our most valuable resource, and what you have to say is important to us!

Not on the Web yet? It's easy to get started with *Dummies 101*®: *The Internet For Windows*® *98* or *The Internet For Dummies*® at local retailers everywhere.

Or let us know what you think by sending us a letter at the following address:

For Dummies Book Registration
Dummies Press
10475 Crosspoint Blvd.
Indianapolis, IN 46256

BESTSELLING BOOK SERIES